Musicking Bodies

MATTHEW RAHAIM

❧

Musicking Bodies

GESTURE AND VOICE

IN HINDUSTANI MUSIC

❧

WESLEYAN UNIVERSITY PRESS

Middletown, Connecticut

Wesleyan University Press
Middletown CT 06459
www.wesleyan.edu/wespress
© 2012 Matthew Rahaim
All rights reserved
Manufactured in the United States of America
Typeset in Galliard by Integrated Publishing Solutions

Wesleyan University Press is a member of the Green Press Initiative.
The paper used in this book meets their minimum
requirement for recycled paper.

We gratefully acknowledge the AMS 75 PAYS Endowment of the American Musicological Society, funded in part by the National Endowment for the Humanities and the
Andrew W. Mellon Foundation, for assistance with this publication.

The press also would like to thank the College of Liberal Arts at the University of
Minnesota for assistance with this publication.

Library of Congress Cataloging-in-Publication Data
Rahaim, Matthew.
Musicking bodies: gesture and voice in Hindustani music / Matthew Rahaim.
p.   cm. — (Music culture)
Includes bibliographical references and index.
ISBN 978-0-8195-7325-4 (cloth: alk. paper)—ISBN 978-0-8195-7326-1
(pbk.: alk. paper)—ISBN 978-0-8195-7327-8 (ebook)
1. Singing—India.   2. Gesture in music.   3. Hindustani music—Philosophy and
aesthetics.   4. Raga.   I. Title.
ML2551.I5R35 2012
782.20954—dc23
2012012531

5 4 3 2 1

Contents

❦

Illustrations

～

Acknowledgments

⌒

The heart of this work has been the patient guidance of the many teachers who sat with me over the years, beginning with my parents and brother. In writing a book that comes to focus on the tacit transmission of musical knowledge from teacher to student, I was reminded again and again that everything important here was given to me face to face, *sina ba sina*.

First and foremost, I am deeply grateful to the Hindustani vocalists who have so generously guided me over the last fifteen years, including Mohan Darekar, Harriotte Hurie, Arun Kashalkar, Shafqat Ali Khan, Chandrashekar Mahajan, L. K. Pandit, Rita Sahai, Veena Sahasrabuddhe, and Warren Senders. Most of all, I am grateful to Vikas Kashalkar, who accepted me as a student twelve years ago, when I could hardly sing in tune, apparently out of a simple sense of duty to pass on what he knew. Since then he has sat patiently with me for literally hundreds of hours. His good-humored curiosity about my many mistakes — and his willingness to question his own ideas — provided a model of intellectual discipline that I have aspired to in this book. His stubborn insistence that I commit to a single musical ethos not only paid off musically; it also led me to understand better the dynamics of musical transmission in general. Kashalkarji's warm and inclusive extended community (both his family and his *gurukul*) have provided crucial musical and emotional support in Pune over the past twelve years. In particular, I thank Mukul Kulkarni, Chintan Upadhyay, Makarand Kharwandikar, and Pavan Naik for their hospitality, open-handed musical guidance, and friendship.

As I was preparing this book for publication, the world of Hindustani music suffered the loss of a master whose voice appears in these pages: Ustad Rahim Fahim-ud-din Khan Dagar. His depth of knowledge and his seamless integration of *lakshan* and *prayog*, of theory and practice, was and is a great inspiration. May his spirit live on in his disciples — among whom I am particularly grateful to Irfan Zuberi for his kindness in introducing us, for video-recording the interview himself, and for his friendship and collegiality.

I am grateful to the many scholars who have submitted my work to dialectical critique. Bonnie Wade challenged me to think through points I was inclined to conveniently ignore and helped me direct my writing to a broad intellectual community. Ben Brinner saw the potential of this project even when it was shadowy and purely speculative and has challenged me again and again to refine my questions through careful analysis. Eve Sweetser has consistently made me feel welcome in the world of gesture studies and contributed greatly to my analyses through her willingness to analyze speech performances as music. David Wessel started me on my formal research path, providing both encouragement and logistical support. Jocelyne Guilbault worked hard to help me make my theoretical concerns clear to others. Richard Taruskin (whose formidable teaching prowess is somehow less well known than his scholarship) challenged me to be ever more straightforward about the ethical dimensions of my work. Richard Crocker taught me a great deal about many dimensions of melody through the study of Gregorian neume dialects. Katharine Young and Harry Berger, two of my favorite writers, spent a great deal of focused time and energy helping me refine my phenomenological excursions. Parker Smathers at Wesleyan University Press trained his scalpel on the clunkiest parts of this writing, always reminding me that, in the end, someone will be reading this. Tomie Hahn contributed many pages of valuable suggestions about how to render the intricacies of movement readable in prose. I thank my wonderful colleagues at the University of Minnesota: Diyah Larasati for her help in reading bodies; Bill Beeman for his insights into the voice; Gabriela Currie, David Grayson, Sumanth Gopinath, Kelley Harness, Peter Mercer-Taylor, and Karen Painter for their constant support and collegiality; Scott Currie, Erkki Huovinen, Alex Lubet, and Guerino Mazzola for their suggestions about how to think about improvisation; David Myers for his institutional advocacy; and Lars Christensen for his brilliant, sustained engagement with the theoretical puzzles in this book.

The Berkeley Gesture Studies Group enthusiastically welcomed my first theoretical sketches and raw video footage. Shweta Narayan and Nathaniel Smith in particular helped me to be clear about the degree to which song gesture is metaphoric. Adam Kendon, in addition to providing a great deal of the theoretical scaffolding for this project through his scholarly work, patiently and meticulously edited an early article that grew into this book. Martin Clayton, whose wide-ranging interests include gesture in Hindustani music, has been an exceptionally generous colleague. He invited me to give my first talk on gesture, to contribute to a collaborative book chapter (Fatone et al. 2011), and to share his own valuable data, some of which appears in this book. Nikki Moran, Laura Leante, and Gina Fatone have likewise been wonderful collaborators in working to understand the role of the body in music. Ingrid Le Gargasson graciously made her interviews with Vikas Kashalkar available to me. Doug Leonard and Juana Berrio patiently worked with video and photographs to render them clearly in line illustrations. Dileep Chinchalkar generously made the cover illustration (by his late father, Vishnu Chinchalkar) available to us. My dear friends Max Katz and Justin Scarimbolo, fellow scholars of Hindustani music, have done more than anyone could expect from mere colleagues over the last ten years: they alerted me to dozens of historical accounts of gesture, introduced me to important historical sources, and generously offered valuable critique at many levels — from theoretical moves to sentence structure to the fine details of *svara lagao*.

This project has required translation from Hindi, Urdu, German, Marathi, Sanskrit, and Tamil, and I have relied a great deal on my learned colleagues to supplement my own limited language skills: Surajit Bose, Gautam Tejas Ganeshan, Harriotte Hurie, Max Katz, Srinivas Reddy, Simona Sawhney, Chintan Upadhyay, Homayra Ziad, and Irfan Zuberi. Rupert Snell, in addition to providing invaluable materials for understanding medieval Hindi, offered valuable advice about how to transliterate Hindi-Urdu in Latin script. Lys Weiss's patience and care in rendering diacritics, Devanagari, and Urdu script made it possible to render this transliteration system clearly. Lee Rothfarb and Nils Boltmann spent a great deal of time and energy, out of sheer intellectual curiosity, in untangling Ernst Kurth's thorny German (which, to paraphrase Milton Babbitt, should cost a hundred dollars a paragraph to translate).

Jon K. Barlow, my first mentor in world music, laid the foundations for this project long before the formal research started. Our ongoing dialogue over the past fifteen years has moved me again and again from not knowing what it is that I do not know to knowing what it is that I do not know. He pointed me to the gestural performance of melody, the neumatics of physiology, the physics of playing piano, and the phenomenology of baseball — all of which, in different ways, led me to work on gesture. His *mudra* is evident throughout this book.

The many trips to India that formed the basis of this book would not have been possible without the generous financial and institutional support of the Fulbright Program, the American Institute for Indian Studies, the Qayum Family Foundation, the UC Berkeley Center for South Asian Studies, and the UC Berkeley Department of Music. A Berkeley Graduate Fellowship, a Mellon Post-Doctoral Fellowship, and an early research leave from UMN supported me during periods of intense writing, study, and travel.

Jenna Dawn Rice has supported this work in ways no one else could, and surely in ways that I myself don't even realize. She has stood by me in the field and at the computer; she has smoothed out my unruly sentences and made the beds for visiting musicians. Her contagious warmth, curiosity, and laughter have made writing a delight. *Shukran kteer, habibti.*

A final thanks — in advance — goes to the scholars who will do *upaj* on this book, sprouting new and better work from its ambiguities and contradictions. Despite all the help I have received, I alone am responsible for the mistakes in this work. May they be productive mistakes.

Credits

Figure 6.1 and Figure A.1, "Planes of the Body," include illustrations by Douglas Leonard. Figures 2.4, 2.7, and 5.7 include illustrations by Juana Berrio.

Some material in this book has been excerpted by permission of the publishers from my "Gesture and Melody in Indian Vocal Music," *Gesture* 8, no. 3 (2008): 325–347; "Music" in the *Encyclopedia of Hinduism* (Leiden: Brill, 2010), 2:574-584; and "Imagery, Melody, and Gesture in Cross-Cultural Perspective" (with Martin Clayton, Gina Fatone, and Laura Leante), in *New Perspectives on Music and Gesture*, ed. Anthony Gritten and Elaine King (Farnham, UK: Ashgate, 2011).

A Note on Transcription

꥓

The notation system used throughout the book is designed to be easily readable by both Hindustani and Western musicians and also accessible to readers with no musical training. It is based on the Hindustani *sargam* system, akin to *movable-do solfège* (in which C, D, or any note may be considered *do*). Sargam names seven scale degrees: *shadaj (sa)*, *rishabh (re)*, *gandhar (ga)*, *madhyam (ma)*, *pancham (pa)*, *dhaivat (dha)*, and *nishad (ni)*. Note that these are scale degrees, not absolute pitch values: shadaj is taken to be any note convenient for the instruments and voices at hand and is reinforced by a continuous drone. The remaining scale degrees are measured relative to shadaj. The system of names repeats at the octave, so that *ni* ascends to *sa* (see figure N.1). In general, *sa* serves as both a point of melodic return and the note emphasized by the drone of the tanpura. *Sa* and *pa* (the tonic and fifth, respectively) are never raised or lowered, but *re*, *ga*, *dha*, and *ni* have lowered (*komal*) versions. Only madhyam (the fourth scale degree) ordinarily is raised (*tivra*); it is ordinarily not lowered.

Most of the transcriptions in this book plot this sargam system onto a staff: a set of horizontal lines corresponding to *sa*, *re*, *ga*, and so on. This combination of sargam and staff notation makes pitch contour visible (very important when correlating gestural shape and melodic shape) while maintaining the primacy of *sa* in the sargam system. As it avoids the complexities of key signature and absolute pitch, it will also, I hope, be easy for readers who are familiar with sargam (but not with traditional five-line staff notation or rhythmic notation) to read. Figure N.2 shows the concordance between sargam notation, five-line staff notation, and the sargam staff.

Traditional flat (♭) and sharp (♯) signs indicate lowered and raised notes, without the intended implication of any uniform system of intonation — tuning varies widely in practice (see Jairazbhoy and Stone 1963; Mark Levy 1982). When the raga at hand has consistent komal or tivra notes, these are indicated on the left side of the staff next to the names of the notes they modify, like a key signature. Thus "M♯" indicates that all instances of the

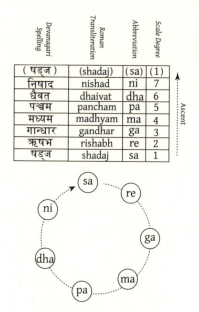

Devanagari Spelling	Roman Transliteration	Abbreviation	Scale Degree
(षड्ज)	(shadaj)	(sa)	(1)
निषाद	nishad	ni	7
धैवत	dhaivat	dha	6
पञ्चम	pancham	pa	5
मध्यम	madhyam	ma	4
गान्धार	gandhar	ga	3
ऋषभ	rishabh	re	2
षड्ज	shadaj	sa	1

Ascent

Figure N.1. Sargam scale.

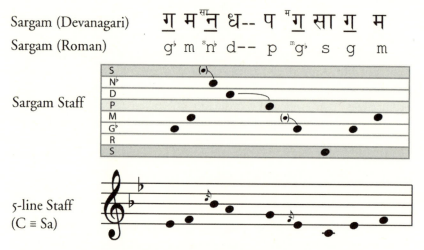

Figure N.2. Concordance between sargam notation
(in both Devanagari and Roman scripts), five-line staff, and sargam staff, shown
notating the same sample melodic phrase.

note madhyam will be raised unless marked otherwise; "N♭" indicates that all instances of nishad will be lowered unless marked otherwise. Other raisings or lowerings refer only to the particular instance of a note. Only the spaces on this sargam staff are used, not the lines, in order to ease reading for those familiar with sargam but not with staff notation. Much of the vocal action analyzed in this book consists of melismata on continuous vowels, thus there is usually some continuity between pitches. Extended glides between notes and other particularly salient intertonal action are approximated by curved lines extending from the notehead; horizontal lines indicate extended notes. Slurs and other phrase markings are indicated by curved lines above or below noteheads. Lightly touched notes are indicated in parentheses. When the full staff is shown, the space corresponding to *sa* is darkened for ease of reading, and where appropriate, the space corresponding to *pa* is as well.

A Note on Languages
and Terminology

∾

Many of the technical terms in this book are borrowed from the Hindi-Urdu lexicon of Hindustani music. Hindi and Urdu are mutually intelligible to such an extent that they can be considered a single language, and their grammatical flexibility has allowed an easy flow of loan words from Sanskrit, Arabic, Persian, Portuguese, and English. Thus musical terms are spelled variously in various scripts (Devanagari, Roman, Bengali, Tamil, Persian, etc.) and in many cases are even pronounced differently. My aim has been to smoothly integrate these terms into English prose alongside Indic words such as *jungle* and *guru*, just as once-foreign words such as *chai* and *sitar* have been smoothly adapted into Indic languages. Thus these words are italicized only when they first appear, or in extensive translation from Hindi-Urdu. The English plural suffix *-s* has likewise been used instead of Indic plural forms. For ease of reading, I have generally tried to avoid the prefixes *Ustad, Pandit,* and *Doctor* for musicians and scholars.

In the main text of this book, I have used nondiacritical Latin transliterations of Indic words that are widely known and, I hope, intuitive for both native speakers of Hindi-Urdu and readers with no background in Indic languages. In most cases, the context should leave little doubt about the word in question — for example, whether *kala* is *kalaa* (art) or *kaalaa* (black). The precise pronunciations of Indic terms and proper names, indicated with diacritics and their equivalents in Devanagari and Urdu scripts, can be found in the glossary, alongside technical terms from gesture studies and other fields.

Musicking Bodies

Introduction

❧

A singer reaches a crucial moment in her performance. As her voice spirals
upward, her index fingers swerve lazily through the air, tracing gentle but
purposeful ascending curves. Her gaze is tilted slightly upward, searching the
space between her hands. She finds what she is looking for: a note. She grabs it.
Her eyes close and she tilts her head to the left. She holds the note between her
thumb and index finger for what seems like a full minute, then suddenly tosses
it aside with a twist of her wrist as her voice drifts back down.

What does gesture have to do with music?

This question came from an All-India radio executive, over tea and bis-
cuits. She was trying to persuade me to stop thinking about how bodies
move and focus on the real stuff of music: sound. She placed her teacup
aside and spread her arms wide, palms facing up. "It's as though you have a
grand feast set in front of you," she said, then picked up a tiny virtual object
from the virtual table and squinted at it. "And you insist on studying the
silverware!"

Her analogy seems quite apt. Isn't sound the main dish of music? Isn't
gesture just a shiny distraction? The answer, as this book aims to demonstrate, is no: just as the gestures of the radio executive were an integral part
of her utterance, the intricate shapes traced by singers' hands are an integral
part of melodic rendering. But in an age in which sound recordings have
become the dominant means of engaging with music, both in India and
elsewhere, it is easy to confuse music with sound. While the pan-Indian
term *sangeet* once indicated the coordinated art of dancing, singing, and
playing instruments, it has now, like the term *music*,[1] come to refer strictly
to the sonic traces of these actions.

What do we miss if we reduce music to sound? People, for one thing.
And when people make music, they move: a finger slides along the neck of
a violin, a palm whacks a drumhead, a laryngeal cartilage tilts back and forth

I

as air is pushed through the vocal folds. But musical action also includes inaudible motion. Flamenco singers heighten the rhetorical impact of their performance with dramatic movements of the hands, arms, and eyes. Singers of Beijing Opera assume stylized gestural dispositions according to specific role types. And systems of hand gesture have long been part of Coptic, Jewish, Byzantine, and other liturgical chant practices.

This book is about the intertwining of vocal and bodily action in North Indian (hereafter, *Hindustani*) music. Various traditions of Hindustani voice production call for specific postures of the head and neck, disciplines of the tongue and jaw, and intricate systems of visualizing sound placement. More conspicuous is the elaborate gestural motion produced alongside vocalization, which ranges from subtle flicks of the wrist, to dramatic movements of the whole upper body, to the manipulation of virtual materials, to moments of concentrated stillness. Vocal forms such as *dhrupad*, *khyal*, and *thumri* in the North (and *ragam-tanam-pallavi* in the South) feature disciplines of improvisation[2] that give rise to ever-novel melodic utterances. This improvisation includes tightly coordinated gestural and vocal action. Although the hand and the voice work together to articulate melody, this gesture does not amount to a systematic code for vocalization. Unlike the elaborate systems of postures and handshapes mastered by Indian dancers, movement in Hindustani music is not explicitly taught, deliberately rehearsed, or linked to specific meanings. Melodic gesture embodies a special kind of musical knowledge, transmitted silently from body to body alongside the voice: a knowledge of melody as motion.

The term *musicking body*,[3] as I use it in this book, refers to just such a trained body in action, engaged mindfully in singing and/or playing an instrument. The special quality of a body in music is easiest to see when it comes alive at the beginning of a performance. When a singer begins to sing — confidently adopting a familiar posture, forming her jaw and tongue into resonant shapes, tracing melody in the air with her hands — it is as though (to paraphrase vocalist Sameer Dublay) some entirely different person has replaced the person who was there a moment before. The activity of this body is not reducible to muscle and bone; it is the product of years of discipline and practice. The musicking body may seem to disappear while chatting on a train or riding a bike, but it springs to life again in concerts, in practice, and in lessons.

I started attending to how singers move when I began studying Hindustani vocal music with Vikas Kashalkar in Pune in 2000. I noticed that when Kashalkar was singing, his way of moving took on a rather different quality from his way of moving while walking, speaking, or riding a bus. From our earliest lessons, he moved his hands extensively to indicate the shape, structure, and texture of improvised melodic passages. I found that I could make better sense of these passages if I imitated not only what he sang but also how he moved. Often I would struggle to piece notes together into melodic phrases while sitting still with my eyes closed in concentration, but when I opened my eyes and moved my hands as I sang, melody sprang to life in the space before me. As I attended more and more concerts, I was surprised to find that my teacher was not alone in moving while singing. Indeed, every Hindustani vocalist does. Over time, it became clear to me that gesture and voice work together to embody melodic ideas.

Scholars of human interaction have long been fascinated by the ways in which the hands operate alongside the speaking voice. The movement that accompanies improvised singing has much in common with the movement that accompanies improvised speech. Speech-affiliated gesture acts as a stream of dynamic, imagistic discourse, complementing, but rarely duplicating, the information carried by the voice (McNeill 2005: 33). Gesture analysts have observed this complementarity in a wide range of social situations and linguistic groups, as when a person opens up an empty space to indicate lack (McNeill 1992: 154), a person with a complex question holds it like an object (ibid.: 149), a person specifying a precise topic among several possibilities grips it between her fingertips (Kendon 2004: 236), or a person refusing a suggestion pushes a virtual object away from in front of her (Calbris 1990: 154). My account of the radio executive's gestures at the beginning of this chapter (in which the broad, generous strokes depicting the "grand feast" of musical sound contrast vividly with the nitpicking grip on the "silverware" of bodily motion) is in this tradition of gesture analysis. Similarly, I have come to see the gestures of singers as a stream of melody parallel to the voice. This disciplined motion is neither random flapping about nor a coded restatement of what is being sung. Gesture complements vocal action without duplicating it, revealing knowledge about the shape, texture, and motion of melody.

Furthermore, the musical knowledge embodied in this physical action is transmitted from body to body through teaching lineages. I first became aware of this several months after my studies with Kashalkar began, when a young musician surprised me by guessing who my teacher was from the way I moved while singing. Although my teacher had been passing on his methods of rendering raga music, he had never mentioned gesture. I had imagined that the knowledge he was imparting was invisible; I certainly was not aware of how I looked when I sang. These disciplines of sculpting novel melodic forms consist of more than neural and laryngeal processes hidden within the throat and skull. They are also ways of moving in space, understood and manifest through the musicking body.

The Scope of the Book

This book focuses on the performance of *khyal*, the best-known genre of North Indian raga-based vocal music. (For a thorough overview of the genre, and its cultivation in Indian courts and cities in the eighteenth through twentieth centuries, see Wade 1985; Bagchee 1998; and Brown 2010.) In cities throughout North India, and particularly in the rich music scenes found in Bombay, Calcutta, Delhi, Lahore, and Pune, the vast majority of Hindustani vocal concerts are centered around khyal performance. The rigorous training required for singing khyal emphasizes large-scale, imaginative melodic and rhythmic elaboration of song material. Although the compositions that serve as the seeds for this improvisatory elaboration are quite short (usually consisting of four-to-eight-line poems set to simple tunes), the unfoldment of a composition in performance often extends to thirty or more minutes of novel material. The phonetic vehicles for vocal improvisation in khyal largely consist of nonlexical vocables ("aa," "re," "eh," etc.) and short phrases drawn from the composition at hand. Significantly for studies of gesture in khyal, extensive melodic gesture is more often found in sections of improvisation than in sections of pre-fixed melodic material. Spontaneous melodic action in khyal, as in extemporaneous speech, takes place within conventional structures even as it requires the creation of novel material in the moment of performance. It unfolds within melodic and metrical frameworks (*raga* and *tala*, respectively), which are discussed extensively in chapters 3 and 4. Talas are metrical cycles that provide a measured, periodic place of return for melodic elaboration. Ragas are distinctive modal spaces for melodic action. While allowing for infinite possibilities for elaboration, a raga features a set of prominent melodic motives, a hierarchy of important pitches, and, most importantly, characteristic ways of moving among them.

For readers unfamiliar with khyal, figure I.1 offers a rough outline of the form of a typical performance. The structure of khyal performances, however, vary widely, and techniques of raga development are linked closely to musical lineages, individual style, and the particular setting. There are many fine recordings of khyal performances available online at sarangi.info, musicindiaonline.com, and parrikar.org.

Khyal is a soloist-dominated musical genre.[4] The melodic soloist controls virtually all of the structural aspects of performance; the tabla accompanist follows the singer's lead, and the melodic accompanist (on sarangi, harmonium, or violin) quickly recognizes and follows after the soloist's improvised melodies. For the purposes of this book, interaction between musicians in the course of performance has been deliberately backgrounded

Alap		1-5 min	The singer sketches the melodic contours of the raga at hand, free of rhythmic accompaniment or metrical reference. Non-lexical vocables such as "aa," "ee," "ri," etc. are used as vehicles for melody.
Vilambit Khyal	*Vilambit Bandish* (Slow Composition)	1-2 min	A slow-tempo *bandish* (composition) is sung once or twice. The tabla (drum) marks the metric cycles of tala.
	Improvised Elaboration	15-30 min	Once the bandish has been presented in its entirety, the singer spontaneously elaborates on its melodic and textual materials, within the bounds of raga and tala. Every 15-30 seconds--at the end of each metric cycle--the singer returns to the first phrase of the bandish to meet the first count of the metric cycle. The texture gradually gets rhythmically denser, more emotionally intense, and higher in pitch. Fragments of the bandish text as well as vocables are used as vehicles for improvised melody.
Drut Khyal	*Drut Bandish* (Fast Composition)	1-2 min	A second, faster bandish in the same raga is presented.
	Improvised Elaboration	3-10 min	Similar to the elaboration of vilambit khyal (above.) Emphasis on rhythmic play and fast, virtuosic note runs.

Figure 1.1. Outline of typical khyal form.

to focus attention on the extensive improvisation of the solo performer. This is not to say, however, that solo performance is a radically individual act in which a singer is cut off from the social world. Surely, the social setting of a public performance, the presence of connoisseurs, the chemistry between singers and accompanists, and the discourses that embed all of this in a system of meaning matter greatly. But even in solitary practice, the musicking body of a singer is always already social: it bears the imprint of its training.

The singers I discuss in this book have all been trained extensively in Hindustani music. They come from a wide range of backgrounds — hereditary and nonhereditary, Muslim and Hindu, singing dhrupad and khyal, from various musical lineages, who belong to regions stretching from southeast Maharashtra to Pakistani Panjab. I have, however, focused most of my research on a dozen or so singers centered in Maharashtra (shown in Appendix B) who are students and grandstudents of two important teachers: Gajanan Rao Joshi (1911–1987) and Jitendra Abhisheki (1929–1998). The majority of these singers are Maharashtrian Brahmins, and many of them live in the city of Pune, a hub for classical music located a hundred miles southeast of Bombay on the Deccan plateau. This was done partially out of convenience, as I have for the last decade spent a significant part of my time in Pune studying music from Gajanan Rao Joshi's student Vikas Kashalkar.

But it also comes out of a fascination with how these two influential teachers (who figure in the musical heritage of many young khyal vocalists) served as melting pots of musical knowledge from diverse lineages. Both Joshi and Abhisheki sought out training from several teachers, and each developed a distinctive style from his eclectic training. Moreover, the stylistic differences between the two singers defy conventional categorization by *gharana* (musical school). Although each nominally received training from singers from the same three gharanas (Jaipur, Gwalior, and Agra), their vocal and gestural styles are so different as to seem diametrically opposed along many dimensions. In this way, the two lineages, though closely related, have served as an ideal field to investigate very different ways of embodying music. Of course, no matter how eclectic these singers are, the broad, diverse worlds of Indian music could not possibly be exhausted by the specific, situated claims I make about musical gesture and the several dozen examples given in this small work. Carnatic vocal music offers one broad unexplored field of improvised vocal-gestural performance; vocal lineages in Bengal, Benares, and Panjab (both in India and Pakistan) also deserve further exploration.

In addition to this focus on a particular group of singers, this book focuses on a particular kind of gesture. This is not a study of bodily movement as such, but a study of spontaneous gestural action that is coperformed with spontaneous vocal action: tracing curves in space, stretching virtual materials, sculpting virtual objects. There is also, of course, physical movement in the course of performance that is not directly affiliated with melodic action. Singers, as one might expect, occasionally adjust their sitting position, drink water, and carry out other physical actions that are unrelated to sound production in the course of performance. Also, during parts of the performance in which precomposed material is being sung, many singers fall back on conventional gestures in which an open hand reaches out toward the audience. This kind of gesture is found in support of vocal performance in many Indian genres, such as didactic *bhajans*, sentimental *fados*, and heroic *maands*. (Indeed, it is common to singers from many traditions beyond India as well.) In genres of music that focus on song texts rather than improvised melody — and particularly in performances in which the words of a song may be sonically or linguistically obscure to the audience — singers may mime the words of a song as they sing. For example, while singing of a distant beloved, a singer may point far off with an open palm; while singing the word *one*, a singer may hold up a single finger. Highly stylized gesture of this kind is akin to the redundant gestures produced between speakers of two different languages trying to communicate, as it tends to reproduce the meaning of the words very closely. In this sense, these conventional gestures differ markedly from the

special, spontaneous gestures that arise when singers of raga music improvise, and I therefore discuss them very little in this book. Although sitarists
and other instrumentalists also perform characteristic gestural patterns in
the articulation of melody (Tzanetakis et al. 2007), these gestures typically
are more directly implicated in the physical production of sound (i.e., the
stretching of a string across a fret) than are the gestures of vocalists. I also
deal very little with the specialized, conventional gestural signs that allow
Hindustani musicians to communicate with each other. These signs mark
the progression of metrical cycles, guide accompanists, and indicate tempo.
For example, a singer who wants to rein in a tabla player who is playing
too fast might make a repeated pulling gesture in the air. As Clayton (2007)
has shown, performers communicate with each other and with audience
members via gesture. Audience members — particularly in intimate musical
gatherings — gesture in conventional ways to encourage the performers,
and musicians often pause for a moment while performing to greet well-
known connoisseurs as they arrive.

The study of individual singers, paradoxically enough, has led to a broader
view of the inherent sociality of the musicking body. The apparent tension
between autonomy and sociality highlights a key question in gesture studies: to what extent are gestures produced for the benefit of the speaker (i.e.,
as a part of cognition) and to what extent are they produced for the listener
(i.e., as part of communication)? To insist that the answer is one or the
other is to suppose a clear split between individual cognition and the social
world of communication, imitation, and mutual influence, but as David
McNeill points out, gesture bridges the two (2005: 151–163). The idea that
melodic gesture would be produced strictly for the sake of a listener is hard
to maintain in light of the fact that singers move while practicing alone in
very much the same way as they do in a concert (just as people produce
gestures while talking on the phone). As singer Shaunak Abhisheki once
told me, "When you become one with the music you naturally move, even
when you're by yourself." On the other hand, to "become one with the
music" requires a great deal of training. Thus, even a singer practicing alone
in a room bears the impression of many other singers, through both formal
and informal training. Therefore, we also cannot maintain the idea that
gesture is completely idiosyncratic. Dard Neuman's work on music transmission among hereditary professionals shows that the spontaneous knowledge and explorations of raga space "are not epiphanies; they do not emerge
as ideas or mental images that just happen, as if by divine inspiration. They
are rather nurtured through and created by the body instruments, instruments trained to be several steps ahead of the comprehending mind" (Dard
Neuman 2004: 165). As Marcel Mauss (1973 [1934]) and Pierre Bourdieu

(1977) remind us, even the habits of a bounded, individual body (such as posture, gait, and silverware technique) require training and indicate much about the positioning of a body in a social matrix. Gestural and vocal motion likewise are highly disciplined, refined techniques of the musicking body that are nurtured through years of sitting in front of a teacher and extended daily practice. I thus treat lessons and practice sessions — no less than formal concerts — as performances in which the whole body works to articulate melody.

Thinking about the Musicking Body

To take the role of the body in music seriously, we need a path through the disciplinary thicket that divides the voice from the body. Ordinarily, the voice is recorded either as a sequence of words (if speaking) or as a sequence of notes (if singing). The body, on the other hand, is ordinarily approached rather differently: as an organic assemblage of tissues, as a nexus of signification, as a site of subject formation, and so on. Thus we are ordinarily left with two entities that seem not just separate, but incommensurable. In the moment of performance, though, the voice and the body are united in melodic action. I attempt to highlight this consubstantiality of voice and body by transcribing bodily action, no less than vocal action, as music, and by bringing phenomenology, physiology, and ethics to bear on the whole singing body. In doing so, I have drawn inspiration from the many scholars that worked to describe the body in performance. A survey of the literature on bodily practices (like a survey of an elephant in the dark) reveals not a single, unified body, but a multitude. One encounters the "wrestler's body" (Alter 1992), the "recitational body" (Hirschkind 2006: 80), the "ballet body" (Wulff 2006), and the "body in a state of music" (Bowman and Powell 2007), just to name a few. This diverse array of body after body does not amount to a pile of cadavers. Instead, they are various dispositions of the self in various situations, various aspects of that living, complex bodily whole for which words are otherwise inadequate.

In this book, two "bodies" (i.e., aspects of a singer's body-mind in action) become particularly important: the *musicking body* (the body that comes alive in the moment of musical performance) and the *paramparic body* (the disciplined disposition of a particular singer's musicking body, developed over many years of training and practice). Neither, I argue, reduces to what I call the *flesh-body* (the aspect of the body as an object known to biology: muscles, bones, voltages across membranes, etc.).[5] While I am singing, for example, you could measure aspects of my flesh-body (taking my blood pressure, tracking the position of my tongue, measuring my neural activity), observe the patterns of my musicking body (noticing, as my teacher did on one particular morning, an easy grace in my lower vocal register, but an evident introversion, and a reluctance to open my voice), and/or analyze my paramparic body (noting ways in which I seem to have inherited gestural-vocal techniques from my various teachers). The first would yield figures, the second would engage with action, and the third would envision a variegated but more or less static disposition. This would mean not that there are three singers on stage, but rather that there are three rather different ways of making sense of a singer. If I were to break a rib, I would go to a medical doctor for an examination of my flesh body; for musical disorders, I trust my teacher to diagnose the bad habits of my musicking body; in time, with training, I have come to recognize the imprint of my teacher's teacher on my teacher, and the imprint of my teacher on myself — that is, I recognize the transmission of paramparic bodies.

Because we encounter a singer through so many ways of looking, it is easy to understand why an observer might think that the voice and the body were utterly separate. From the point of view of an audience member, vocalization and gesture seem to be detachable into separate streams of sensation. One can cover the eyes and still hear the voice; one can block the ears and still see the body moving. The former seems airy, insubstantial, filling the hall; the latter seems to be made of flesh and bone. The voice, like the mind, is hidden from view, and may seem to be purely subjective; gesture, like the flesh, is plain to see, and may seem to be purely objective. But whether a musical action is hidden inside the sheath of skin that enfolds the body (like stretching the vocal cords) or is perfectly visible (like sweeping the arm upward), further reflection shows that no musical action is, in itself, either radically objective or subjective. Raising vocal pitch, for example, occurs inside the throat and is ordinarily invisible; on the other hand, it could be studied as an object in the world (say, by measuring the contraction of the cricothyroid muscle) or in relation to the lived experience of a particular subject (say, the person singing). As Ken Wilber (1995) points out, ordinarily invisible actions (such as silently discerning the notes in a melody) have observable "exterior" neural correlates, even if these correlates are evident only on an MRI; ordinarily visible actions (such as gripping a note) are also lived as "interior" experience by a musician, even if they are plain to see. For this reason, the *musicking body* at issue in this book could just as easily be called the *musicking body-mind*.

We do not, after all, go to a concert to take objective readings from a knot of humanoid flesh, or to experience a series of subjective visual and aural sensations. We go to see a *singer* perform: to see a body and voice like ours whose music moves us. Engaging with this performance is not simply a matter of sitting back and letting our sensory neurons register light and sound. We strain with it as it reaches for high notes, feel elation as it effortlessly soars through rapid melodic runs, focus where it focuses, are moved by its motion. This is a special, sympathetic way of knowing, largely reserved for other humans. (We do not feel for the crash of a breaking window as we do for a child's cry of pain; we do not feel for the broken shards as we do for the child's broken arm.) This special sympathy between bodies is part of what makes performance so powerful.

When we are thus engaged in singing, either as listener, performer, teacher, or student, vocalization and gesture are a single process. The unity of this action was once forcefully demonstrated to me by Shaunak Abhisheki. I had been struggling to sing a phrase properly, note by note, when he interrupted me, telling me to yell, "What's the matter with you?" angrily at him. As I did, I extended my open palm forcefully from my body; he pointed at my open hand, smiled, and said, "*That's* music." Of course it is possible to thrash about randomly while singing; the hand is not determined by the voice in the way that the position of a marble on a track is determined by gravity and friction. But to do so is like patting your head and rubbing your belly at the same time: doing two different things at once. Tracing a gentle, meandering ascent with both the voice and the hands, by contrast, is a single, unified action. Only with difficulty can this action be analyzed into its constituent parts. As my fellow vocal student Mukul Kulkarni put it:

> You can't sing like this [*sitting stiffly*], like a pillar. When you start singing, you start moving your hands . . . because it is natural, you can't do anything against it . . . because [*sings without moving*] is not good. You are not free to sing. Hand movement makes you free.

In this light, it does not work to see the body as a constraint holding us back from a prior, unqualified world of musical freedom. As Suzanne Cusick puts it, music "does not exist until bodies make it" (1994: 10–11). Far from being constraints, the physical disciplines of music are vehicles without which music would not happen at all.

What is this musicking body? The words may seem to evoke something fleshy, heavy, and solid — perhaps in contrast to a chalkboard covered with music notation. But if the musicking body has to do with muscle and bone, it has equally to do with the immaterial curves it traces in the air, dynamic melodic action every bit as abstract and massless as a series of notes on a page. The body that musicks is neither a heavy cadaver waiting to be dissected, nor a frozen token waiting to be positioned within grids of race, gender, and other axes of signification (Massumi 2002: 2). In contrast to a word or a hunk of flesh, the musicking body thinks, feels, and — most importantly — moves.

Every body, furthermore, moves differently. Each musicking body has unique patterns and habits which cohere in teaching lineages like family resemblances. These patterns and habits are often described in terms that are not only aesthetic but also ethical. The dominant body of psychological research on the implicit transmission of behavior tends to focus on the unconscious imitation of aggression (Bandura et al. 1961) rather than the cultivation of, say, humility or chastity. Building on critical histories of music and dance reform in the twentieth century (Quinn 1982; Subramanian 2006; Soneji 2012) and various approaches to embodied ethical affect (Mauss 1973 [1934]; Bourdieu 1977; Wolf 2000; Hirschkind 2006), I have worked to show how these dispositions are imprinted with various aesthetic and ethical values.

The last three decades have seen a gradual acceleration of ethnographic work on bodily practices, inaugurated by John Blacking's (1977) call for an "anthropology of the body" that would link biology to social life and Thomas Csordas's (1990) call for a paradigmatic focus on "embodiment" that would help to resolve subject-object dualities. Dance ethnographers bring a great deal of expertise to bear on the social life of the performing body, as for example in Roderyk Lange's work on the articulation of social structures through various ways of dancing Polonaise (1977), in Helena Wulff's study of the "Irish dancing body" (2006), and in Tomie Hahn's work on the bodily transmission of Japanese dance from teacher to student (2007). Music scholars have taken a variety of approaches to physicality in music performance. Three recent collected volumes (Godøy and Leman 2010; Gritten and King 2006, 2011) survey approaches to musical gesture ranging from the ancillary gestures of clarinetists to the motion of the hands in *guqin* performance. Some have focused on the bodily technologies of music making, as in Mark DeWitt's account of the connection between accordion fingering and melodic idiom (2003), John Baily's comparison of the ergonomics of Afghani *rubab* and *dutar* technique (2006), and Elizabeth Le Guin's "carnal" reading of Luigi Boccherini's cello music (2006). Others have studied systems of gestural repertoire, such as the specialized handshapes used in the transmission of Samavedic chant (Howard 1982) and the persistent gestural codes of nineteenth-century melodrama (Smart 2005; Randall 2009).

Several other scholars have already published valuable work about the bodily action of Indian musicians, drawing on a wide range of disciplines. Nikki Moran (2007, 2011) has studied communicative movement in raga performance, such as the implicit coordination of tempo between sitarists and tabla players. Martin Clayton (2007) has written about entrainment and the gestural mediation of attention and temporal awareness, with a special focus on khyal performance. Laura Leante (2009) has developed a method of examining the anaphonic connections between sound and movement in Hindustani music. The current work draws quite explicitly on all of this scholarship.

Another body of scholarship has used the methods of phenomenology to address the musical life of the body. Ruth Stone's pioneering work on temporal awareness in Kpelle performance events (1982), Jeff Todd Titon's account of musical being-in-the-world in an old-time string band (2008: 31), Dard Neuman's account of practice rituals in Hindustani music (2004), Gina Fatone's analysis of meta-gesture in Scottish piping (2010), and Harris Berger's close studies of embodied musical experience in various Ohio music scenes (1999, 2010; Berger and Del Negro 2004), among others, have paved a path for the rigorous study of musical experience. This book shares a philosophical lineage with these works, drawing special inspiration from the phenomenological tradition of Edmund Husserl (1964 [1928]), Maurice Merleau-Ponty (2002 [1945]), Alfred Schutz (1976), and Don Ihde (2007).

A related music-theoretic tradition has studied the enactment of kinetic forms in music as gesture (Zuckerkandl 1969; and Mersmann 1922/23, Becking 1958 [1928], etc., cited in Schneider 2010). The classic work in this field is Ernst Kurth's evocative theoretical account of musical motion as the buildup and release of energetic potentials (1922). Robert Hatten has recently developed Kurth's esoteric theory into methods of musical analysis that take the gesture ("significant energetic shaping through time") as a fundamental unit of analysis (2004). This literature has developed a way of understanding melody as energetic motion, rather than principally as sound or as discrete notes. It thus helps to open an interpretive space in which vocalization and physical motion work together in the performance of melody.

Many of the above works are part of a larger movement across disciplines, from literary criticism to computer engineering, that aim to shift scholarly attention away from the processing of abstract systems of symbols and toward the life of the body in the world. Although this work has been profoundly influential on my own, *Musicking Bodies* is not intended as a radical alternative to conventional music analysis. As I explain in chapters 2 and 3, analytical techniques that focus on note sequences are an indispensable, time-honored part of Indian music practice. Nor is this project founded on a preference for either the physical or the metaphysical, or a conviction that one reduces to the other. Although very few Hindustani musicians are also authoritative spiritual masters, many draw on discourses of contemplation and devotion to describe the processes of musicking (see Slawek

1996). Studies that have addressed the bodily techniques of yoga (Sarukkai 2002; Alter 2004), sufism (Qureshi 2006; Schimmel 1994; Shannon 2006), and vedanta (Chaudhary 1959; Sinha 1985) are especially useful in this connection.

The musicking body at issue here, then, is not to be understood as a material, visible replacement for an immaterial, invisible (and lately somewhat unfashionable) musicking mind. As Murphy Halliburton points out in his study of psychopathology in Kerala (2002), the very framing of the "mind-body problem" as a relation between precisely two terms implicitly excludes liminal faculties such as *atman* and *bodham*. Though both Indian and Western philosophers may sometimes invoke a dualistic mind-body heuristic, one is hard-pressed to think of any practical tradition in which any two divisions of self exhaustively account for the whole of human Being (Staal 1993.) For example, in cosmopolitan English-language discourse, consider the differences and overlap between "soul," "heart," "spirit," and "mind." In the register of Hindi-Urdu shared by Hindustani musicians, the point may be illustrated by comparing the faculties of *dimagh* and *man*, both of which apply to discussions of musical performance. Though each is commonly translated into English as "mind," they are rather different.[6] *Dimagh*, typically located in the head, is the faculty that analyzes, conflates, distinguishes, and reproduces for evaluation; *man*, by contrast, is typically located in the chest, receives and cultivates aesthetic impressions, imagines, and is the seat of more or less permanent affect, particularly enchantment and devotion. Likewise, singers' descriptions of the dynamics of *kundalini*, *naad*, and other liminal body-mind activity cannot be adequately addressed either as purely subjective mental noumena or as purely objective physiological phenomena. Even the most transcendent descriptions of mystical experience are shot through with descriptions of spinning, ascent, expansion, and other physical processes; even the most technical advice about vocal production is directed toward freedom, sincerity, and other metaphysical attributes. Musicking, perhaps more than any other familiar activity, defies the handy distinctions between subject and object, mind and body, matters of concern and matters of fact. Throughout, I have tried to find a way of describing the musicking body that harmonizes the evident physics of performance with the musical metaphysics that is so central to descriptions and experience of musical action, transmission, and power.

Overview

The chapters in this book split Hindustani vocal performance into a sequence of discrete parts, for the same reason that a student may split a melody into discrete notes: analytical convenience. But singing is always an integrated whole: melodic action (chapter 2) is undertaken by a musicking body (chapter 5) in spatial (chapter 3), temporal (chapter 4), and ethical contexts — both discursive (chapter 1) and paramparic (chapter 6).

Chapter 1 attempts to account for the current commonsense view of gesture as haphazard, sensual, and extramusical by tracing a history of gesture in Indian music. It surveys ancient and medieval music treatises, films, recent critical histories of gender and performance, and the vast music-theoretic and music-critical literature of the late nineteenth and twentieth centuries. Chapters 2 through 4 turn to analysis. Chapter 2 investigates the parallel performance of melodic motion as gesture and vocalization. Chapter 3 explores the most important context for melodic action in Hindustani music: *raga*. Ragas, I argue, serve not only as grammars for combining discrete pitches but also as spaces for melodic motion. Chapter 4 deals with the relationship of gesture to time: *tala* (metrical cycles), phrasing, and thematic development. This includes the relationships of kinesic hierarchies with hierarchies of phrasing, and the gestural articulation of musical themes as objects.

By chapter 5, the analytical separation of gesture and voice has been superseded by a unified view of a singer moving and singing in a stream of unified musical action. The chapter begins with a consideration of the ontology of this *musicking body*, including posture as well as gestural and vocal motion. The analytical examples focus on the interaction of singers with virtual objects in the course of performance. It addresses the melodic functions of holding, manipulating, and releasing objects, as well as the more perplexing question of what exactly is being grasped. Chapter 5 closes with a consideration of various stances that the musicking body may take in relation to the musical materials at hand.

Chapter 6 returns to the social world described in chapter 1 by exploring the formation of the musicking body. It begins from two complementary observations: (1) students tend to gesture recognizably like their teachers, and (2) the gestural repertoire of every vocalist is nonetheless unique. I will suggest some ways of understanding how gestural dispositions, and their attendant disciplines of melodic improvisation, may be transmitted through teaching lineages, producing lineage-based gesture dialects. The Sanskrit word *paramparik* indicates something that is passed on again and again through generations of teachers and students. *Paramparic bodies*,[7] then, are trained bodies from the point of view of their construction and education in musical lineages. The insights gleaned from studying the transmission of gestural-vocal disciplines from body to body provide a way of thinking about bodies that accounts for their social embeddedness as well as their autonomy. Musicians' bodies in the moment of performance, though recognizable and unique, are links to traditions of melodic knowledge and ethical affect that are muscular as much as cognitive — traditions that find new expression in each performance but are older than any living musician.

CHAPTER ONE

A History of Moving and
Singing in India

◡

A murmur of conversation rises from the audience between performances at
Shantiniketan, Rabindranath Tagore's university in West Bengal. A music teacher
and I are excitedly discussing the different styles of two classical singers that we
admire. We compare their styles of voice production, their divergent approaches
to raga development, their preferences for different tempi and metrical cycles.
Then I mention their differences in gestural dispositions. The flow of our
conversation is interrupted. She sits upright, furrows her brow, and says, "But
gesture is a *dosha* [fault], not a *guna* [virtue], isn't it?" As she drops technical
terms from authoritative Sanskrit music treatises into her vernacular mix of Hindi
and English, the tone of the conversation shifts abruptly. We interrupt our
discussion of singers, performances, and musical training in favor of a discussion
about authoritative texts, terms, and categories. It is only when the singer
interrupts our conversation with a compelling phrase in Rag Jhinjhoti that
we turn our attention back to the body on stage.

Somehow, it is in discussions of gesture — where the body and the voice
work together in the most obvious way — that music scholars insist most
emphatically that the body and the voice are, in fact, separate. The body
serves as a discursive pivot that modulates from matters of aesthetics
(beauty vs. ugliness, grace vs. awkwardness, elegance vs. excess) to matters
of ethics (chastity vs. promiscuity, sincerity vs. ostentation, spirituality vs.
sensuality). This can be explained in part by the moral burden borne by
singers. This burden, a residue of centuries of discourse in Sanskrit and
Persian, Hindi and English, continues to shape thought about the role of
the body in music. As we will see, music scholars of all kinds, writing in
Persian, Sanskrit, Tamil, and English, writing for courtly feudal and urban
bourgeois audiences, drawing on the jargon of yoga, sufism, theosophy,

16

and secular romanticism, have found remarkable agreement when it comes to the gestures of vocalists. The consensus is that gesture is bad: uncouth, antispiritual, or at best incidental to real music. The goal here is not to summarily debunk these claims as fanciful "projections onto an empty screen" (Latour 2004: 242) — indeed, the coming chapters will make the case that the movement of singers, in the moment of performance, is anything but empty. I am not urging music connoisseurs to take pleasure in gesture; nor am I urging singers to reject received wisdom and gesture *more*. Nothing here is evidence that gesture in itself is a sign of good manners, that movement is necessarily and inherently spiritual, or that the hand is more important than the voice. But for those who are interested in the role of the body in music, the processes of melodic improvisation, and the transmission of musical practices, there is much to learn from gesture, posture, and the physicality of vocal production that cannot be learned from sound alone.

Readers who are eager to get on with the analysis of gestural performance may wish to skip this chapter for now and move on to chapter 2, which addresses the relationship between vocalization and gesture. First, though, in order to understand why the melodic knowledge embodied in gesture has been largely ignored by music theorists and, eventually, to understand the ethical import of gestural inheritance in teaching lineages, it is helpful to look carefully at these streams of discourse — even where we cannot draw conclusions about the details of gestural practice.

Gesture in Ancient and Medieval Indian Music Literature

The earliest lengthy discussion of performance conventions in the extant Sanskrit literature is found in the dramaturgical manual *Natyasastra* (ca. 200 CE). Here movement is mostly treated in connection to drama and dance. In its discussion of drama, for example, the *Natyasastra* suggests three ways in which gestural dispositions can indicate a character's social standing. First, gestures made higher on the body indicate high rank; second, frequent gestures indicate low rank; third, while characters of high social rank move according to canonical rules, actors playing characters of low social rank merely emulate the spontaneous gestures of daily life (Bharatamuni 1998: 9:61–66, 191). Thus begins a long tradition of placing spontaneous gesture in opposition to prestige and nobility. The notion that gesturing according to prescribed rules is suitable for high-status performance helps to explain why conventional, systematized systems of gesture — such as the conventional patterns of claps and waves that mark metrical cycles, the intricately prescribed motions of classical dance, and the handshapes (*mudras*) that correspond to melodic formulas in Sama Veda recitation — have traditionally been considered morally neutral. These systems, unlike the spontaneous melodic motion of singers' gesture, prescribe fixed, prefigured hand movements. Indeed, it seems to be precisely this explicit systematicity that exempts these gestural systems from moral condemnation. Among the very few descriptions of bodily motion in connection to melodic action is the prescription that a good female singer should be capable of "maintaining disposition"; among the bad qualities of a singer are *sandasta*, or singing with teeth clenched (Bharatamuni 1998: 32: 450–454, 467).

The *Sangitaratnakara* (thirteenth c. CE), perhaps the most influential Indian music-theoretic treatise of all time, deals extensively with the bodily processes of singing. The author, Sarangadev, served as an ayurvedic physician at the Seuna court in Devgiri. Accordingly, the first substantive section of the book is a detailed description of human anatomy, from bones to chakras, running to 163 verses. This virtuosic survey of the body is capped by the following summary statement: "Such is the body, a heap of filth surrounded by all sorts of impurities of all sorts; and yet intelligent people utilize it as a means for worldly enjoyment and for salvation [*mukti*]" (Sarangadev 1991 [13th c.]: I.2.163c–164b). This by itself is a fairly conventional statement of a tantric view of the body (i.e., it is both inherently filthy and a potential vehicle for liberation) that would have been well known in Sarangadev's Kashmiri scholarly lineage. More surprising, however, is the following verse, in which he asserts that practicing and contemplating music is one way his readers might use the body to save themselves from the horrors of incarnation. After considering various means of salvation in turn, Sarangadev concludes that music is the best method for most people, as it is more immediately appealing than austere, purely contemplative practices (I.2.167–168b). Thus Sarangadev justifies the extensive discussion of music that follows on the grounds that it offers an easily accessible means of liberation from the flesh. In his decidedly unfleshy account of voice production, for example, the voice finds its origin in the atman, or individuated soul:

> Desirous of speech, the atman impels the mind, and the mind activates the *vahni* [vital fire] stationed in the body, which in turn stimulates the *prana* [vital breath]. The vital force stationed around the root of the navel, rising upward gradually manifests *naad* [vibration] in the navel, the heart, the throat, the cerebrum, and the cavity of the mouth as it passes through them. (I.3.3–4)

Unlike the *Natyasastra*, the *Sangitaratnakara* specifically mentions hand movements produced while singing. As the music described in the *Natyas-*

astra was largely through-composed, it is possible that the singing practices described therein featured little spontaneous gesture. By the time of the *Sangitaratnakara*, the prevailing melodic system seems to have featured melodic improvisation within ragas, and it seems that, as in modern practice, improvisatory singing was accompanied by improvisatory gesture. In any case, we can be reasonably certain that singers were moving while singing because Sarangadev criticizes them for doing so. Such movements appear in lists of *doshas* (faults): "involuntary shaking of the limbs" and "stretching the limbs." Other physical faults, such as displaying the bulging veins of the neck or face (III.3.25–38), are listed as well. Significantly, there are no corresponding descriptions of approved bodily movement on the list of musical virtues.

Subsequent Persian and Sanskrit music treatises used the *Sangitaratnakara* as a model. As in the *Sangitaratnakara*, the visible motion of the musicking body typically appears in later music treatises only in formulaic lists of bad qualities, alongside bad posture and harsh vocal timbre. For example, the list in Faqirullah's 1666 treatise *Rag Darpana* (Faqirullah 1996 [1666]: 157) includes "throwing right and left of the limbs and causing jerks to the voice when singing," stretching the neck "as a camel does," singing in such a way that veins protrude, and showing the teeth. Indeed, showing the teeth while singing seems to have been a feature that distinguished high-status musicians from low-status ones in North Indian courts. This was stated explicitly in Mirza Khan's encyclopedic 1675 *Tohfat al-Hind*, which specifically mentions that a well-mannered singer should not show the teeth while singing. Indeed, in court paintings of this period, *dhadhis* (low-status musicians) are often depicted with visible, misshapen teeth; the teeth of *kalavants* (high-status musicians), are typically concealed inside their mouth (Brown 2003: 160 n. 68). Mughal court paintings of singers often depict singers with a distinctive upturned hand, though no details of gestural patterns can be gleaned from these (Wade 1998: 195). In lists of singers' good qualities, gesture is typically not mentioned, except when prescribing its avoidance, as when the *Tohfat al-Hind* recommends that a singer should maintain a "calm demeanour when performing, and an open and cheerful countenance" (Brown 2003: 138). The preference for a "calm demeanour," as we shall see, is in tune with the bulk of discourse about gesture that prefers stillness to motion.

One later treatise, the *Ma'dan al-Musiqi* (1856) of Hakim Mohammad Karam Imam, goes into some detail in its description of gestural practice at the Awadh court of Wajid Ali Shah. Imam not only rehearses the standard lists of bad gestural habits (including using the hands to indicate melodies that the voice cannot reach), but also names specific contemporary singers who display these bad habits. He also breaks from tradition to mention some singers who move subtly and beautifully while they sing, such as "Babu Ram Sahai, whose eyes, eyebrows, and hands just quivered to highlight the nuances of his song." He includes a rare nondenigrative description of singers gesturing, asserting that

> it is very difficult to keep one's body straight and still when one sings. There should be slight movements of hands, eyes, and eyebrows to highlight the beauty of the song. Because such well-measured actions of the body, according to the bhava [affective] nuances bring added charm to the music. (Imam 1959 [1856]: 9–10)

Although Imam, like his predecessors, disapproves of spontaneous gesture, he also describes the potentially "charming" effect of "well-measured actions." The *Ma'dan al-Musiqi*, containing both formulaic restatements of tradition and a humanistic concern for the particularities of performers and performances, anticipates the rich archive of gesture discourse provided by the literature of music reform in the late nineteenth and twentieth centuries. There is likely a good deal more to learn about the history of musical gesture in the vast body of yet unedited early modern Sanskrit and Persian music literature (Pollock 2011). For now, all that is certain from the era between the *Sangitaratnakara* and the first films of singers is (1) that it was perfectly ordinary for singers to have moved their hands while singing and (2) that this motion was understood as faulty in the prevailing courtly and spiritual discourses.

Gesture, Gender, and Music Reform in the Nineteenth and Twentieth Centuries

Many recent histories of Indian music have focused on the institutional, music-theoretic, and educational consequences of Indian music reform in the late nineteenth and early twentieth centuries (Dan Neuman 1990; Bakhle 2005; Subramanian 2006, etc.). Recently some scholars of dance and music have extended this history to include changes in the presentation and reception of bodies on stage (Dard Neuman 2004; Weidman 2006; Krishnan 2008; Soneji 2012). Janaki Bakhle (2005), for example, reports two fascinating cases in which reformers seem to have insisted on reforming the conventional postures of singers — but in opposite ways. In Bengal in the 1850s, "popular singers were condemned for singing while standing" (273, n. 71); half a century later, Maharaja Sayajirao Gaekwad III of Baroda asked that his court musicians "break their habit of singing while seated." In this latter case, the musicians were specifically asked to "emulate the tradition of vocal performance in Western high art music" (33). Despite evident regional variation, the music reform movement transformed the conventions of bodily comportment on stage.

Although there are few documentary films of vocal performances from this period, some picture of the ethical power of these corporeal reforms can be gleaned from depictions of singers in fictional films. In *Tansen* (1943), *Baiju Bawra* (1952), *Basant Bahar* (1956), and many other early Indian films that feature classical music, singing gesture is depicted in film as a token of clownish, showy virtuosity in contrast to devotional (and usually Hindu)[1] piety (Booth 2005).

Sant Tukaram (1936), among the best-known and most influential of Indian films, develops the gesture-denigrative discourses found in medieval music treatises into embodied norms for modern politics, gender, and devotion. When *Sant Tukaram* was released in 1936, it ran for fifty-two straight weeks. Today it is shown again and again on Marathi TV and plays to full houses in movie theaters, even outside Maharashtra. It was also the first Indian film to win international acclaim, winning third place in the Venice International Film exhibition. Though the film is filled with Marathi devotional songs known throughout Maharashtra, its power and popularity far exceed its linguistic reach and literary content. Indeed, the near-unanimous critical praise of this film focuses almost exclusively on its powerful musical performances and visual language. The power of this musical and visual language derives from a play of various modes of embodiment — gestural and vocal dispositions that carry profound moral and political weight.

In the opening sequences of the film, gesture operates alongside elocution, dress, song style, and posture as a sign of the main opposition represented in the film: between the hierarchical, elite Brahminical religion and the populist, devotional spirituality of the Marathi singer-saint Tukaram. These extremes are enacted in the performance styles of Tukaram and the vain, hypocritical priest Salomalo (figure 1.1). Tukaram sits on the ground and hardly moves at all as he sings his simple, unadorned songs — transported, as it were, beyond his body. Salomalo, on the other hand, marches about and gestures wildly as he peppers his devotional songs with florid, distracting melodic runs. At one point he nearly smacks an audience member in the face with his flailing arms.

Later in the film, a courtesan in the service of Salomalo is converted to Tukaram's devotional path, and her piety is depicted dramatically through a transformation in her gestural disposition (figure 1.2). Salomalo sends Sundara, the courtesan, to tempt Tuka into abandoning his devotional life. She approaches Tukaram's house dressed in glittering ornaments, singing

Figure 1.1. Tukaram (left) and Salomalo (right) performing the same song with radically different gestural dispositions.

an erotic song about Radha's yearning for Krishna. Tukaram emerges, playing his *kartal* (wooden clappers) along with her, in a rhythm typical of the devotional genre *kirtan*. Oblivious to her flirtatious glances, he praises her voice for "carrying to the heavens." In contrast to Salomalo, who earlier in the film had listened to Sundara while chewing *paan*, praising her performance in conventional courtly verbal formulas, Tuka participates by musicking along with Sundara, as though they were performing kirtan together. Thus Tuka converts a courtly, worldly performance into a devotional occasion. But, crucially, Tukaram also converts Sundara. Although Tukaram's words serve as an important instrument of conversion (he advises her not to waste her beauty on temporary pleasure), the results are most immediately visible in her gestural disposition. She renounces her former ways and becomes Tukaram's disciple. She throws herself at his feet and immediately adopts a new manner of singing. After the conversion, she sits down on the ground and accompanies herself on kartal with her hands folded palm to palm, singing a devotional song, with her eyes closed,[2] and quite still. In short, she inhabits a new musicking body.

In 1936, at the height of the music reform movement in Maharashtra, this cinematic conversion signified more than the transformation of a fictional woman. It was perfectly in tune with a role transformation already under way for female singers. While the image of the converted female singer was projected on the movie screen, the image of the female singer off the screen was being converted as well. A female singing body was not to reach out to the audience with glances and gestures but was to remain self-contained, pious, detached, still. As a place was gradually prepared for respectable female classical singers on the public concert stage in the late nineteenth and early twentieth centuries, the image of the prototypical female singer grad-

Figure 1.2. Sundara, a courtesan from the film
Sant Tukaram, before (left) and after (right) conversion.

ually shifted from a courtesan who sang and danced in private rooms to a
respectable middle-class woman who sang in public but, crucially, sat on
the floor, quite still. Through most of the nineteenth century, professional
female performers in India both sang and danced (Quinn 1982). This dance
ranged from complex rhythmic footwork to subtle mimetic gestures performed while seated and singing. In many cases, these female performers
were courtesans (called *tawa'ifs* or *baijis*) or temple dancers ritually wedded
to a temple divinity (*devadasis*). The precise relationship between sexual
economies and musical performance varied widely across individuals and
regions (Srinivasan 2006: 162), but dancing while singing nonetheless carried the stigma of nonconjugal sexual practices. This stigma was a particular
focus of the so-called anti-*nautch* (i.e., anti–"dancing girl") campaign that
extended from the 1880s through the 1930s. This movement was spear-
headed by Methodists, theosophists, and social reformers — both British
and Indian — who sought to outlaw the institution of the *devadasi*. Although the moral force of this campaign derived from outrage about child
prostitution, rape, and the spread of venereal disease, its advocates tended
to construe any kind of salon-based dance as immoral (Coorlawala 1992:
130). Reformers developed systematic, classicalized dance traditions such as
Bharatanatyam that were detached from court and temple contexts and
made available to middle-class students (Soneji 2012). Though eighteenth-
and early-nineteenth-century dance scholars had attempted to document and
standardize dance practices (Krishnan 2008), modern Indian dance reformers were specifically concerned with dance as a vehicle for moral reform.

The visible break from courtesanry was apparent in many ways, from
posture to dress to song genre to performance setting, which increasingly
was centered on concert halls and *sabha*s rather than urban private residences

or courts. Reformed dancers, unlike *devadasis*, were not to sing, and they performed with a minimum of representational gesture (Weidman 2006: 131).[3] Likewise, reformed female singers (like Sundara) gestured very little, even going so far as to restrict their eye movements (Quinn 1982: 91–92). By the early decades of the twentieth century, opportunities for paid musical performance (though still quite rare) were increasingly on public stages in Bombay, Calcutta, and other cities, attracting performers who had theretofore made their living singing and/or dancing for small, private gatherings of men. To perform in these newly established public spaces, female singers had to reshape themselves for presentation before an urban middle-class audience: they had to distance themselves from any suggestion of courtesanry. Singers changed their concert attire from dress associated with dancing girls to dress more typical of urban middle-class women (Pradhan 2004: 343). On the Carnatic music stage, the new concert attire of female singers was characteristic of a well-dressed (but not opulently dressed) family woman — the very antithesis of a courtesan (Weidman 2006: 132). This necessity grew as public distaste for courtesanry became codified in law in the years following independence: first the ban of devadasi temple performances in 1947, followed by a 1956 amendment that banned performances by devadasis even at private events (Soneji 2012). In the north, All-India Radio forbade performances by any women "whose private life is a public scandal," and once the Suppression of Immoral Trafficking Act came into effect in 1958, police raided courtesans' salons, forcefully stopping even private performances (Qureshi 2006).

Song genres also changed. Female singers deemphasized *thumri, dadra, lavani*, and other song forms associated with dance and courtesanry in favor of more austere classical genres like *khyal*. One consequence of this was that song texts became less intelligible. Pradhan points out that the older courtesan-dominated song genres presented song texts clearly, making them well suited to mimetic gesture, whereas in *khyal*, the texts of songs are often obscured by elaborate melodic action (Pradhan 2004: 341–342). Also, while thumri performance often included moments in which the singer would intersperse the singing with elaborate dance steps (which survive today as *laggi* sections performed on tabla), the varied rhythms of *khyal* are ill suited for dance accompaniment. It is also likely that the rise of *khyal* (in which the focus is on extensive melodic improvisation rather than textual ornamentation) as the major vocal genre minimized text-referential gesture in favor of melodic gesture. But as there was no discursive distinction between these kinds of gesture at this time, there was likely pressure to diminish even this melodic gesture as a means of downplaying the role of the female body in performance. Later, female singers of khyal often accompanied themselves on tanpura, which not only required a sitting posture to balance the large instrument on the lap, but also kept one hand engaged while singing. Thus a combination of gestural disposition, the physical requirements of instrumental performance, song genre, and performance setting produced a dramatically different mode and manner of female vocal performance.

In the south, where singers visibly kept *tal* (marking metrical cycles with patterns of handclaps and waves) as they sang, critics and musicians alike encouraged women to sit still, as these gestures were considered inappropriate for women. As singer Vina Dhanammal famously put it, "Women should not be slapping their thighs like men" (Viswanathan and Allen 2004: 74). South Indian female singers were also encouraged to sing fixed pieces rather than improvising (Weidman 2006; Viswanathan and Allen 2004: 73). As melodic gesture seems to be most overt during improvisation, and practically disappears during through-composed sections, this would have implicitly reduced gesture among female singers. Anthropologist Amanda Weidman goes further to argue that gesture was explicitly suppressed among southern female singers:

> For female musicians in particular, a convention of music performance developed in which the body was effaced; too much physical movement or "show" on the stage was seen not only as extraneous to the music but as unseemly. . . . The ideal became a kind of performance of nonperformance: nothing visible was supposed to happen on the music stage. (2006: 131)

In all of these ways, the paradigmatic image of a female singer shifted dramatically from the middle of the nineteenth to the middle of the twentieth centuries.[4] The most gesturally significant change was that the new kind of female singer sat on the ground, relatively still, like a male singer in a classical vocal lineage.

To this day, classical dancers do not sing while dancing, and classical singers do not dance while singing.[5] Female singers, on the whole, gesture less dramatically, and in smaller gesture space, than male singers. Once a young female student of the austere (and usually male-gendered) vocal genre *dhrupad* commented bitterly to me about the dramatic gestures of a male dhrupad vocalist on stage — not because she herself found the gestures repugnant but because "gestures like that make people think that women can't sing dhrupad."

One striking picture of the subtle, ethereal song gestures expected of a properly reformed female singer appears in the film *Chashme Baddur* (1981), in which Neha, the female lead, is shown leaving a classical vocal lesson in a modest *salwar-kameez*. While standing at a bus stop, she continues practicing what she learned in the lesson. Though her voice is inaudible, her hands continue to trace curves in the air as she stands with her eyes closed, oblivious to bystanders giggling at her gestures. Significantly, though she is an object of bemusement here, she is decidedly not an object of sexual desire as a singer. Her gestures, restricted to a small space in front of her torso, are sufficiently abstract and restrained that she appears as a devotee of music, withdrawn from the world and absorbed in melody, rather than a courtesan figure reaching out seductively to others with her eyes, hands, and voice. It is only when her love interest pulls up on a motorcycle that she stops singing, opens her eyes, and flashes him a flirtatious smile. While most Hindi film songs sung by women are routinely full of flirtation, the bodily disposition of classical singing is here distinguished sharply from the bodily disposition of courtship.

On the other hand, many other song genres, discursively and spatially separated from the classical stage, do feature prominent gesture and dance. The folk song genre *biraha*, popular in Uttar Pradesh, often features women singers who make characteristically male gestures, such as slapping the thighs; indeed, some folk singers seem to embrace this challenge to gender norms (Marcus 2006). *Tamasha*, *mujra*, and other female performance genres often include both singing and mimetic gesture. Though forms such as these once enjoyed aristocratic patronage, they are now performed primarily for men as part of small-scale stage shows in which sexuality is foregrounded. Overtly physical performance genres such as these are occasionally brought to urban concert stages as folk curiosities, but none typically share the stage with classical music.[6]

The Separation of Voice and Body

The separation of voice and movement in classical performance was related to a more general discursive separation of the voice and the body. The late nineteenth century saw several scientific developments that enhanced the sense that the voice was independent of the body. One was the development of scientific phonology, which, in its early days,[7] studied the vocal mechanism of the larynx, pharynx, nose, and mouth as a separate entity from the rest of the body. The shock of the late-nineteenth-century physiological view of the voice is illustrated by this excerpt from the *Reminiscences* of poet and composer Rabindranath Tagore, describing his boyhood in Bengal in the 1870s:

> One day [our teacher] brought a paper parcel out of his pocket and said: "I'll show you to-day a wonderful piece of work of the Creator." With this he un-

tied the paper wrapping and, producing a portion of the vocal organs of a human being, proceeded to expound the marvels of its mechanism. I can still call to mind the shock this gave me at the time. I had always thought the whole man spoke — had never even imagined that the act of speech could be viewed in this detached way. However wonderful the mechanism of a part may be, it is certainly less so than the whole man. (Tagore 2004 [1912]: 49–50)

Another new field that implicitly abstracted the voice from the body was psychoacoustics, which from the beginning drew comparative data from Indian intonation (Ellis 1885) and isolated the arithmetic relations of perceived tones from the physical mechanisms that produced them. A third, related field of study was the rise of scientific linguistics (inspired, in part, by studies of Sanskrit), which emphasized the structural relations of words quite apart from the details of their performance in speech. Coincidentally or not, the rise of these analytic methods seems to have accompanied the steady decline of gesture in British public speaking practices (Kendon 2004: 356–357), which no doubt, in turn, influenced the public speaking conventions of the Anglo-Indian political public sphere in the early twentieth century.

In the 1920s and 1930s, listening to phonograph records, which became quite common in middle-class urban homes in the early decades of the twentieth century, further strengthened the sense that gesture was separate from the voice.[8] The phonograph, as Amanda Weidman says, "operated as though music consisted only of sound and not of gesture" (2003: 464). This erasure of the body in music conditioned the early reception of live singers, as phonographs were widely available in India decades before concert hall performances became common. Dard Neuman argues that when middle-class audiences accustomed to phonographs first saw the body of a beloved singer on stage, they had already developed a mode of listening that focused on the voice to the exclusion of all else. The unfamiliar presence of the singer in live performance, Neuman argues, led audiences to attend to the sound of the voice as "undead," floating separate from the visible body. But even as the body was erased from vocal production, certain singers' bodies were sacralized as public landmarks in a national landscape.[9] After independence, music critics began to refer intimately to the familiar sight of a singer's body around town, and photographs of great musicians began to find a place alongside those of saints and political leaders in middle-class homes. But this newly configured public role for the bodies of great singers, crucially, was still utterly separate from the singing voice (Dard Neuman 2004: 354, 392–393).

Weidman understands this separation of voice and body rather differently: as a separation of interiority (audible as the voice) and exteriority (visible as the moving body). The interiority of voice would be "unseemly" in a dancer; excessive motion would "interfere with the singer's projection of interiority" (2006: 214). The discursive action that divided the voice from the body around the turn of the century seems to have been part of a larger process of imagining the Indian nation. As Partha Chaterjee argues, "anticolonial nationalism . . . divid[ed] the world of social institutions and practices into two domains" — an interior spiritual domain (to be preserved as uniquely Indian) and an exterior material domain (to be reformed in accordance with European modernity) (1993: 6, 120.) In an era when nationalists and romantics worked so hard to distinguish Indian vocality and intonation from the West (Rahaim 2011), it is remarkable that gesture — as an apparently external, incidental epiphenomenon of music — was treated as an uncomfortable marker of Indian distinction, a difference to be smoothed out rather than exaggerated. Of course, the implicit separation of singing and moving, as we have seen, is much older than modern music reform. The Natyasastra has separate chapters for music and dance; the sense of a split between the body and a transcendent world of vibration that offers liberation from the body had likewise been suggested in the thirteenth-century *Sangitaratnakara*, and elaborated in sixteenth- and seventeenth-century treatises. Nonetheless, the practical separation of singing and dancing, previously long integrated in many vocal genres, seems to have been a special feature of the musical processes of the late nineteenth and early twentieth centuries.

The separation of vocal discourse and bodily discourse — and the separation of still singers and silent dancers — was reinforced by a vast new body of music literature in the late nineteenth century. While medieval music-theoretic treatises (written and copied by hand in Sanskrit, Arabic, or Persian) had very narrow circulation, this new writing about music found much wider audiences in the urban middle class. A body of mass-produced music writings in Tamil, Hindi, English, Urdu, Marathi, and other widely known languages emerged to determine new aesthetic and ethical standards for public performance in modern India. This literature included concert reviews, essays about aesthetics, and musicians' biographies. More significant for the history of gesture was the growing body of analytic transcriptions: collections of classic compositions, generalizable rules of melodic behavior in ragas, and speculation about the arithmetic of intonation. Inexpensive editions of compositions and guides to raga grammar have become a common fixture in the houses of music enthusiasts.

The model for much of the theoretical work of this era was the work of North Indian music theorist V. N. Bhatkhande. From the first page of his magisterial survey of Hindustani music theory, *Hindustani Sangit Paddhati*,

Bhatkhande makes it clear that knowledge of notes (*svar-jnan*) is the foundational discipline necessary for music theory. Note that here *svara* refers not to the dynamic articulation of a melodic shape in time but to a named, discrete note of constant pitch:

> Without having suitable *svar-jnan*, one does not understand the classical [*shastriya*] part of music. Proper svar-jnan can be recognized like this: if someone asks you to sing a particular svara, you should immediately be able to sing that svara; in the same manner, on being asked what the svara of a certain sound is, you should instantly be able to name the svara of that sound. Upon possessing such svar-jnan, the entire path forward becomes clear. . . . There are many people who make a living through music but who do not have proper svar-jnan or know the rules of ragas. . . . Without svar-jnan one cannot understand the true secret of the system; nor can one derive real joy. (Bhatkhande 1964: 1)

Bhatkhande drew explicitly from the centuries-old tradition of theorists such as Ramamatya, Kamilkhani, and Venkatamakhi, whose work dealt in detail with tuning systems and scalar classification, but he was the first to insist so strongly that discrete notes are the basic stuff of music. He was also the first to write in vernacular for a wide audience. In Bhatkhande's system, ragas are placed in groups called *thaats* (scalar frameworks) based on their characteristic pitch sets; they are then distinguished from each other primarily on the basis of characteristic sequences of discrete pitches. Bhatkhande based his raga grammars on hundreds of compositions collected from North Indian music masters over many years. He was able to derive a set of rules for each raga by generalizing from a wide range of compositions, rendered by many singers in many ways — thus putting his voice in place of those "who make a living through music but who do not have proper svar-jnan or know the rules of ragas." His method was not only a means of aesthetic apprehension: it was a means of rendering diverse embodied performances commensurable by filtering out the particularities of individual bodies, voices, and performances. Gesture is invisible in a music-theoretic system that consists fundamentally of rules for combining tones, just as gesture was for many years invisible to linguists, who initially considered language to consist fundamentally of rules for combining words (Kendon 2004: 356; Sweetser 2004: 197).

But gesture was anything but invisible to most music writers. Although concert reviewers, like ancient and medieval writers on music and gesture, agreed that singers shouldn't move much, many early critics implied that excessive gesture was not (as traditionally held) a failure to uphold universally valid aesthetic ideals but, rather, a specific failing of Indian musicians in contrast to Western musicians. In other words, the time-honored ideal of effortless singing enshrined in Indian musical treatises became conflated with an imagined ideal of European bodily comportment: restrained, un-obtrusive, urbane. For example, Rabindranath Tagore noted that European singers move less conspicuously than Indian singers when they sing, per-haps because Indian audiences are willing to ignore "uncouthness of ges-ture in the exponent of a perfectly formed melody" (2004 [1912]: 227). If audiences took this "uncouthness" for granted, critics did not. A. M. Chin-naswami Mudaliar bemoaned the "convulsions, grimaces and ungraceful gesticulations, which inseparably accompany the performance of almost every musician in the east" (quoted in Subramanian 2006: 5). Musicologist Chitra Bailur complained that "violent and spasmodic physical movements, either of face or body, on the part of the musician, may have the tendency of ruffling the tranquil atmosphere of the audience or even lending an al-most comical touch" (1955: 40). Some music writers even directly prescribed the suppression of gesture: for instance, the music critic Bhavan Rao Pingle insisted that "the activities wasted away by bodily actions and movements, should be concentrated on the voice and instruments" (1962 [1894]: 103–104). Weidman notes furthermore that gesture was figured discursively as empty imitation, as opposed to originality, and that South Indian critics developed a repertoire of denigrative terms that framed gesture as exten-sions of low-status occupations: "*iyantiram araikkiratu* (a phrase suggest-ing the motions of a machine hulling paddy) and *mallayuttam* (wrestling)" (Weidman 2006: 131).

When music critics do praise singers for their gestural habits, it is usually in praise of restraint and in contrast to a prevailing tendency to overgesture, as in V. H. Deshpande's description of Mogubai Kurdikar: "She rejects an unnecessary taan, a straining for effect in the voice, tiyye [i.e., *tihai*, a form of virtuosic rhythmic play] made to order merely for the sake of response, or futile gestures of the hand" (cited in Quinn 1982: 161). In the following passage, Amir Khan's relative lack of gesture[10] is discursively linked to spiri-tuality. The author achieves this by associating his stillness with both yogic practice and with Sarangadev (the author of the *Sangitaratnakara*), who posited *mukti* (spiritual liberation) as music's primary goal:

> [Amir Khan's] dignified bearing and his upright, yogi-like posture, when per-forming on the stage, was perfectly in tune with the serene grandeur of his music. Acrobatics and contortions of any kind were conspicuous by their ab-sence in his case — and, that too, at a time when "making faces" (as also a be-wildering variety of physical gestures) had already become a specialized art by itself. Here, indeed, was an executant who appeared to live up to the dictum of

Sharngadeva, that distortion of the face and indulgence in physical gestures was a gross disqualification. (Nadkarni 1999: 178)

This chapter will close with two representative examples of how these discourses combine to frame post-Independence accounts of the gestural practices of three classical musicians: Carnatic vocalist S. Ramanathan and Hindustani vocalists Bade Ghulam Ali Khan and Bundu Khan. In the middle of a short celebratory biography of S. Ramanathan, his gestural restraint is compared to the conspicuous gestures of Bade Ghulam Ali Khan:

> Sometimes while traveling by an auto-rickshaw, [Bade Ghulam Ali Khan] would burst into song, spurring it on with lavish gestures of the arm and hand, which would frequently result in the driver taking a wrong turning, since the extended arm looked like a road-direction to him. Withal, Dr. Ramanathan was not given to much body movement while singing. He would say that the voice should indicate all the movement, not the body. (*Sruti* magazine 1989: 30)

While Ramanathan's voice, like a sign, "indicates," Bade Ghulam Ali Khan's voice, like a horse, is "spurred on." His gestures are described as "lavish," implying not just intensity but excess. His gestural disposition also is placed in tension with the space of a modern city. It results in wrong turns down unknown streets navigated by an anonymous auto-rickshaw driver who has to be told the way. The gestures, in other words, are literally misleading. Yet even the suggestion that singers should suppress their gesture affirms the centrality of motion in melody: "the voice" — and not the body — "should indicate all the movement." This suggests that both the voice and the body can and do indeed indicate melodic movement in the course of singing.

Another revealing description of the melodic gesture of a hereditary musician is found in B. R. Deodhar's account of a discussion with Bundu Khan:

> I asked Khansaheb [i.e., Bundu Khan] to tell me more about different varieties of tanas [i.e., melismatic vocal runs]. I tried my level best to make him concentrate on this one question, but it was not to be. . . . He soon lost his interest in that subject too and began to expatiate on how a vocalist should conduct himself during a recital — his posture, the importance of restrained and correct gestures, etc. His demonstration of how the singer's arm should move during an ascending tana, how he should express what he had in mind or was planning to do . . . [his] mobility of features, posture and gestures was most beautiful and absorbing. (Deodhar 1993: 185)

The blend of admiration for the master's virtuosity and condescending bemusement at his inability to "concentrate" on musicological questions is typical of such accounts of hereditary musicians by music reformers. That he "lost interest" in the subject at hand and instead talked about something apparently irrelevant suggests the gulf between Deodhar's concerns and those of the musician. Where the musicologist asks about the taxonomy of *taans*, the singer prefers to talk about performance.

But perhaps there is more to read in this account than Bundu Khan's sheer inability to answer Deodhar's question in conventional musicological terms. After all, it is unlikely that a master like Bundu Khan would have been simply unable to analyze the various kinds of taans as note sequences. Perhaps Bundu Khan was in fact answering the question that Deodhar posed. Could this gestural demonstration of the shapes of melodic runs have been a demonstration of the connection between hand and voice? The next chapter will investigate just this connection.

CHAPTER TWO

Gesture and Melodic Motion

❧

Sitting in the front row of a vocal concert one night, I am distracted by a
scratching sound to my right. An up-and-coming young musician sits with a
notebook in her lap and a pen in her hand, writing so furiously that the friction
of pen against paper is audible above the singer's voice. She is rapidly, and with
astonishing accuracy, transcribing the singer's improvised melodic passages, note
for note. Every few minutes, after a particularly difficult phrase, the scratching
stops. She drops her pen, raises her hands to her face, and traces the contours of
the phrase in the air before her eyes. Seeing the phrase clearly in front of her, she
returns to her pen, and the scratching resumes.

Melody is motion; melody is notes. The young singer at the concert
switched smoothly between these two ways of understanding. In this, she
showed a mastery of two complementary models of melody among Hindustani musicians. One model, embodied in the young musician's note-by-
note transcription, sees melody as a sequence of independent units, as a
necklace is made of beads. The other model, embodied in her hands moving in space, sees melody as motion.[1]

The note-sequence model is expressed in a precise, explicit, centuries-old
notation system. Like movable-do solfège, this system names seven notes:
sa, re, ga, ma, pa, dha, ni. This model, called *sargam* (*sa/re/ga/ma*), analyzes
melodic action in terms of these stopping points. These stopping points
retain their names even if their sonic referents are slightly raised or lowered,
bent or oscillated. The English word notation is sometimes used for this
analytic process of breaking a melody into units and naming them according to these seven notes. For example, the melody of "Happy Birthday"
could be roughly notated as shown in figure 2.1.[2]

This model is precise and simple, and it is used widely by both musicians
and theorists to describe melody. It allows for compact printed notation,
straightforward classification of ragas according to scalar content, and the

> **Hap-py birth-day to you, Hap-py birth-day to you,**
> *pa   pa   dha   pa   sa   ṇi , pa   pa   dha   pa   re sa,*
>
> **Hap-py birth-day dear Pa-van, Hap-py birth-day to you.**
> *pa   pa   pa   ga   sa   ṇi   dha,   ma ma   ga   sa   re sa.*

Figure 2.1. "Happy Birthday" in sargam.

analysis of hierarchies of pitch importance. It also enables rigorous analyses and comparisons of ragas in terms of note sequences (for example, Bhat-khande 1964), and has become the dominant tool of musical analysis in both North and South India.

The second model, which understands melody as motion, lends itself more readily to physical movement than to writing. Its tradition therefore seldom leaves a written trace. The idea that melody moves is familiar even to un-trained musicians, who might perceive, for example, that "Happy Birthday" begins low, jumps to "to" before settling on "you," ascends to its apex on the third "birthday," and drifts down to "you" in its closing phrase. This chap-ter will focus on the gestural articulation of melody as motion. By the end, we will see that the two models are complementary and interconnected.

Melodic Trajectories

Trained musicians need not picture every note they sing as they improvise. Instead, they rely on nuanced models of motion and melodic trajectory. Vocalist Veena Sahasrabuddhe, for example, says that while improvising, she is generally thinking not about individual notes (*svaras*) but about cur-vilinear motion:

> If there are four or five notes, I will say this is one unit, because that's how I practice every day. So if I want to reach from *rishabh* [i.e., re] to the upper rishabh, in the meanwhile, all the svaras in the middle, {*re ma pa ni*} [*waves hand dismissively*] I don't care. I know from rishabh to rishabh. I'm just going to put the [*moves hand in curve*] just like a curve. I know I'm perfectly going there. I have full confidence. So {*re ma pa ni sa*} or {*ni sa re ma pa ni sa*}, what-ever it is . . . I see rishabh there waiting for me [*laughs*]. And I will just go there. . . . I make all kinds of designs, and the designs are in my mind. But at that time, I'm not putting any efforts, "Now after *re, ga*, these are the svaras." No. Instead of svaras, I'm just thinking about the curves and the lines. (Inter-view courtesy of Martin Clayton, Bombay, 2004)

This is echoed by vocalist Arun Kashalkar:

> It's like ascending or descending the steps. So you need not think of each and every step. You know the goal, you know the direction. . . . You can just climb up or climb down. It happens like that, not thinking of each and every note. . . . At *times*, you may think in that manner [i.e., thinking of notes]. But as far as taan [intricate melodic runs] is concerned, you are thinking of the phrases. . . . It's like drawing the straight lines. You don't think of the points. . . . So many points together in one direction make the line. So if I am thinking of a line, all points come together in one direction. . . . When it comes to forming the difficult designs, then I am thinking of designs, and the designs that I have already practiced, during my day-to-day practice.

Many widely used terms for melody in the lexicon of Hindustani music imply motion (e.g., the characteristic movements [*calan*] of a raga, leaping [*laghana*] over pitches, ascent [*aroh*]). Further, the conception of melody as motion does not seem to be limited to any particular lineage. Arun Kashalkar's training from Gajananrao Joshi and Baban Rao Haldankar was centered in the forceful, rhythmic Agra style, but his conception of melodic trajectories agrees fundamentally with Sheila Dhar's account of the style of the Kirana training she received from Niaz and Fayyaz Ahmed:

> One outstanding feature of the Kirana gharana is the refined sculpting of the melodic line. The practitioners of the Kirana style tend to regard the entire scale as a continuous flow of musicality and not a series of separate notes. Conceptually every phrase in a raga is represented by a flowing line which passes smoothly through all the gradations of the participating notes without revealing the joints. The extremely fine tuning of the intonation of the line conveys the emotional intention, subtly and enduringly, as though it were not a string of notes but a single musical sound with a distinct expression. (Dhar 2001: 22, 27–28)

One of the first obstacles I myself faced in learning to sing raga music was my fixation on discrete notes and my inability to apprehend melodic trajectories. I was singing stiffly, rendering one note after another. My teacher, Vikas Kashalkar, insisted again and again that I needed to "connect the notes." I struggled for months with my eyes closed, but it wasn't until I opened my eyes and noticed his hands moving while he sang that I understood that these curves were also manifest in gesture as he sang. Once, when practicing with Vikas Kashalkar's student Mukul Kulkarni, I was having trouble with precise pronunciation of a particular swooping phrase. Mukul instructed me to "think of the curves" instead of individual notes, while tracing curves with his hands. Later, he described the rendering (*lagao*)

Figure 2.2. Velanti/U-turn/change in direction.

of such melodic trajectories: "The design is important as that image is created in your brain, and you start singing the same phrase, the expected phrase. Because it is not only the [*sings very rigidly, sitting still*]. The lagao is [*sings smoothly with curvaceous gestures*]." Furthermore, he said, "if at times you don't get the notation [i.e., if you aren't able to model the design as a sequence of notes], you can show the shape." For example, Mukul demonstrated the shape of the following phrase in Shree Raga, which follows an abrupt ascent from *re* to *pa*. The phrase ascends from *ma* to *dha*, turns around, and descends, as shown in figure 2.2. Mukul called this trajectory a *velanti*, a technical term for the curving Devanagari script vowel sign indicating that a given syllable should be pronounced with a long /i/ ("ee") sound (figure 2.3).

This velanti, he said, "tells that you go and come back. . . . This suggests that it is a curve." After singing this phrase, he traced the velanti in the air several times without singing, in the same space as it had occupied while singing. This form — rather than individual notes — was the salient element extractable from his vocalization, traceable by both voice and hand. Mukul also linked this explanation to another kinetic domain: driving. The phrase is "like going to that note and taking a turn backwards. Here in this phrase, when singing this phrase, you get a feeling of U-turn." He went on to distinguish between two different kinds of U-turn: "In singing *ma dha ma dha ma ga* the feel is of taking a U-turn. . . . Had I sung *ma pa dha ma ga re* (another valid phrase in Shree), you could have easily understood the U-turn taken at Shivaji statue!" (personal email, November 27, 2008; my

Figure 2.3. Velanti, shown here as the long /i/
of -*vi*, the third syllable in *bhairavi*.

italics). The statue of Shivaji (a Maharashtrian king) to which Mukul refers
is on Karve Road, near Vikas Kashalkar's house in Pune, and drivers often
make tight, dramatic U-turns around it to change direction. Mukul links
this particularly sharp U-turn to a phrase in which *pa* is included rather than
jumped over in ascent, producing a tight, chromatic change in direction.
Though the range of the phrase is the same, the extra note interpolated
between raised *ma* and lowered *dha* gives a different sense of size, space,
and motion.

In one of the few scholarly treatments of melodic trajectories in Hindustani music, vocalist and musicologist Rabindra Lal Roy asserts that "the
idea of musical curves is always present in the mind of the Indian artist
while he sings in the Hindustani style" (1934: 325). Roy suggests that the
trajectory of the hand in space traces these graphs:

> Observation shows that the singer describes with his hand apparently fantastic
> curves in space, by raising the hand with the rise of pitch and lowering it with
> the lowering of pitch. Sometimes, to avoid bad mannerisms, he makes for-
> ward and backward movements instead of upward and downward movements,
> but in any case the gestures underscore the movement of sound in the proper
> direction. (325)

According to Roy, the hand goes up when pitch goes up, and down when
pitch goes down.[3] He is correct in a general sense: the hand and the voice
work together to coarticulate melody. But video analysis shows that the
correspondences between hand and melody are considerably subtler and
more context-bound than Roy lets on.

Gestural and Vocal Motion

Even a casual look at vocal-gestural performance affirms Roy's basic contention: the hand and the voice work closely together. The shapes of gesture phrases link closely with vocal phrases. Consider figure 2.4, in which
Mohan Darekar sings a series of four descending phrases, reaching lower
and lower in turn. These curves are traced by coordinated motion of the

Figure 2.4. Coordinated traces of curves in the hand and the voice.

hand and the voice. Figure 2.5 shows a similar correspondence. Here, an obliquely ascending melodic curve, {*sa ma ga pa*}, corresponds to the motion of Mukul Kulkarni's left hand.

It is tempting to conclude from these examples that hand motion in the course of performance is merely a map of pitch onto the vertical axis. However, further observation shows that this is not the case. First, even in cases where there is a clear correlation between pitch and hand position, pitches do not have consistent locations in space the way that they do on a keyboard. (*Sa* is not always in front of the chest, *ma* is not always three inches to the right, etc.) The movement from left to right is context-dependent — each left-right gesture is calibrated to a single phrase rather than corresponding to an exact pitch.[4] This gestural recalibration is often centered around the "goal" note of each phrase, which tends to be located in front of the chest or the abdomen. Thus phrases are oriented around their goals, revealing foresight into where the melody is headed.

Second, it is clear from observing gesture over the course of a performance that the relationship between vocal and gestural shape is not rigidly fixed. Sometimes, for example, the left side of a gesture space is associated with lower notes, while higher-pitched notes are located to the right;[5] sometimes the opposite relationship obtains. Pitch may be mapped onto radial dimensions as well, or onto the relative position of two hands. Sometimes singers conjure an invisible cord that they stretch between their hands, and pitch corresponds to its virtual tension. Figure 2.6 shows an example of one such consistent but nonvertical correspondence between pitch and hand position. Here the relative position of Shafqat Ali's hands along the sagittal axis is closely linked to pitch. A position in which his left hand is in front of his right corresponds with the lowest note of a phrase; his right in front of his left corresponds to the highest; intermediate positions correspond with intermediate notes.

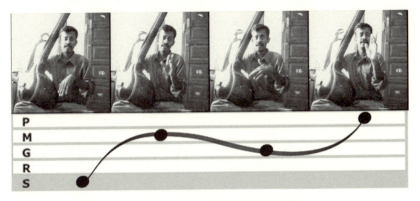

Figure 2.5. {*Sa ma ga pa*} phrase: gesture and pitch vs. time.

It may appear at first that the three hand positions (right-in-front-of-left, together, left-in-front-of-right) correspond to note positions (*sa*, *ga*, *ma*). We would then expect that every instance of these notes is accompanied by these hand positions. But in phrase 3b, for example, the hands do not go two steps forward for *pa* and then one step back for *ma*; instead, they merely move one step forward, approximating the net melodic motion rather than the positions of individual notes. More importantly, when *sa*, *ga*, and *ma* arise in other melodic contexts (e.g., {*ga ma pa sa ni*} — an ascent to high *sa* followed by *ni*), the hands are not sliding past each other at all.

The logics that link vocalization and gesture are temporary and contingent, not deterministic: one cannot discern a vocalization from its affiliated gesture, or a gesture from its affiliated vocalization. One linkage (e.g., forward for higher notes) may obtain for a phrase or two before giving way to another. Thus, identical melodic contours are often articulated quite differently in different melodic contexts. As Adam Kendon demonstrates, gestural-vocal coherence is achieved in the moment of speech performance rather than merely given as a precondition for performance (2004: 151–156). Recall figure 2.5, in which, in the context of a single one-second phrase, Mukul Kulkarni's hand seemed to match the sung pitch. Figure 2.7 shows a contrasting set of stills from the same performance, a minute and a half later, in which Kulkarni is singing a phrase with the same vocal contour (and nearly the same note content: {*re ma ga pa*}) but in a different melodic context, and with a strikingly different gestural articulation.

Here, rather than moving up for high notes and down for low notes, the hand is tracing a circular trajectory in the frontal plane (the plane of the camera frame). In the first two frames, it looks as though the hand is mapping pitch so that pitch height is correlated with position to the singer's

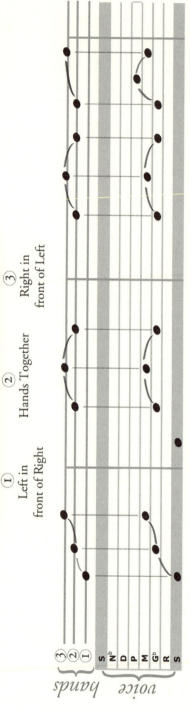

Figure 2.6. Correspondences between relative hand position and pitch.

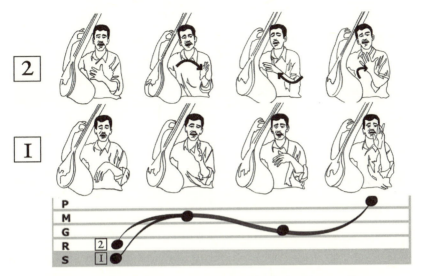

Figure 2.7. Distinction between two nearly identical sequences of notes
in the same performance. Phrase 1 is reproduced from figure 2.5; phrase 2 is from
the same recording, approximately ninety seconds later.

left. In the second phrase, the hand is farther to the left for *ga* than it was
for *re*, indicating that the circular hand trajectory in this phrase is modeling
not absolute pitch, but the alternating pattern of ascent and descent. The
hand turns upward for *pa* as it prepares (in the second case) for a coming
descent to *sa* via *re*.

Even in cases in which a vocal phrase is repeated several times in a row,
each repetition may find different (but internally coherent) gestural expression. This parallels cases of verbal repetition in which gesture is deployed
differently each time to create a novel utterance. Figure 2.8 shows such a
moment in a performance of Rag Bhimplas by Shafqat Ali Khan. Here he
sings three sequential phrases with the same pitch content {*ga ma pa (sa)
ni dha dha pa*} and melodic contour. The repeated vocal material lends
coherence to the melodic utterance. The gestural affiliates of these phrases,
however, are different. In the first phrase, the right hand faces up, and
moves away from the chest on {*dha pa*}. In the second, the right hand faces
to the left, and pulls toward the chest on {*dha pa*}. The third phrase is performed with the opposite hand, placing it in a different gesture space, preparing the way for the next phrase, which culminates in Shafqat reaching
forward with his left hand, as if presenting the note. Correspondences between pitch and space cohere tightly within single phrases but differ from
phrase to phrase.

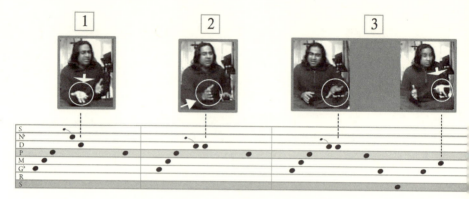

Figure 2.8. Melodic repetition with gestural variety.

Sometimes the melodic motion expressed in hands and voice has to do with parameters other than pitch: the hands may be linked to a changing vowel quality or to the amplitude of the voice. The hands are often used to manipulate virtual objects, during which time there is no such consistent link with any single acoustic dimension. Rather than serving as a link between space and sound, such gestures cohere in the consistent physicality of the virtual object at hand — its viscosity, elasticity, weight, and so forth (see chapter 5).

Although the hands are the most obvious gestural vehicle for melody, other parts of the body often engage as well. The head, shoulders, and even the eyes often enact melody, especially when a singer is playing the harmonium, has both hands occupied, or is deliberately holding their hands still. Figure 2.9 shows Sudhakar Deoley singing with his hands folded in his lap to demonstrate how "unnatural" it is to sing without moving. Though his hands were still, he unintentionally tilted his chin to the left in concert with his vocal ascent to *re*.

Loops, Circles, and Twists

Thus far, we have seen that gestural trajectories, though closely coordinated with vocal action, are not determined by vocal pitch. The logics that link the voice and hand are temporary, vary across repetitions, and sometimes are not connected to pitch at all. The idea that gesture has a purely melographic function is difficult to maintain in the face of these observations. Indeed, to insist that the hand is merely mirroring the pitch of the voice would require us to reduce the voice to pitch and to reduce gesture to a single dimension. A closer examination of gestural motion shows that there is much more going on.

R	●
S	
N	●

Figure 2.9. Chin motion
when hands are still.

   Though it is easy to picture melodic ascent and descent as linear motion, curves are by far the most common gestural trajectories. Given the anatomy of joints, this is not surprising. Joints, after all, produce not linear translation but rotation about a point. Watch the path of your hand as you rotate your forearm about your elbow: it traces an arc. To trace a line in space, on the other hand, is more, not less, complex than tracing a curve: you must coordinate the motion of two or more joints. Try drawing a line in the air: your wrist, elbow, and shoulder joints must work in concert. Given the relative ease of tracing curves, we might be tempted to speak of the "constraints" that joints put on movement. For example, we might say that the wrist joint is constrained to rotate (around a point) rather than to translate (along a line). But to speak of the rotation of the wrist as a constraint assumes an ontologically prior ideal world of unconstrained motion. One might try to imagine, with some difficulty, a fictional joint that translates linearly. One might just as well try to imagine singing without needing to take a breath. But given the staggering variety of designs available to the voice and the hand, it will take us further to consider the abilities of the hand and arm — no less than the abilities of the voice — as a vehicle for music rather than a constraint. The arcs traced by the hands afford melodic loops that intersect themselves in ways that sound cannot, they allow connectedness even across breaks in phonation, and they allow various kinds of looping melodic periodicity.

In figure 2.5, the four notes of the phrase {*sa ma ga pa*} are not merely independent data points with separate pitch values. Nor is the gestural articulation of this phrase merely a sequence of snapshots. (As Arun Kashalkar put it, melodic shape is "musically explained — you cannot explain it like a drawing.") The melodic fragment is performed both gesturally and vocally as a unified curvaceous melodic action. This phrase traces an ascending, serpentine curve — up, then down, then up. The phrase has both periodic and linear components — it changes direction periodically (rotating around the wrist) but maintains a net linear motion (as the shoulder and elbow extend the hand). The technical term for this kind of motion is *vakra* (crooked), a term also used for the meandering progress of a river and for the apparent retrograde motion of heavenly bodies from the point of view of an observer on Earth.

A melographic trace of {*sa ma ga pa*}, as in figure 2.5, meanders like a vakra river; the looping trajectory of Mukul's hand mirrors Mercury's vakra path (figure 2.10). The motion of Mukul's hand, like the vocal motion of the phrase, has both linear and periodic components. Even as the shoulder and elbow unfold to trace an ascending line, the hand rolls upward and forward about the wrist, describing an ellipse in the sagittal plane. The resultant hand motion in the sagittal plane, then, includes a loop, depicted in figure 2.11.

Looping patterns of melodic motion (e.g., {*sa ga re ma ga pa ma dha pa* . . .}) are learned and practiced repeatedly by singers in training. They are available to singers in the course of performance as modes of motion, like gaits, for which there is no need to think of the constituent notes. The attention to individual notes, like scaffolding, falls away once the pattern is learned. As Arun Kashalkar says:

> Those designs also come forward instantly — without even my knowledge, I would say. . . . They can just present themselves before you . . . that practice you have been doing for years together — {*sa re ga, re ga ma, ga ma pa, ma pa dha*} . . . that you have been doing for all those years.

The extended melismata that emerge from these patterns often find cyclical gestural articulation like the one seen above. This motion often extends beyond a single loop. An ascending phrase may include eight or more loops on its way up, as the hand describes an extended looping form. A phrase like this in Gaud Sarang would be {*sa ga re ma ga pa ma dha pa sa*}. Such a phrase may also maintain its looping, periodic component while proceed-

Figure 2.10. Vakra motion of Mercury from the point of view of an observer on Earth.

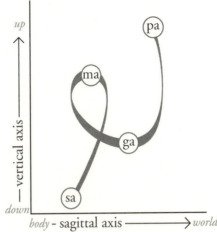

Figure 2.11. Vakra motion of Gaud Sarang phrase, articulated in the sagittal plane.

ing up and down linearly, as in the Bhimplas phrase {*sa ma ga pa ma dha pa dha ma pa ga ma ga pa ma pa*}. That this kind of looping is not merely a mirroring of vocal pitch is shown by the fact that the circular looping motion of the hands begins, in some cases, before the vakra vocal motion. Furthermore, the terms used to describe vakra motion typically reference loops and circles, rather than zigzags or meanders. A voice that has trained itself to render vakra patterns gracefully is sometimes called gol gala, or "round throat." Arun Kashalkar describes certain kinds of melodic motion as "twists" (which are described gesturally as a circle — see figure 2.12). Sheila Dhar describes how a master vocalist melodically "traces delicate three-dimensional arcs, and draws from silence deeply searching spirals" (2001: 22). Rabindra Lal Roy explains how these melodic patterns — which, in a melographic pitch-time plot, is an uncrossed serpentine line — may be conceived as circular.

> [Melographic diagrams] show only a time-order of events in one direction: that of futurity. In space-sensation, the directions are at least both backwards and forwards, and the correct representation of the curve E D F E . . . would be a dynamic circle or ellipse in terms of space-values. . . . The notes occur just as an arrangement of events in space occurs, an arrangement in which measurement in either direction is equally legitimate. (1934: 330)

In light of these vivid accounts of melodic shape, it would require a very strong allegiance to a melographic ideal to insist that the looping motion of

Figure 2.12. "I come across certain twists
of their singing, their designs."

the hand is merely an elaborate way of mapping pitch onto the vertical axis. Even raising and lowering vocal pitch are distinct and often asymmetrical melodic actions. From a physiological point of view, the voice often uses different muscle patterns in ascent and descent (Ewan 1976); from a cognitive point of view, subjects tend to hear falling pitch as vertical descent, while rising pitch is more consistently perceived as acceleration (Eitan and Granot 2006). The shape-based descriptions of melody above refer to melodic action in the course of performance, not melographic reductions of melodic action after the fact. It seems that gesture does not represent pitch any more than pitch represents gesture, and neither by itself fully encapsulates melody.

A loop on a pitch/time graph would imply progress backward in time, which requires attention, memory, and imagination. The apprehension of melodic motion as coherent shapes requires a broad temporal consciousness: the retention of what has just come and the protention of what is to come. None of these are shown in a melograph, and all of these are necessary to apprehend melody as simultaneously sequence and shape, sound and gesture.

Theorizing Melodic Motion

The description of melody as motion is nothing new. The oldest extant Sanskrit treatment of melodic processes, the *Natyasastra* (Bharatamuni 1998 [first millennium CE]), describes svaras moving (*gamana*, 781) and melodic movement between svaras (*sancharam*, 785). The thirteenth-century *Sangi-*

taratnakara describes four basic kinds of melodic figure (*varna*), each of which is described in terms of motion: ascending (*arohana*), descending (*avarohana*), steady (*sthayi*), and wandering (*sanchari*) (ibid.: 234–235). Nor is this conception limited to India. Among the theorists of the ancient Mediterranean, both Pythagoreans (such as Nicomachus) and Aristotelians (such as Aristoxenus) considered vocal action to be a kind of motion (Nicomachus the Pythagorean 1993 [ca. 100 CE]: 37–39; Aristoxenus in Barker 1989: 133). Commonsense descriptions of music in various languages describe melodic action in vivid kinetic terms: speeding up and slowing down; rising and falling; tensing and slackening; cascading, pooling, and swirling (Feld 1981; Zbikowski 2005: 66–67; Eitan and Granot 2006).

"But in a waterfall," we may object, "water moves; as we ascend a hill, our bodies move; in melody, nothing is *actually* moving, is it?" Only if our model of melody is listening to a sound recording. The performance of melodic motion is always linked to some kind of physical motion, whether of the larynx, the finger, the wrist, and so on. Likewise, a feeling for melodic motion is not merely an analytical, visual appreciation of a trajectory (as we might appreciate the differences between two curves). It unfolds over time, rooted in sympathy with motion (as we might feel moved by the grace of a bird, or spun by a dance partner). This is as much the case with listeners as with singers: as Eitan and Granot (2006) have shown, listeners routinely — rather than as a secondary interpretive step — interpret sound as kinetic information about motion: acceleration, approach, ascent, and so on. While we may analytically reduce melodic motion after the fact to a written trace to be apprehended visually (Ihde 2007: 219), melody — as sound, gesture, or otherwise — arises directly as movement in space (ibid.: 69).

This kinetic approach to melody has taken on a special urgency among some music theorists in the past ten years. Robert Hatten, perhaps the most influential and wide-ranging of these theorists, has developed a way of analyzing melodic action as "significant energetic shaping through time" (2004: 301). Crucially, for Hatten, "the gestural energy of a melody is phenomenologically more fundamental than the sequence of pitches of which a melody is comprised" (ibid.: 114). This model of musical gesture draws heavily on the work of music theorist Ernst Kurth. Kurth's major theoretical work, *Grundlagen des linearen Kontrapunkts* (*Foundations of Linear Counterpoint*), begins quite simply with the words "*Melodie ist Bewegung*": "Melody is motion" (Kurth 1922: 1). Kurth locates the essence of melody not in sequences of particular pitches, but in psychological patterns of energetic tension and release. These patterns are realized through sound but are not, themselves, sound. Kurth's theory will become useful later in developing a cognitive model for gesture and melody. For now, however, it is important to make a distinction between Kurth's approach and my own. Kurth saw melody-as-motion not just as a complement to melody-as-tones, but as a revolutionary alternative (1922: 7, 18, and passim). He explicitly rejected the note-based methods of analysis that had come to dominate Western music theory.[6] The evidence from Hindustani musicians, however, suggests that note-based and motion-based models of melody are complementary.

The note-centered model that has dominated modern Indian music theory is the mirror image of Kurth's system. The intellectual hallmark of a modern classical musician is the ability to translate a melodic phrase into a sequence of note-names, and vice versa (Bhatkhande 1964: 3). The precision of this method is part of its allure. In the words of sitarist Sakhawat Hussein Khan, a longtime colleague of theorist V. N. Bhatkhande, note-based analysis serves as a *gayan kaimraa*, a "singing camera," which "creates an exact picture of every movement of the throat" (S. H. Khan 1976 [1952]: 34, cited in Katz 2010: 173). But it is important to bear in mind that neither Kurth's nor Bhatkhande's approach produces an exact picture — they each are models that account for complementary facets of melodic action.

On the surface, these two models of melody seem to be mutually exclusive. Methods of analysis centered on unmoving snapshots of melody are apparently at odds with melodic motion. Yet in many cases vocalization, images of discrete notes, and physical motion seem to blend (Fauconnier and Turner 2003). Recall, for example, Veena Sahasrabuddhe's account of the note rishabh "waiting" for her to arrive. Mukul Kulkarni likewise describes "going to that note and taking a turn backwards," as though the notes were stopping points in space. As we will see in chapter 4, specific pitches inform the spatial relationships that form the architecture of phrases. More importantly, this knowledge of curvaceous motion does not inhibit the ability to sing in tune. Indeed, *sur*, the word used most often used to indicate tunefulness, includes both precise intonation and proper melodic curvature. The mutual entanglement of these two ways of knowing melody was expressed pithily in Vikas Kashalkar's Kaluli-esque admonition one day that I should sing like "water flowing down steps, not the steps themselves." The falling water (the melody) maintains the shape of the steps (the pitch material), but, unlike the steps, it is always moving.[7]

Svara and Neume

This interplay between notes and motion is reflected in the very term *svara*, a term that has appeared in every extant work of Indian music theory for the last two thousand years. One common sense of svara is virtually identical with note: we might say that the scale of a certain raga has a certain set of svaras, or that two svaras are particularly close together in a particular raga. Svaras in this sense are atomic, unchanging analytic units, with no beginning or end. In another sense of the word, however, svaras are always in motion: rising, falling, swaying, or pulling (Mokkapati 1997: 51–52 and passim). An andolit gandhar, for example, is performed with undulating pitch motion but is called by the note-name *ga*; the slide between the seventh and sixth scale degrees in Rag Hameer is ordinarily just called *dha*; the long, gentle glide from the fourth, through the third, to the second scale degree in Rag Bhairav is simply called *re*.[8] Svaras in this sense are what they are by virtue of their motion. Outside music theory, svara can also mean "voice" or "vowel," and accordingly, a given svara is always articulated on a single vowel, even if it varies in pitch.

This ambiguity is not limited to Indian music. The medieval European term *neume*, like svara, indicates continuous melodic action on a single vowel (Mokkapati 1997: 93; Crocker 2000: 223; Taruskin 2010: 1:13). It also refers to one of several kinds of curvilinear melodic notation. These glyphs, found in early Armenian, Byzantine, Gregorian, and other chant notations, prescribe patterns of melodic motion without necessarily prescribing specific pitches. In this sense, they operate much like systems of curvilinear Buddhist chant notation, such as Tibetan *Dbangs Yig* and Japanese *Shyoomyoo*. The shapes of these signs, which in many cases resemble the trajectory of a hand through the air, have led many musicologists to accept a tantalizing though historically uncertain (Hucke 1980; Kenneth Levy 1987) link between curvilinear notation and singers' hand gestures. The connection is so attractive that many chant scholars have taken this connection as a straightforward matter of fact: in Dom Cardine's classic formulation, "a neume is simply a 'written gesture'" (1982: 9).[9] The relationship between melodic shape and hand gesture in Byzantine chant or Torah recitation (Katsman 2007), which has surviving chironomic traditions, is somewhat clearer in a broad sense, if not in the details. Whatever the historical validity of specific claims about the relationship between curvilinear notation and gesture, it is important to note that the three-dimensional motion of the hand through the air — its various handshapes, its rotation about several joints at once — cannot be exhaustively represented on a flat surface (see Seeger 1958.) The relationship between voice and hand, though apparently related to curvilinear notation, is not necessarily mediated by visions of fixed, two-dimensional curves.

There is, however, a somewhat broader sense of the word *neume* that applies well to unified vocal-gestural performance. Music theorist Jon K.

Barlow has developed the term beyond its specific historical sense (in reference to chant) to encompass a much broader range of dynamic action, both audible and inaudible — a phrase played on a vina, the trajectory of a bird, the motion of a dancer. This expanded term accounts well for the unified vocal-gestural melodic shapes performed in Hindustani music, which, inasmuch as they are neumes, are "perceivable through the various sensory modalities and/or through bodily movement" (Barlow 1998–2000). Further, a neume in this sense is intimately tied to the perceptual process (noted earlier) of retaining and anticipating the course of melodic action: "Because we can hear, see, and otherwise feel the whole neume in its parts, we can know where a neume is going while it is still in the process of going there" (ibid.). This accords closely with Victor Zuckerkandl's subtle reversal of Kurth's *"melody is motion"* formula: "Musical motion is at the core of every motion, [and] every experience of motion is, finally, a musical experience" (1969: 138). Motion, in this view, is melody.

The Relationship between Gesture and Vocalization

The foregoing theoretical excursion has only demonstrated that it is possible to think of melody as motion (and vice versa), not that it is necessarily helpful to do so. Let us now return to our observations and see how thinking in this way may help us make sense of gestural-vocal performance.

We have seen that the coperformance of gesture and vocalization is both tightly coordinated and nonredundant. Ordinarily, we might assume that this motion is merely a metaphoric representation of sound (see Johnson 2007: 248). And to be sure, in a few special cases, singers sometimes *do* imagine notes and represent these notes with their hands. For example, a teacher may deliberately "sketch" notes in the air along a clearly delineated linear axis for the sake of a student who repeatedly fails to reproduce the pitch sequence of a phrase. There are even rare moments in performance when singers seem to be using such representations to aid themselves in visualizing the relationships between a particularly complex series of pitches. In ragas with difficult grammars, in which special versions of certain svaras are used in particular situations, singers occasionally point at notes as if pointing at objects floating in the air, as they work their way through difficult phrases. Beginning students who are improvising in unfamiliar ragas often gesture in this way as well, evidently struggling to produce acceptable sequences of notes.

Apart from these special, distinctive cases, however, there is no evidence that the spontaneous flow of gesture in the course of masterful singing *represents* vocalization in general. Of course, vocalization is fundamental in one obvious sense: if you perform khyal, you call yourself a singer, not a gesturer; one typically does not gesture extensively without singing; and singing — not gesturing — is usually billed as the main attraction in a performance. But none of this qualifies sound itself as the sole target domain in the course of vocal improvisation, during which gesture is found almost ubiquitously.

As we have already seen, the same vocal figure may have very different gestural affiliates. Preparation phases of coming gestures reveal that a hand-shape or gestural form is sometimes chosen before the sonic content begins, and gestural phrases likewise often continue smoothly across breaths (see chapter 4). As we shall see in chapter 6, teachers sometimes gesture silently while a student is singing, guiding the rhythmic flow of a phrase. Likewise, some singers (particularly elderly singers whose vocal ranges are narrower than they once were) sometimes continue articulating a melodic phrase in gesture when their voice cannot reach the heights or depths of the melodic phrase at hand. Were gesture merely a representation of sound, the trajectory of the hands would change abruptly when the voice gave out. Nor does it seem to be generally the case that vocalization is a representation of gesture. The same gestural motion may be cotimed with different vocal action (as shown in figure 2.6). Even though singers may imagine sweeping trajectories for their improvisation without having to plan each individual note, they are, crucially, singing in tune. Were a swooping gesture merely represented by the voice, it would be a continuous glide, not a sequence of precisely tuned notes. Neither gesture nor the voice, then, under ordinary circumstances, seems to point to the other.

Instead, in most cases of vocal performance by trained singers, vocalization and gesture seem to act as complementary, parallel channels for melody. If we are prepared to think of motion as melodic, this is unsurprising. More remarkable is that this seems to be precisely the relationship between vocalization and the gestures that accompany speech. These, too, are precisely cotimed, and preparation strokes frequently reveal that a speaker has a gesture prepared before vocalization begins. The motion of the hands does not refer to the voice or to the words that are spoken; instead, vocalization and gesture amount to a single action, showing different aspects of the same thing (McNeill 1992: 35 and 2005: 105; Kendon 2004: 127). While singing, as Mukul Kulkarni once put it, "you know the design in your brain, and it is sung as well as shown." Gesture and voice, to put it in Barlow's terms, perform a neume simultaneously. In Kurth's terms, they are the "outer layer" of music (1922: 4). Taken together with McNeill's and Kendon's analyses of coexpressive gesture and vocalization and Barlow's theory of synaesthetic neumes, this offers an alternative to seeing gesture as a representation of the voice, or vice versa. This allows us to understand the otherwise puzzling concurrence and nonredundancy of vocal and gestural improvisation. They are simply parallel aspects of melody.

On the other hand, Kurth's analytic reliance on a distinct surface between external physics and internal psychophysics may lead us to imagine a one-way melodic street from inside to outside. In the case of Hindustani vocal music (as with any music, notated or not, in which students learn through the examples of great performers), melodic imagination is crucially informed and shaped by melody in the world.[10] The creative source of vocalization and gesture does not hide behind the ramparts of the skull, insulated from the world outside. Hindustani vocal training requires thousands of hours of sitting face to face with a teacher, striving to both understand and perform disciplined melodic action. In the moment of musicking, Kurth's sharp line between internal psychological process and expressive performance dissolves; melodic imagination is both performed in the world and informed by the world. As the following chapters will reveal, melody is always performed in specific modal, metrical, social, and moral contexts.

CHAPTER THREE

Ragas as Spaces for
Melodic Motion

～

I am sitting before Vikas Kashalkar. He is teaching me Rag Hameer, but he hasn't
said a word about it yet. Instead, he is tacitly communicating a crucial feature of
its structure: again and again, he follows the same crooked pattern of descent
when bringing his phrases back home to *sa*. After repeating five phrases like this,
I grasp a simple rule: sing {*ga ma re sa*} to close phrases in Hameer. But my
rendering still sounds awkward — I am tentatively moving from note to note, as
though exploring a path in the dark. It is only after following his graceful lead
down this path twenty or thirty times that I begin to get my footing. He sings an
ascending phrase and cues me to finish the melodic sentence, making a small
downward spiral with his left hand; I descend along the crooked path to *sa*. By
the end of the lesson, Kashalkarji has shown me more ways to move: a propul-
sive, energetic ascending route from gandhar to shadaj that leaps over pancham;
a rapid forceful jump from below that touches nishad and hangs on dhaivat; and a
region of tight, twisted maneuvering around pancham. Later, walking home, my
mind wanders here and there, but I am surprised to find that I am humming
Hameer to myself. Just as I needn't think about the individual steps that lead me
to my flat, I needn't think about the individual notes on the paths of Hameer.

The heart of Hindustani music training is learning to render melody freely
and spontaneously in various ragas. Ragas are distinctive melodic worlds
full of characteristic color, affect, and motion, encompassing many compositions and a wide scope for improvised elaboration; a well-trained musician will have mastered dozens of them.[1] To sing in a given raga requires an
understanding of both melodic models outlined in the previous chapter: an
analytic sense of appropriate note sequences and a kinetic sense of appropriate melodic motion. Many music theorists have discussed raga in terms
of the first melodic model: they treat ragas as grammars that organize notes.

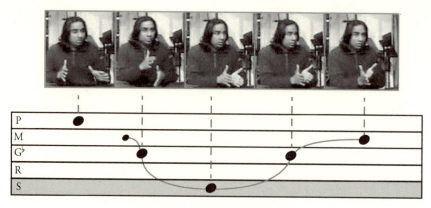

Figure 3.1. Bhimplas hand-slide.

This chapter proposes a complementary vision of ragas, appropriate to the second melodic model: ragas are distinctive spaces for melodic motion. A fuller discussion of raga will come later in this chapter; for now, an example will illustrate how raga performance unfolds in both vocal and gestural space.

Consider the performance of Rag Bhimplas by Shafqat Ali Khan referenced in figure 2.6. The alap begins with a few melodic figures near the low part of his range and gradually moves upward in large, swooping gestures over the course of several minutes. To a trained listener, his melodic action fills the room with the unmistakable color of Bhimplas. To a listener unschooled in raga, he may merely seem to be wandering up and down a scale. Over time, however, an attentive listener, schooled or unschooled, would notice that there are patterns in his melodic wandering. Every minute or so, for example, Shafqat Ali returns to a familiar groove: his right palm slides past his left while he sings a slow, sliding phrase in the middle of his vocal range (see figure 3.1).

While we might otherwise expect this gesture to correspond to melodic ascent in general (so that pitch is mapped onto the sagittal axis), it is rather more specific. The hand-sliding zone is reserved for vocal action that rises from shadaj to come to rest on madhyam. These rising, madhyam-tending phrases are not identical — they may be timed differently, may be preceded (as in figure 3.1) by a descent to shadaj (during which the hands are not sliding past each other), and may even momentarily touch other notes. But all of these phrases are articulated by vocal action in a well-defined vocal region and by gestural action in a well-defined gestural region.

Once we notice this region for melodic motion, we begin to notice others. Shafqat approaches nishad and gandhar from above with a gradual, pulling vocal glide that is often matched by a physical pulling gesture. Rapid ascents to high shadaj skip rishabh and dhaivat (e.g., {*ni sa ga ma pa ni sa*}), and often his hands move quite far upward in these motions — sometimes even above his shoulders. When he does descend to shadaj via rishabh or pancham via dhaivat, he pauses (both vocally and gesturally) for a moment before dropping down to the goal pitch. We begin to see the space in front of the singer's body not as a cube of empty air in which any melodic action will do, but as a landscape of regions, dynamic fields, and pathways for motion: as raga space.

Raga

Hindustani music is raga music; indeed, the bulk of Indian music theory amounts to raga theory. For musicians, each raga serves as a melodic template, including a set of pitches, characteristic phrases, relationships between notes, and architectures of melodic weight, energy, and tension. Songs are said to be "in" ragas, and musicians familiar with a raga can improvise melodies in it. Thus the term *raga* is used to refer to a specific performance ("he is going to perform Rag Saraswati") as well as the melodic entity that is the basis of an improvisation or composition ("here is a composition in Rag Saraswati"; "his alap in Rag Saraswati was very long"). Musicians and nonmusicians alike typically experience a raga as a gestalt, sometimes described in terms of color, taste, or affect. Many ragas evoke extrasonic entities: seasons, places, festivals, moods, persons (Brown 2003: 178–179).

The most rigorous work in Indian music theory, however, has tended to focus on rules for sequencing notes (see Jairazbhoy 1971; Bhatkhande 1964; Magriel 1997; etc.). These rules prescribe which notes are to be used in ascent and which are to be used in descent, and which key phrases, omissions, and emphases will generate acceptable melodies characteristic of that raga. For example, suppose a vocalist were moved to sing an ascending phrase to come to rest on *taar sa* (the high tonic). Depending on the raga at hand, there would be certain appropriate ways to carry this out. In Hameer, the melodic phrase {*ga ma (ni)dha ni sa*} would be a grammatically appropriate ascent whereas in Bihag (which has roughly the same pitch set) {*ga ma pa (sa)ni sa*} would be correct (see figure 3.2). Either phrase would, in general, be inappropriate in the other raga context.

Seeing a raga as a grammar is a consequence of seeing melody as a sequence of notes. If notes are discrete items, they can be ordered into meaningful sequences according to the rules of ragas, just as words are sequenced into meaningful sentences according to the rules of grammar. Sequences of notes are easily translated into sequences of symbols on a page, and these

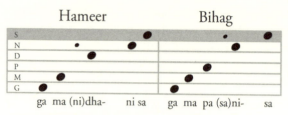

Figure 3.2. Appropriate ascending routes
to *sa* in Hameer and Bihag.

sequences can be juxtaposed for analysis. A printed, typeset handbook on raga can hardly avoid dealing in sequences of discrete symbols — typically notated by the extraordinarily space-efficient means of sargam notation, which in its most condensed form only requires seven distinct symbols, one each for *sa, re, ga, ma, pa, dha,* and *ni* (see Note on Notation). This notation is easy to read at a glance, and many musicians routinely consult printed books on raga to learn a basic grammatical outline of a raga.

Raga as Space

When the book is closed, however, and a musician turns his or her attention to performance, other ways of understanding raga become more useful than grammar.[2] Musicians often describe a raga at hand as if it were a space. For example, "in" Rag Bihag (*Bihag mein*), the rishabh is "leapt over" (*langhana*) in "ascent" (*aroha*) to the gandhar; this movement in the "lower part" (*purvang*) is also followed in the "upper part" (*uttarang*) by "leaping over" the dhaivat. In Rag Bhimplas, {*ma pa ga ma pa (sa)ni ni sa*} is a "launch vehicle" for approaching the upper regions (Parrikar 2001). A common way of speaking about the proper intonation of a note is to describe its *svarasthan* — literally, the place of the svara. Musicians often call distinctive spaces within ragas *jagahs* (spaces). As Sheila Dhar puts it, "Each *jagah* or place in the scale of a raga is not a point but a musical area that must be explored anew each time and brought to life in the living moment" (2001: 22). For example, the jagah between *dha* and *sa* in Mian ki Malhar, which contains four separate svarasthans, is especially dense. Rajan Parrikar (2001) has coined the hybrid Indic-English term *svaraspace* to describe the total distribution of notes in a raga, as for example the "crowded" svaraspace of raga Jaun Bhairav, or the "busy" svaraspace of Hamsakinkini. Music theorist and sarodist Parag Chordia has visualized relationships between ragas spatially, though the spatiality that he investigates is primarily the "perceptual distance" between related ragas, rather than the spatial layout of individual ragas, and their affordances for melodic motion (Chordia and Rae 2007).

Singer and musicologist Rabindra Lal Roy's evocative description of Hindustani music as "movements in musical space" (1934: 325) follows naturally from his description of melodic trajectories described in chapter 2.

While a simple visualization of pitch space in which pitches of lesser frequency are placed lower than pitches of greater frequency may seem commonsensical, it yields a scale, not a raga: a homogeneous, one-dimensional melodic space in which any path up or down is equivalent. Proceeding as though melody simply fits into an up-or-down, one-dimensional slot makes it difficult to attend to other dimensions of motion in space (cf. Zbikowski 2005: 66–68). Knowledge of this multidimensional space, full of learned paths and distinctive turns, is achieved only through training and practice. As Dard Neuman explains in his ethnography of hereditary Hindustani musicians, learning a raga is, in part, an extensive tour of a melodic geography. The student "is made to become familiar with the twists and turns of the neighborhood, the aesthetic territory of the raga, before he needs to know the names of the neighborhood streets" (2004: 202). Although prescriptions about melodic action in raga can be reduced to grammatical rules after the fact, patterns of melodic action in the moment of performance function more like paths. Hindustani musicians practice the routes within ragas repeatedly, so that they may move smoothly within them without having to think about note sequences. Such patterns of melodic motion are called the calan (movements) of a raga. As one master explained to Dard Neuman, the calan is a guide to "how we can walk in the paths of this raga" (ibid.). While in the space of a raga, one walks on certain paths, briefly touches certain points, stops to rest on others.

Knowing a raga requires knowing its paths. Simply moving wildly up and down a raga's scale flattens out its sense of space. This is not only true for highly trained Hindustani musicians. Even children seem to understand tunes as "action-paths" (Bamberger 1991: 10). Jazz pianist David Sudnow describes the difference between knowing a set of interchangeable pitches and following paths with the hand: "It became apparent after a while that any of the twelve notes 'can be played' with any of the chords. . . . Finding that any note would do, however, was tantamount to having no path to take whatever" (1995: 28). The difference between singing a familiar raga and an unfamiliar one is like the difference between navigating a path that one has walked hundreds of times and trying to pick out a path that one has only seen on a map. Though I may be able to sing the scale of an unfamiliar raga, merely stringing the notes together produces no sense of consistent spatiality. Making the space of the raga palpably present requires hours of practice, walking its distinctive paths over and over. To sing the phrase {ni re(♭) ga ma(♯) dha} in Rag Marwa, for example, seems difficult if performed cold, without practice, conceived step by precarious step: seventh, lowered second, third, raised fourth, sixth. With practice, though, I learned to feel this phrase as a familiar route ascending to dhaivat, as though dhaivat were "there waiting," as Veena Sahasrabuddhe put it in chapter 2. The intervening steps became easy, as though they were a pentatonic pathway projected downward from dhaivat itself. Paths do not just appear in the middle of a jungle — they lead somewhere, and one walks them with a goal in mind. With repeated trips, the paths become clearer. With more practice, the individual steps blur out of consciousness like the individual left and right turns on a familiar route, and the ascent to *dha* becomes a single melodic gesture.

It also matters *how* one walks these paths. Vocalist Veena Sahasrabuddhe, for example, links the spatiality of a raga with the pacing of melodic action, describing a preference for "expansive ragas one can sing in a leisurely fashion" (Navras 2004). Even ragas that share a common pitch set, such as Paraj and Basant, are distinguished by the quality of melodic motion that each requires. Mukul Kulkarni once explained this to me both vocally and gesturally: while Rag Paraj is *cancal* (trembling, shaking, volatile), Rag Basant is *gambhir* (heavy). While describing Paraj, his hands bounced rapidly through the air; while describing Basant, he slowly stretched the air in front of him, as though there were springs between his hands. Many other pairs of ragas with similar tonal content are contrasted according to this cancal/gambhir distinction — for example, Adana/Darbari, Deskar/Bhupali, Bahar/Mian ki Malhar (Martinez 2001: 322).[3] Just as one walks and talks differently in a mosque than in a crowded bazaar, raga spaces call for different gaits, tones of voice, and gestural bearings. In the midst of the slow, contemplative development characteristic of Raga Darbari, a sudden, rapid melodic move in the upper range of the voice can shatter the raga space even if the notes of the phrase are in proper order. This demand that raga music places on a singer is both aesthetic and ethical: one is not merely required to do what is beautiful in a given moment, but also what is necessary to establish the space of the raga.

Disciplined melodic motion establishes a raga's inside. Being "inside" a raga in this sense is not like being inside a box — it is more like being in a groove or in a game. This is not merely a question of reproducing sequences of notes or putting one's hands at objectively verifiable three-dimensional coordinates — someone who does so is no more in a raga than a toddler who wanders onto a cricket pitch is in the game. To sing inside a raga is a matter of walking its paths with its characteristic gaits. This inside implies an outside, and a common way of describing an inappropriate melodic act is that it has gone "outside the raga." This may refer to a grammatical violation (e.g., an inappropriate {*ni re ga*} ascent in Bihag) and may be described in grammatical terms. But moving inside and outside a raga does not reduce to following rules. Even the strictest melodic grammarians agree that competent musicians can sing phrases that violate grammatical rules and yet remain inside the raga. As Dard Neuman points out, this is often considered a mark of musical mastery. Consider Baha-ud-din Dagar's praise of Vilayat Khan's rendering of Marwa, below. The performance is seen to be good precisely because it includes note sequences characteristic of a closely related raga and yet remains in the "circle" of Marwa:

> He's going "Ni Ma Ma Ga Re" [7 ♯4 ♯4 3 ♭2]. [Some people will say,] "hah, yeh to Puriya hai (this is Puriya [because he is emphasizing Ma, a characteristic of Puriya])." But it's not happening to be Puriya. He's not leaving the pattern of Marwa. He's within the circle of Marwa. (Bahauddin Dagar in Dard Neuman 2004: 220)

The spaces of ragas are sometimes described as having a certain inherent pattern of movement structured into their shape. In certain ragas that call for crooked melodic motion (such as Kamod, Nayaki, and Gaud Malhar), not only individual phrases but the raga itself is described as crooked (*vakra*) (Roychaudhuri 2000: 189). Rahim Fahim-ud-din Dagar explained to me once that the raga Darbari is itself andolit (undulating). The conventional wisdom about Darbari is that two isolated notes (gandhar and dhaivat) are rendered by moving the voice up and down around the pitch without quite touching the pitches on either side. Dagar, however, explained that in a proper rendering of Darbari, the raga itself is andolit:

> "Dhaivat andolit hai aur pancham andolit nahi hai." No. Yah khyal galat hai. ye gandhare ke liye baat nahiye. Poora raag darbaari jo hai andolit hai.

> [Some say,] "Dhaivat is andolit and pancham is not andolit." No. This idea is wrong. This is not only a matter of gandhar. The whole of Rag Darbari is andolit.[4]

While saying the word *poora* (entirety), he opened his arms wide, encompassing a wide space. He went on to describe a kind of raga knowledge that answers "where" questions about location and action in raga space — "Kaha dirgha hai? Kaha sphuta hai? Kaha khincit hai? Kaha alp hai?" (Where is it elongated? Where is it opened up? Where is it stretched? Where is it small?). These terms have specific, conventional meanings in reference to the treatment of various notes, but Dagar Sahab's repeated use of *kaha* (where) highlights that these terms also refer to spatial, kinetic knowledge. Knowing a

"steam rising"   "lightning crashing down"

Figure 3.3. Vikas Kashalkar's
descriptions of motion in Malhar.

raga, then, does not mean merely knowing its boundaries or its texture — it also means knowing its spatial layout.

Sri Raga is another raga with a long tradition of extrasonic associations. Singers associate it with a bewildering array of characteristics — high status, stillness, devotional surrender, a warriorlike spirit, reaching out with longing, standing on a hilltop, standing before an ocean, a lover's quarrel, and so on (Leante 2009). In an incisive analysis linking these associations to the gestural performance of Sri Raga, Laura Leante suggests that many of these characteristics may in fact find a common origin in an "upward arm gesture" associated primarily with a distinctive *re–pa* glide (2009: 203).

But raga space also seems to invite melodic richness precisely because it embraces radically different kinds of motion in a single *sva-roop*, a single melodic gestalt. For example, Vikas Kashalkar once described two key oppositional phrases in Raga Mian ki Malhar, as illustrated in figure 3.3. {*Ma pa dha ni sa*}, he said, is "the steam rising from trees"; {*(ni) pa (ma) ga*} is "the lightning crashing down from clouds."

A general link between the many Malhar ragas and rain is repeated many times in folklore (most famously in the widespread legend of Tansen's daughter summoning rain with Megh Malhar). But this specific link between the characteristic movements of water and the melodic gait of Malhar ragas seems likewise to obtain for some musicians. For example, B. R. Deodhar describes Bade Ghulam Ali Khansahab singing Rag Mian ki Malhar along with the motions of the Arabian Sea during a rainstorm in Bombay:

> We came to Marine Drive [in Bombay] and Khansaheb asked the cabbie to stop his vehicle at a spot where there is a cement-concrete projection. The waves of the turbulent sea at this point were thirty to forty feet high. Khansaheb said, "Deodharsaheb, the time and this place are just right for doing riyaz [practice]. Listen." And he began to sing. Whenever a particularly massive wave broke and water spouted up, Khansaheb's tana [i.e., taan] rose in synchronization and descended when water cascaded down. Water rose in a single massive column but split at the top and fell in broken slivers; so did Khansaheb's tana in raga Miyan Malhar. Sometimes, if his ascending notes failed to

keep pace with the surging water, he was angry with himself but tried again till it synchronized perfectly with the surging water. (Deodhar 1993: 250)

Another raga with strong rain associations is Megh. Once, in a lesson, Mukul Kulkarni linked deep, heavy oscillation in Raga Megh (articulated vocally with deep, swooping *gamak*, and gesturally with loose shaking of the hands from the wrist) to thundering clouds and the "unclear atmosphere" of mist. He contrasted this with the noontime raga Madhmad Sarang, which has the same scale as Megh but which, he said, is to be sung like the "straight rays" of light at noon, in clear, straight melodic motion. Rahim Fahim-ud-din Dagar showed me once how touching rishabh and returning to shadaj in Raga Bhairav (a raga traditionally performed in the early morning) suggests the first light has appeared in the sky; ascending from rishabh to gandhar, he said, suggests that the sun has risen. While the descriptions of individual raga spaces vary widely across singers, ragas nonetheless consistently function in performance as spaces.

Raga Space

What kind of spaces are these? Raga spaces are both sonic and gestural: just as motion fills space, so does sound. Close your eyes and snap your fingers: you can hear your space. Even when apprehended visually, space shares many of the same properties attributed to sound: we feel certain spaces to be open or closed, vast or small, bright or dark, straight or curved. Raga space is not the kind of radically objective space that is measured with demonstrable accuracy on maps; nor is it the radically subjective space of dreams, relevant to no one but the dreamer. Instead, it arises intersubjectively, palpably real to all involved in the moment of musicking, built for and by performance. These spaces are defined not by the absolute position of the limbs or the voice at any given moment, but by a coherent range of potential actions. In the same sense in which one might need a certain space to take a particular shot when playing billiards, or a certain flat area to chop vegetables, raga space is defined and shaped by its purposes. A cup of tea on the table to your right affords a space of potential motion between your body and the cup that is not there to your left; a tea stall across the street affords a route for foot traffic even without a crosswalk.

Gesture space, in speech and song, is likewise dynamically shaped by potential action. In speech, regions of gesture space are often linked to characters in a story (McNeill 1992: 171), or distinctive discursive functions, such as mediating turn-taking (Sweetser and Sizemore 2008). But these regions are not floating in the air when you get up and walk away. They are ephemeral extensions of the body that appear and disappear according to the needs of performance. People who are singing while walking carry raga space with them; when they sit down, the space of potential gestural action remains around their body like a fog. Unlike the homogeneous, interchangeable points of Euclidean space, raga spaces have distinctive landscapes, relative to the current melodic needs. They serve as extensions of the body, regions of potential kinesis.

Dard Neuman observes that with rigorous training, Hindustani musicians can think not of the individual notes that are appropriate to a raga, but rather of places within a raga:

> We confront an epistemic order that has transcended epistemological categories (with rules and their infractions . . .) to "points" and places (jagah) of ragas, places traveled and "pushed" by the hands, spaces of melodic movement that are aural as well as tactile, melodic as well as material, effective as well as physical. The musician makes music not by playing notes but by "sculpting silence" and "weaving patterns out of nothing." At this point we are no longer dealing with notes, note-names or rules, just places traveled by the hands. (2004: 221)

These places are flexible but stable topographies that singers explore through both melodic and gestural action. Singers navigate the space of a raga in the space around their body while elaborating on melodies, moving through particular regions via particular melodic paths, with particular textures and topographies. By performing a raga, a singer transforms a continuum of pitch into a flexible but stable terrain in which the musician moves. The space around the body is likewise transformed into a landscape with consistent features. These landscapes are not given or fixed, but simultaneously created and explored through consistent melodic action, as paths are created in a forest through repeated use. Singers maneuver in this space while improvising, moving through particular regions via particular melodic paths articulated by both sound and gesture.

Pakad and Catchments

Ragas are often ascribed sets of catchphrases, or pakads ("catchings"), which are important in identifying ragas. While a singer moves (calna) through a raga to understand it, a listener attempts to catch (pakadna) the motion to identify the raga at hand. In this sense, a pakad is a musical analog of what David McNeill calls a catchment[5] in the performance of speech. A catchment is a consistent gestural form that links together recurring themes in discussions, even if these themes are separated by digressions. In one example given by McNeill, a woman uses four distinct catchments in describing her house: she performs two-handed symmetrical gestures whenever talking about the front doors of the house, reserves the space above her right knee for the kitchen at the back of her house, and so on (2005: 165–172). In raga performance, singers perform catchments that seem to involve subspaces within raga spaces: consistent regions within the raga that have distinctive tonal and kinesic potentials.

One clear example of this is found in a performance of the Raga Ramkali by the eminent singer Girija Devi. Ramkali is a close relative of one of the best-known ragas in Hindustani music: Bhairav. Ramkali is one of a group of ragas that is closely related to Bhairav through shared tetrachords or melodic motion (e.g., Ahir Bhairav, Jaun Bhairav, Basant Mukhari). Bhairav and Ramkali share the same basic pitch set: all natural notes except for a lowered rishabh and a lowered dhaivat (second and sixth scale degrees). In both Bhairav and Ramkali, these lowered notes tend to be approached from above and are sometimes rendered andolit (i.e., undulating: with a subtle, slow vibrato). From a grammatical point of view, there are several phrases, such as {ga ma (ni)dha pa} and {ga ma pa ga ma (ga)re sa}, that distinguish Bhairav from the several other ragas, such as Kalingda, which share a scale with Bhairav — Ramkali uses all of these distinctive phrases as well.

Ramkali is distinguished from Bhairav, however, by an occasional, very distinctive introduction of a *tivra madhyam* and *komal nishad* (sharp fourth and flat seventh).[6] I call the introduction of these distinctive notes a "Ramkali shift" (see Rahaim in Fatone et al. 2011). Figure 3.4 shows an example of how a Ramkali shift might be fluidly inserted into an otherwise Bhairav-ish sequence.

In terms of pitch sequences, the Ramkali shift is the primary feature that distinguishes Ramkali from Bhairav. The subspace of Bhairav-like melodic action in Ramkali will be called "quasi-Bhairav" to distinguish it from the subspace of Ramkali shifts.

Gesturally, Girija Devi delineates two subspaces that correspond to these vocal subspaces: one, which is used most of the time, for quasi-Bhairav space; and another, which is only used occasionally, for Ramkali shifts.[7]

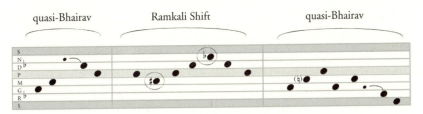

Figure 3.4. Ramkali shift.

Figure 3.5. Sketch of Girija Devi articulating
the Ramkali shift subspace.

The space of Ramkali, then, is evident both vocally and gesturally. While
the quasi-Bhairav melodic motion is generally performed only with her
right hand, the Ramkali shifts are two-handed and are restricted to a small-
ish sphere in front of her solar plexus. While quasi-Bhairav melodic action
moves freely within a larger gestural space, the Ramkali melodic action
always curves in on itself. Moving in this space, her hands curl around each
other without touching, as though tracing a curvaceous three-dimensional
figure. Figure 3.5 is a sketch of the space of the Ramkali shift subspace.

While moving within the Ramkali shift subspace, Girija Devi's hands
curl around a small empty spherical region, about the size of an apple, without touching. This motion is parallel to the sonic action of the Ramkali
shift, in which the notes center around the stable fifth scale degree. The
Ramkali shift is also enacted with heightened shoulder tension. In the performance analyzed here, the melodic action of Ramkali shifts is dramatically and consistently contrasted with quasi-Bhairav action by the spatial and
movement features of the hand gestures accompanying them. Figure 3.6
shows the distinctive features of the quasi-Bhairav and Ramkali subspaces.

Note that here, as in the hand-sliding space in Shafqat Ali's Bhimplas, the
space of a raga is not merely a range of frequencies or a three-dimensional
region of objective space. The frequency range between *ga* and *ni*, for example, is used in both the Ramkali shift subspace and the quasi-Bhairav
subspace; likewise, Girija Devi's hands move through the Ramkali shift subspace while articulating linear motion in the quasi-Bhairav subspace. The
distinction lies not in absolute position or frequency but in path and man-

	Quasi-Bhairav	Ramkali
Notes	Same as Bhairav	Tivra Madhyam, Komal Nishad
Gestural Region	In front of trunk	In front of solar plexus
Hand Motion	Free	Curls around small sphere
Vocal Motion	Free	Pivots around Pancham
# of Hands	One	Two
Tension	Slack	Tense

Figure 3.6 Table of quasi-Bhairav and Ramkali shift subspaces.

ner. This subspace, then, is defined not only by its boundaries, but also by the special contours along which gesture is performed.

Although the contours of a raga space, once established, tend to remain in place over the course of one rendering of a raga, it will not necessarily be the same for every rendering. Some patterns cohere across certain lineages, while others seem to be idiosyncratic; most seem to last only as long as a single performance. For example, although the gestural pattern above is very consistent in the particular performance of Rag Ramkali analyzed here (of thirty-four sung Ramkali shifts, thirty follow exactly the pattern described here in her 1991 Savai Gandharva performance), Bhimsen Joshi's performance of Ramkali at the same festival one year later shows no trace of these curling gestures.

However, the few cases in which I have made many video recordings of a single raga by the same performer suggests that at least some features may remain the same from performance to performance. For example, in every performance of Vikas Kashalkar's Mian Ki Malhar that I have seen, whether in lessons or on stage, he generally performs the common phrase {*ma re pa*} in a special curved subspace. This phrase is performed with a curving, upward swoop of the hand, led by the fingertips, in which the hand inclines backward toward the top of the forearm. This swoop is coordinated specifically with the *r–p* segment of the phrase. The *(m)r* segment of the phrase often involves a churning motion in this space, coordinated with one or more cyclical churns of {*ma re ma re*}, depending on the context. Figure 3.7 shows a lesson with Vikas Kashalkar in which he first sings this phrase, then tacitly gestures along with his students as they repeat it, and then sings the phrase again. This same subspace, and its affiliated gestural action, is found in Kashalkar's performances of other ragas of the Malhar family that feature the {*ma re pa*} catchment: Nat Malhar, Gaud Malhar, and so on.[8]

Although the logic and consistency of spaces and subspaces[9] is shown through correspondences like the one above between Ramkali shifts and the small curvilinear subspace, these rules are not ontologically prior to

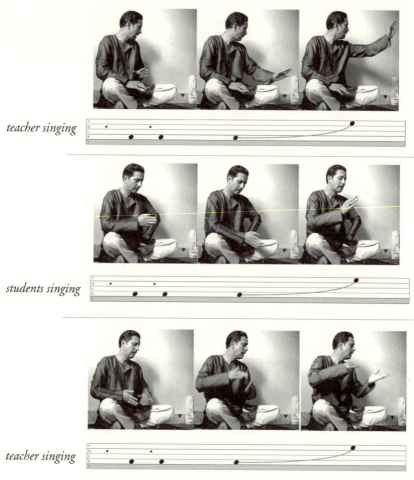

teacher singing

students singing

teacher singing

Figure 3.7. Three articulations of swooping {*ma re pa*} pattern.

performance. They also seem to be constructed in the course of performance. If raga space is not empty, nor are the features of raga landscapes made of granite. Instead, like clay, they are malleable yet hold their shape long enough to sculpt recognizable, plastic forms. Furthermore, spatial features sometimes linger during the transitions between ragas. After the performance of Bhimplas analyzed in figure 3.1, Shafqat Ali Khan sang Rag Bagesri. Bagesri and Bhimplas have the same pitch set: a flat third and a flat seventh. Recall that Shafqat had just established the hands-sliding-past-each-other catchment alongside {*sa ga ma*} in rag Bhimplas. As one would expect, Bagesri had a different landscape despite having the same pitch set. However, the Bhimplas hand-slide did appear once, at the very beginning, the first time that Shafqat Ali sang {*sa ga ma*}, a phrase that appears in both Bagesri and Bhimplas. Once he was more firmly established in the space of Bagesri, this gestural catchment from the previous raga space melted away.

We have already seen that the paths traced within raga spaces needn't reproduce pitch trajectories. In Shafqat Ali Khan's rendering of Bhimplas, for example, we saw a case in which the hands corresponded to the net motion of the voice rather than every single note the voice sang; the inverse happens as well, particularly when the voice is constrained by raga grammar. In Rag Rayasa Kanada, a descent from *ni* to *pa* is typically connected by a smooth glide. But Vikas Kashalkar reports that he often feels an ascent before the descent, even though singing {*ni sa pa*} would be prohibited by the raga. This melodic curve is nonetheless articulated gesturally:

> *Ni* to *pa* is not a straight line. So when I do it, I feel that whatever I could not sing, that has come out from [the gesture] . . . how it should be. *Ni* to *sa* is a small touch which sometimes is not allowed in the raga . . . in that context. But it is my intention. Innermost intention is, if it touches *sa* also, it may look fine. But while singing [the grammar of the raga] doesn't allow me to do that. . . . So that is done with gestures. It would not go {*ni dha ni pa*}, so *ni* should not be straight only; this is shown by the hand actions.

Figure 3.8 shows the contrast between the hand motion and vocal motion marking this melodic phrase.

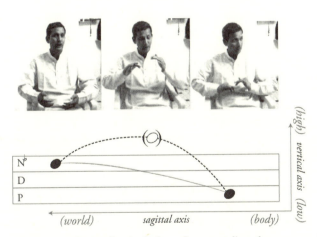

Figure 3.8. Gestural articulation of an ascending-then-descending phrase (dotted line) performed in conjunction with a straight vocal descent (gray line).

Raga Space and Raga Grammar Are Complementary

These metaphors of space and exploration, on the surface, may seem merely poetic, lacking the rigor and replicability of note sequences. But a conception of melody as motion is no more fanciful than its widespread conception as a sequence of discrete objects; conceiving a raga as a space for melodic motion is likewise no more fanciful than conceiving of a raga as a grammar for melodic sequences.

Hindustani vocalists routinely practice in ways that develop a sense of moving-within-space so that thinking of individual notes is unnecessary. Dard Neuman's ethnography of music pedagogy emphasizes that it is possible to move fluently in ragas without knowing which notes one is singing. The sons and daughters of hereditary musicians who were trained in their youth, but stopped before their teenage years, provide an example:

> Their musicianship, therefore, was a product of stunted training and practice; their formal musical practice froze, if you will, at an early level. . . . They could all sing wonderfully and easily. They all possessed a fabulous repertoire of compositions, exercises and ragas. What we call talent was evidenced in the ease and fluidity through which they could sing even the most intricate phrases and *bandish*. . . . But they did not know the names of the notes they were singing. (2004: 174 n. 100)

That this knowledge is not necessarily a foundational level of musicianship is evidenced by the fact that the reverse is also possible: one can learn the grammar of a raga in terms of discrete note-names but be unable to sing it freely and convincingly. Indeed, recitals of school-trained young singers are filled with this kind of singing: blocky and disconnected, like someone speaking a newly learned language, piecing sentences together word by word. And just as the singers described by Neuman master sargam after having been trained to move fluently in raga, singers who learn a raga beginning from note sequences only later, with practice, come to understand a raga as a space in which one moves freely.

Thus spatial and grammatical models of raga are not mutually exclusive, but complementary. Philosopher Michel de Certeau (1984: 100), for example, points out a crucial isomorphism between language and motion: the geometry of a fixed space serves as a "proper meaning" against which the life of a moving, walking subject is the "drifting of figurative meaning." Likewise, the most rigid features of a raga space (avoiding *ga*, for example, in Rag Brindavani Sarang) operate rather like grammar; the improvisation of melodic motion within raga spaces operates much in the same way as, say, the improvisation of spontaneous, stylized, rhetorically potent speech within the grammatical conventions that scaffold mutual understanding. Thoroughly trained Hindustani musicians rely on both spatio-kinetic and note-combinatoric knowledge of raga. Neither one serves as a necessary pedagogical fundament for the other, as evidenced by the fact that either one can be learned first. Even a highly refined knowledge of the space of a raga cannot do the work of *svara-jnan*. It cannot articulate the precise, rational, intervallic relationships between the individual notes of ragas; it cannot provide a common tonal ground for instrumentalists and singers; it cannot explicate crucial distinctions in note sequences that distinguish ragas. Likewise, even a sophisticated knowledge of svaras is no replacement for the grace, sense of melodic purpose, and kinetic freedom enabled by a knowledge of raga space.

CHAPTER FOUR

Melodic Motion in Time

Ustad Iqbal Ahmad Khan is singing a fast composition in Rag Purvi. I am sitting just to his left, accompanying him on the harmonium. While he improvises fast, elaborate melodic runs, I follow close behind him, trying in every moment to play what he just sang. But what he just sang is also here now, as the basis for ongoing, repeated patterns; thus he establishes melodic grooves for me to join. When he returns to the fixed part of the composition, singing the repeated first line three or four times in a row, I lock into unison with him. How do I know where he will end an improvised section and return to the composition? Part is convention: I know that the composition picks up from the twelfth unit of the metrical cycle, that he won't let a whole minute pass before returning to the precomposed melody, and that his cadences occur within the space of Rag Purvi. But it is also evident from how he moves. When his hands start to come together at the end of a phrase, I feel him closing an improvisational episode. When he seems to be holding something and starts to put it down, I feel him finishing what he is doing. When I sense his body and voice moving somewhere, I try to meet him there. To accompany him is to feel both where he is going and when he will get there.

If Iqbal Ahmad Khan was improvising, how could I know what he was going to do? This apparent paradox is rooted in a conflict between two ideas of how a musician moves in time. On one hand, each moment is new: the musician continuously generates new melodic material. On the other hand, each moment touches the past and the future: the musician continuously elaborates on what has come before and reaches toward melodic goals yet to come. Musicians devise melodic patterns with a culminating moment already in view, drawing on just-performed melodic patterns as materials. They work within recurring metrical cycles, using memory and imagination, the known and unknown, to unfold melodic motion in time.

Melodic motion, like all motion, can never appear in an infinitesimal moment: just as a photograph of a runner is not in motion, a frozen instant of melodic action is not, by itself, melodic.[1] Melodic motion emerges only when the present is connected to the past and future (cf. Schutz 1976: 37–38). This applies in principle to any of the melodic motion analyzed in chapter 2 — recall that "we can know where a neume is going while it is still in the process of going there" (Barlow 1998–2000). It also, however, applies to the temporal organization of time structures longer than a single breath. After briefly touching on the conventional gestures that mark the progress of *tala* (metrical cycles), this chapter will investigate the ways in which extended gestural phrases shape musical time into long moments of melodic action and temporal attention.

Tala

Talas, ordered metrical cycles, provide the sturdiest temporal structure in Hindustani music. In the midst of various kinds of rhythmic play, the progression of tala is unambiguous; the rules of tala have become conventional and well established (Bagchee 1998; Clayton 2001; Kippen 2006.) Talas are marked both by fixed cycles of drum strokes and by fixed cycles of handclaps and handwaves that mark metrical progression. Their measure is so clear and verifiable that violations of tala are one of few cases in which the authority of a tabla accompanist can supersede the authority of a soloist. The fundamental unit of tala is the *matra*, and a key characteristic of a given tala is the number of matras it contains (*ektal* has twelve, *jhoomra tal* has fourteen, etc.). In principle, consecutive matras are of equal length, but the range of possible tempi in performance varies greatly. During a slow composition, a matra might last as long as four seconds; at the climax of a fast composition, a matra might be as short as an eighth of a second. Individual matras have no particular kinetic affiliate; indeed, they are not always of a length that corresponds to the comfortable range of foot- or finger-tapping, or stepping. At relatively fast tempi, matras at key structural points are marked with claps (or slapping the hand on the thigh) and waves of the hand. For example, *tintal* contains sixteen matras, divided into four parts, with a clap on the first, fifth, and thirteenth and a wave on the ninth. Tintal, like all talas, starts from and ends on the first matra, called *sam*. It repeats periodically, so that the sixteenth matra is followed by *sam*. One full cycle of tal is called an *avartan*. *Jhaptal*, another common tala, has ten matras in each avartan. Its characteristic gestural sequence follows the same "clap, clap, wave, clap" pattern as tintal but is divided differently (figure 4.1).

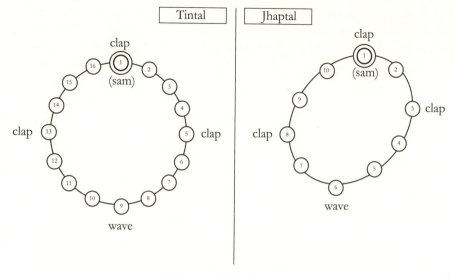

Figure 4.1. Tintal and Jhaptal.

These tala-marking gestural signs are usually implicit and are most often used when the progression of tala is ambiguous, as in a tabla solo, or when first presenting a composition. In the South, singers and knowledgeable audience members alike often continue articulating the tala patterns with claps and waves throughout a performance. In the North, audience members seldom keep tala apart from marking sam,[2] and performers almost never do. The hands are free to do other melodic and rhythmic work.

Phrasing

Within the strict metrical frameworks of tala structures, singers freely articulate melodic phrases in time. Unlike tala cycles, the subtle rhythmic organization of melodic phrases follow no explicit rules. Some general features of gesture apply, however. As with speech-affiliated gestures (Kendon 2004: 112), melody-affiliated gestures follow a predictable trajectory: the hand travels from a resting position (preparation), performs one or more focused movements (stroke), and comes back to rest (recovery). Though the voice likewise has preparation and recovery phrases (in which the larynx, tongue, and other articulatory organs align themselves for vocalization before vocalization and return to rest afterward), these phases are both inaudible and hidden from view. The hands are different. Even the simplest manual gestures — for example, giving someone a thumbs-up sign — requires both that the hand be lifted to a visible position and that the hand be placed into the correct shape before the communicative part of the sign is given. Afterward the hand travels to another position or returns to rest.

The preparatory phrase of a gesture, which generally precedes vocalization, often already contains a plan for the coming action. For example, the index fingers may be extended, or the arms may begin reaching for a virtual object while the singer is still taking a breath. The hand, in other words, reaches for the sound before the voice begins. Martin Clayton vividly describes a case in which singer Vijay Koparkar anticipates a melodic ascent by raising his hand into place to prepare for the vocal ascent (in Fatone et al. 2011). Again, this is not a specific feature of Hindustani music — David Sudnow recalls how the hands of improvising pianists form shapes during silences that lead the melody smoothly into the next phrase (1995: 116–117).

Typically, once the hand is in position, the melodic stroke of a gesture is cotimed with vocalization. However, Vikas Kashalkar once demonstrated to me that a note may begin in gesture before the vocal cords are engaged. On this occasion, I was not singing the *shuddh gandhar* (the third scale degree) of Rag Malgunji correctly. The pitch was correct, but still Kashalkarji was not satisfied with the way I was articulating the svara. Then I noticed that he was initiating the motion of his hand before vocalizing. He said, "There is this pronunciation" and moved his open palm toward his chest for two seconds before saying *ga*. I was perplexed — I heard only silence. He repeated this several times — first the hand gesture, then the *ga*, until it became clear to me that the svara was beginning before the sound. I then was able to do it: I moved my hand, soundlessly manifesting the svara before engaging my vocal cords. Kashalkarji sounded his approval, as did all of the other students in the room.

The aerobic necessity of stopping phonation while inhaling every fifteen seconds or so requires periodic silences, and Hindustani vocalists time their breaths so that these breaks are melodically effective as phrase markers. A pause between melodic movements provides a moment to breathe, a point of repose from which to consider the next move. My own teacher instructs his students, as a rule of thumb, not to interrupt a break or a phrase with a breath. Indeed, for most singers, the hands come to rest during long breaks in vocalization. But sometimes singers continue the course of a gesture while inhaling, articulating macrophrases longer than a single breath. Gestural breaks vary in weight. Singers may fully disengage from musical gesture (buttoning their shirt, resting in their lap, drinking tea) or merely pause for a moment in midair.

But phrasing is not merely a concession to the physiological constraints of lung capacity. Breaking a melody into phrases allows a singer to articulate melodic depth, affording some notes greater melodic significance than

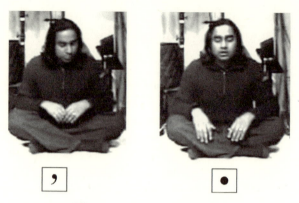

Figure 4.2. Partial and full rest.

Figure 4.3. One phrase in a Bhimplas alap.

others. Hierarchies of phrasing that are longer than the breath are perceptible in gestures and correspond roughly to hierarchies of vocal phrasing. Figure 4.2 is a short excerpt of an alap (unmetered melodic exposition) in Rag Bhimplas by Shafqat Ali Khan. The symbols in circles shown in figure 4.3 indicate different levels of gestural phrasing at breaths and other breaks in vocalization. Commas (,) indicate that the hands come partially to rest, stopping in the air in front of the body. Periods (.) indicate that the hands fully disengage from melodic action (resting in the lap, drinking water, etc.).

The point of greatest gestural repose (represented by the period in the above diagram) occurs on the *sa* that concludes the phrase above. *Sa* is ordinarily the point of greatest melodic repose as well. Resting on *sa* after a long excursion often serves as a major structural point that marks the boundary between two sections. More surprising, however, is that the points of gestural repose spell out a key Bhimplas phrase: {*ga re sa*}. As it turns out, the gestural markers in this performance spell out a series of distinctive Bhimplas phrases. Figure 4.3 shows the first macrophase of this alap (see figure 4.4 for a reduction of the full alap), in which the phrasing markers are placed on the staff according to which note was the end of the phrase. Note that, in addition to periods and commas, ellipses (. . .) are used to

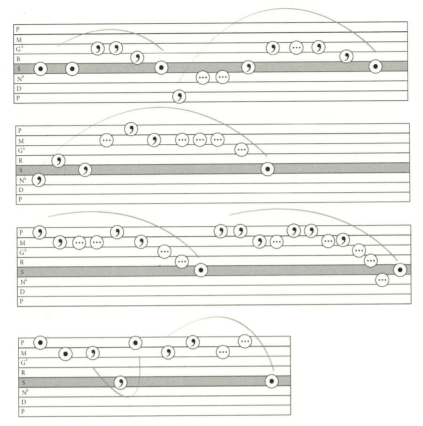

Figure 4.4. Bhimplas alap macrophrases.

indicate that the hands continue moving even when the singer stops phonation for a moment to take a breath.

In this alap, descent to *sa* is always marked with a full gestural rest, and every full gestural rest falls on *sa* — with one interesting exception. The three penultimate macrophrases of the alap find full gestural rest on *pa, ma,* and *pa,* respectively. This functions something like a modulation as the gestures are temporarily centered around pancham.

Remarkably, the ending notes of the gestural phrases (marked above by commas, ellipses, and periods) also trace phrases that move along the paths of Bhimplas: {*sa sa ga ga re sa, pa ni ni sa ga ga ga re sa, ni re sa ma pa ma ma ma ma ga sa, pa ma ma ma pa ma ga re sa, pa pa ma ma pa pa ma ga re sa*}. Phrases that are ordinarily prohibited in Bhimplas, such as {*sa re ga, re ma pa, ma re ga*}, are conspicuously absent from these macrophrases. Gesture and voice work together to articulate the calan of Bhimplas on two self-similar, hierarchically nested levels at once.

Phrasing in Vilambit Khyal

A *vilambit khyal* is a khyal performed in a slow tempo, usually with fifteen to forty seconds per twelve-, fourteen-, or sixteen-matra avartan. The last beat or two of each avartan is given over to a small fragment of the composition that leads to sam. This fragment is called the *mukhra*. Mukhras are recognizably similar from one instance to the next, if not identical. Unlike repeated melodic patterns, which are sometimes affiliated with different gestural forms, mukhras tend to be more gesturally consistent from one instance to the next, in line with their function as a point of return.

But the recurrence of the mukhra also provides a temporal structure for melodic improvisation. The art of improvising melody in vilambit khyal lies largely in looking forward to the arrival of the mukhra and blending one's improvised phrases seamlessly with it so that the return of the mukhra seems like an inevitable outcome of spontaneous melodic play. Consider Veena Sahasrabuddhe's description:

> The perfect avartan maintains a close relation between the swaras and phrases of the alaps on the one hand and the progress of the [tal] on the other hand, so that the listener can feel the mukhra and sam coming. The end point appears so natural, so logical, that the listener is moved to giving out an immediate expression to her joy. (Sahasrabuddhe in Clayton 2001: 141)

Vikas Kashalkar sometimes instructs students to fill tala cycles as though they were moving within a room. He uses the joints of the fingers on his open palm as a map of tilwada tal, a sixteen-matra cycle, counting four matras on each finger. He often instructs students to see the sam coming, as if at the end of a hallway. As we progress through the tal, he narrates his thinking: "Okay, here we are halfway through [at the ninth matra], so we can take a breath. Here we have only four matras, so we should bring our upaj to a close."

Improvisation in vilambit khyal, then, occurs not moment by infinitesimal moment, or along a rigorously predetermined timeline, but within a continuous, thick "field of presence" (Merleau-Ponty 2002 [1945]: 483–484) in which the musician intentionally retains the past and reaches out to the future. I needn't painstakingly call to mind the melodic pattern I just sang, as though it had disappeared into oblivion; instead, "I still have it in hand, and it is still there" (ibid., after Husserl 1964 [1928]), ringing in the field of presence. Likewise, I needn't schedule my future melodic trajectories, note for note; I am already feeling where I want my melody to go, aligning my improvisation within metrical structures as certain as "the back of a house of which I can only see the facade" (ibid.). In the musical field of presence, the past and the future may be invisible, but they are nonetheless present as phrases-in-hand (which appear as seeds for melodic growth) and approaching metrical landmarks (which appear as destinations for melodic motion). This retained past and aimed-for future serve as the ever-present context for melody. In retrospect, a transcription of an alap may present time as a line on the page, but for a musicking body, time is a continuous flow, retaining and reworking past melodic patterns, reaching toward a point in the future.[3]

The pattern of returning to *sa* at structural markers, noted above, is particularly strong during the long metrical cycles of vilambit khyals. This form typically consists of twenty- to forty-second metrical cycles (avartans), each of which culminates in a short melodic formula (mukhra) leading to the first matra of the cycle (sam). Between the mukhras, the singer elaborates on the melodic and textual materials of the raga and composition at hand, drawing these improvised segments to a close in time for the mukhra. One typical pattern is that each improvisation will descend to *sa* before the mukhra begins. Vikas Kashalkar explicitly recommends to beginning students that they end every phrase on *sa* as a rule of thumb. In one lesson he told his students, "All the time you should come to *sa*. You should end your alap [i.e., your improvisation leading to the mukhra] on *sa*." This is a common admonition given to students who improvise aimlessly, without clearly articulated phrasing, and then just sing the mukhra at the proper point in the tala. But, as Kashalkarji's speech gestures show (figure 4.5), this return to *sa* also corresponds to a kinesic sense of putting something down,

All the time...   ...you should   You should end
                    come to sa.   your alap on sa.

Figure 4.5. Gestural affiliates of descriptions of returning to *sa*.

Figure 4.6. Gestural affiliates of several returns to
sa immediately preceding the mukhra.

or joining two things together. The analyses that follow compare the gestural affiliates of Kashalkarji's explicit recommendation of this pattern with the gestural affiliates of this pattern in performance.

The spoken phrase "come to *sa*" is affiliated with both hands in a pinching precision grip, coming together at a point. "You should end your alap on *sa*" is affiliated with a push downward and to the right. (What it is that is pushed aside is a somewhat trickier matter and will be discussed in chapter 5.) His gestures here closely resemble his gestures in performance. They tend to move down, to his right, and toward closure. Figure 4.6 shows the gestures of the concluding phrases just before the mukhra in four consecutive avartans in a performance of Bhimplas.

Although Kashalkar himself sometimes ends his improvisational segments by returning to the low *sa* before the mukhra, there are other methods available as well. Often, even after a return to *sa*, a short melodic fragment (called *amad*) leads the singer back to the pitch level of the mukhra. In compositions that have a high mukhra, and especially in ragas like Sohini and Adana that tend to focus on the upper register, phrases leading to the mukhra often end on the high *sa*. Another possibility is to blend

	1	2	3	4	5	6	7	8	9	10	11	12
1st	ā	-	en	-	ge	mo -	hana	pyāre ra-ha	-	ta kahata	bha – i -│ya mo - rā│	ka-ba ghara
2nd	ā	-	en	- ge	mo -	ha - na pyā - re		ra-ha - ta kaha- ta		bhaī - ya │mo - rā│		ghara
3rd	ā - en		ā -		-	en	- ge	mo -	ha - na	│mo - ha - na│	pyā - ...	
4th	...-(ā)	-	re	mo - ha - na py - ā		│ā - │		pyā-re mohana	pyāre	kaba ghara		
5th	ā - en		ā -		-	enge	ā - en		│ā - enge│	ā - enge	ghara	
6th	ā...											

Figure 4.7. Curling gesture in performance. Shaded boxes
mark a curling gesture cotimed with a Ramkali shift; the unshaded box
marks a curling gesture without a Ramkali shift.

the improvisation seamlessly with the mukhra of each avartan so that it springs organically out of the preceding phrase. Some singers produce sudden gripping gestures on sam, as if grabbing the end of the rhythmic cycle. (I have heard one singer refer to this disparagingly as "pouncing" on the sam.) Another way was demonstrated in chapter 3: Girija Devi's curling, two-handed gestures that were coperformed with the introduction of tivra madhyam and komal nishad. On one occasion in this performance, Girija Devi performed the curling gesture (figure 4.7) without a Ramkali shift. This suggests that the gesture is not merely a mechanical reaction to odd pitches but that both Ramkali shifts and curling gestures have a place in a larger metrical context. In this performance of Ramkali in particular, the Ramkali shifts are distributed evenly, one per rhythmic cycle, tying off the improvisation before proceeding to the mukhra. The one anomalous curling gesture performs this function as well: it closes the rhythmic cycle, right before the mukhra.

These gestural patterns of rest, tying off, dismissal, and putting down affiliated with repose are not mere *signs* of phrase markers, like periods. They free the hands and voice for new action. Accordingly, a point of major melodic repose — whether on *sa* or on another resting point within the space of a raga — is sometimes called a *nyaas* svara: literally, a "putting-down" svara. Although the echoes of the last avartan are still distantly available for recollection, they are no longer retained as vividly as the melodic action in the current avartan.[4] While building a new pattern, I retain in hand and mind what I have sung since the last mukhra even as I am finding a path to the next one. Conceived as mental work, this may seem like an enormous cognitive burden; in practice, it is no more mysterious than carrying on a coherent conversation. These effortless retentions of past phrases and protentions of metrical culmination, marked by periodic and partial dismissals, produce a nested melodic hierarchy that is articulated through both vocal and gestural action.

Upaj, Bharna, Purnavad: *Growth, Filling, Wholeness*

As a performance progresses and phrases are strung together more densely, the fine details of raga exposition explicated in the beginning of a performance are less recognizable, and rhythmic action is foregrounded.[5] This can be explained in part by the density of melodic action. In these later segments of performance, the hands twist, flap, and shake, generating a rhythmic groove rather than tracing the spatial relationships between svaras. Where slow motion can be traced by broad sweeps of the arm, faster vocal action is marked by repetitive motion of the wrists or digits. Rapid taan patterns, in some cases is affiliated with digital motion that resembles rapid fretting on a sitar, though the movement is correlated with rhythm rather than with precise pitch locations.

As the density of melodic action increases, directed motion and exploration are backgrounded in favor of texture, growth, and building. When improvised melody suggests a large-scale pattern longer than individual breaths, musicians often revert to metaphors of growth and building. This is obvious in the first place in some of the technical terms used to describe improvisation: for example, *barhat* (increase), *vistar* (expansion), and *upaj* (sprouting). The English term *well-knit* is sometimes used as well to describe an avartan that is coherent, smooth, and self-similar.

There are various approaches to structuring improvisation within tala cycles. Singers that specialize in the extremely slow *bada khyal* style developed by Wahid Khan and popularized by Amir Khan rely on the processes of *svar vistar* and *mirkhand*, in which each svara is thoroughly explored in turn, systematically shedding light on it from above and below. This kind of raga development is commonly described in architectural terms:

> This introspective approach is also reflected in [the Kirana gharana] style of raga development. The base of the edifice they build up, that is the *sa* and the mandra saptak [lowest octave], claims the greatest attention. Once the foundation is laid, the angles of the rising structure are gently indicated while the apex is often left to the imagination of the listener, in deference to the underlying philosophy that a mere human does not have the ability to perfect or complete anything. (Dhar 2001: 22)

Gwalior, Agra, and Jaipur gharana singers, on the other hand, who tend to sing bada khyals in somewhat faster, shorter metrical cycles, tend to treat each avartan as a separate architectural unit, giving rise to a series of long moments delineated by avartans, as described above. I will focus on this second approach here.

"avartan baraabar bharo"   ...   "proper way"   ...   "avartan bharna"

Figure 4.8. Gestural affiliates of descriptions of *avartan bharna*.

Arun Kashalkar, a performer in this second tradition, describes an architectural approach similar to that mentioned by Dhar above, but oriented in this case to the individual avartan:

> We are trained in that fashion: "*Avartan baraabar bharo*" [Fill the avartan evenly] — just arranging it in a proper way. This is a proper arrangement, not dumping. That is *avartan bharna* [filling the avartan]. Our training is like that only. I mean for years together we just crave for this . . . how to be more able to complete the avartan properly.

Baraabar means "equal, even, balanced." *Avartan baraabar bharo* means "fill the avartan evenly, fill it in a balanced way." This stands in contrast to haphazardly dumping material: using a dramatically different density in the beginning and end of the avartan, or a sudden, surprising melodic move with no internal structural relation.[6] The gestural affiliate of baraabar bharo here is a quick, tense shake of both clenched hands, as though testing the firmness and solidity of an object. While saying the words *proper way*, he emphasizes the beats by repeatedly setting a virtual object into its proper place with both hands. While saying *avartan bharna* (the infinitive form — "to fill the avartan"), he traces a complete circle in the air with his right index finger (figure 4.8).

Kashalkar gesturally links three physical attributes to the proper, even structuring of melodic improvisation within an avartan: (1) firmness/solidity/resistance to shaking, (2) proper placement, and (3) circularity. The second gesture, placing a virtual object into place ("in a proper way"), recalls the usual gestural affiliate of the container metaphor (McNeill 2005), in which an idea is an object and words are a container. Accordingly, in spoken discourse, good "content" is a common term of praise for a singer — meaning patterned, organically arranged design — even if their voice is not sweet.

Figure 4.9. "It's a cycle."

Kashalkar's third gesture, indicating circularity, is echoed in a description of how patterns emerge in phrases over time as described by Mukul Kulkarni. The gestural affiliate of "It's a cycle" is shown in figure 4.9.

> Always there is a feeling of a circle in every phrase, that something is getting completed, then putting another statement, then *it* is getting completed. Then, you are putting your thought this way, in that avartan, in small period of thirty seconds. . . . There is a feeling of completion at the end when you come to sam. So again in the second avartan you start with something, again the cycle starts and ends on sam. So it's a cycle. And whole khyal is again a cycle. In this music, we call it, that everything is a circle, is the theory. . . . *Purnavad*, it is called. There is feeling that something has started at a point and ends at the same point. That is essential. You should give that feeling to yourself as well as to the audience.

In the context of this discussion of *purnavad* (roughly, "holism"), the relevant feature of tracing a circular trajectory in space (which in other contexts may highlight periodicity, flow, or continuity) is its wholeness.[7] The ordering of the phrases in this particular style shows organic self-similarity and nearly always proceeds in the direction of growth rather than reduction. This is most evident in the technique called *upaj*. Upaj is used informally by many musicians and dancers to refer generally to improvisation or elaboration. Sometimes, however, upaj is used in a more specific sense, more in tune with its literal implications of organic growth. Upaj in this sense implies developing a short phrase by progressively appending melodic material before or afterward.

Mukul gives an example of upaj that is reproduced in figure 4.10. Note that at the end of each of these phrases, Mukul closes by showing both palms

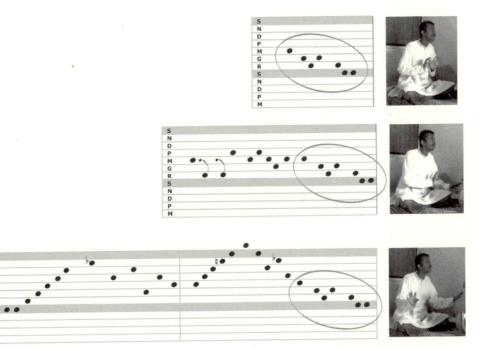

Figure 4.10. Upaj process and the gestures marking the close of each segment.

forward, as though pushing something away that has been completed. The gestures get progressively farther from him, so that by the culminating phrase, in which the upaj has progressed the farthest, the entire process is finished before the mukhra. These pushing-away gestures correlate closely with those of his guru, Vikas Kashalkar, but demonstrate that phrasal organization is multileveled and nested, as in Shafqat Ali Khan's Bhimplas alap. These segments become reified as melodic objects in the course of performance.

The Musicking Body as a Model of Temporal Awareness

Thus far, I have largely focused on a first-person view of musicking: what an individual singer does in the course of improvising raga music. Now, anticipating the investigation of the social and ethical life of the musicking body that will drive chapter 6, I will briefly suggest a few ways in which the musicking body of a performer may serve as a model of temporal awareness for others.

One distinguishing feature of the temporal awareness required in Hindustani music is its remarkably large timescales. Martin Clayton (2007: 92) points out that the length of a tal cycle in a vilambit khyal (usually in the range of fifteen to forty seconds) is "hypermetric" — far too long to capture in a recurring pattern of periodic foot-tapping. Instead, he suggests that tal cycles of this length are more akin to "narrative" timescales — for example, the length of a brief episode in a story. Thus, he argues, the performance conventions of vilambit khyal "support the kind of long-term attentional periodicity that allows performers and listeners to focus some of their attentional resources on this higher-level structure." He further suggests that "one of the functions of the [performance] itself is precisely to facilitate this sharing of attention and of temporal expectations within an intimate group" (ibid.: 93). The shared release of tension on sam, marked by audience members as well as performers, is the most visible example of this shared attention and temporal expectation. The importance of this attentional skill is attested to by the fact that many complaints about Hindustani music from uninitiated listeners center on its elusive temporal structure: to a listener who cannot discern tal cycles, a performance seems to go on and on interminably. Attending to these large-scale temporal patterns requires a special sort of time consciousness, a special style of engaging with a field of presence — one that must be carefully cultivated.

Both in lessons and performance, the musicking body provides a model for a dynamic field of presence within these time frames. As Judith Becker puts it, "Most of our styles of listening have been learned through unconscious imitation of those who surround us and with whom we continually interact" (2004: 71). Holding a note very still in space focuses attention on that moment; continuing a melodic phrase across breaths expands temporal attention to include long phrases; putting aside a built melodic object at sam directs attention to something new. In slow khyals, mukhras serve as periodic culminations of melodic action and horizons of temporal attention.

One important relationship to time within a cycle of tal, particularly within the Gajanan Rao Joshi lineage, is flow, or *pravaha*. As Shafqat Ali Khan once said to me of singers in this lineage, "They have this approach," while tracing a steadily undulating, flowing, serpentine curve in the air toward me. Vikas Kashalkar brought the importance of flow to my attention while we were listening to a live recording of his guru, Gajanan Rao Joshi. He said that although critics sometimes had trouble with Joshi's singing while his voice was warming up, once his voice was flexible and he moved on to medium-tempo melodic motion, people were able "get into the flow of his singing." While saying so, Kashalkar traced circles in the sagittal plane. Musicologist and singer Ashok Ranade, who also learned from Joshi, claims that this approach — which strove to "maintain a musical flow in a medium tempo" — was passed to Joshi's father and guru, Anant Manohar

Joshi, from Rahimat Khan (Ranade 2011: 109). Mukul Kulkarni links the continuous flow of musical motion to a stream, saying that musical elaboration is "a pravaha, or a stream flowing." Arun Kashalkar stresses that flow takes time to develop in musical performance: "It's like the flow of an orator. Once he starts speaking, until some point, he has to preconceive. . . . But as he goes on, the ideas instantly occur, and the expressions also instantly occur." The term *bahlava*[8] is sometimes used to describe these flowing sections of performance. Gesturally, bahlava is often conveyed through continuous, undulating hand motion, in which there is both a periodic and a linear component. Bahlava tends to consist of long melismata (as opposed to short, dramatic phrases delineated by many syllables), continuity of vakra motion (see chapter 3), and a consistent, moderate rhythmic density that tends to fall in between strong beats. As the melodic motion snakes between the metronomic fall of matras but strictly retains its own internal tempo, bahlava appears texturally to be both cohesive and free, both steady and curvaceous — like a flowing stream. This flow, according to Mukul, is entered not only by the singer but also by the audience. When I asked why one shouldn't switch rapidly from one flow to another while singing, he responded: "They are aesthetically different. . . . You take people with yourself. They also are singing." Maintaining this flow for the sake of the audience, then, is both an aesthetic and an ethical responsibility.

The musicking body may also serve as a model for stillness. One of the most dramatic points in performance (and one that has become nearly obligatory in khyal performance in the twentieth century) is when a vocalist grips a note and holds it still for a long time. The hold may last as long as twenty seconds; it typically occurs on the high *sa* and with a closed vowel such as "oo" or "ee." The svara is held carefully in place as the vowel melts into the drone of the tanpura, the tabla fades into the background, and the flow of time, which had hitherto been marked by melodic motion within tal cycles, comes to rest. In nearly every case, this note is not only held by the voice but also held in the hand, like an object. This moment typically marks the longest break in melodic motion in the whole performance: motion nearly ceases as the hand holds the note still in the air. Yet it serves as a key marker of vocal skill. For young singers, holding an extended note is one sign of *tayyari*, or readiness to perform: if a student is to provide vocal accompaniment in a concert, he or she must at the very least be able to sustain the high shadaj reliably, and students often are called to fulfill this duty in a performance. The power of these moments is illustrated by a story of a performance by legendary vocalist Mallikarjun Mansur in which the allure of his sustained shadaj caused the tabla player — who otherwise would be marking the passage of time — to forget to play altogether. Though this story was told to me secondhand and was likely embellished, the features of the story that the narrator foregrounded are instructive: (1) that the tabla player was compelled to stop by the intensity of this grip and (2) that this was, despite the lack of any melodic motion, an outstanding musical moment. A caricatured cinematic vision of this shared time freeze is depicted in the song "Lapak Jhapak Tu Aare Badarva" in the movie *Boot Polish* (1954) — while the singer sustains *sa*, the camera pans past an audience that sits completely still, frozen in time, with their attention focused on the singer, their jaws hanging open. Both of these stories accentuate the social nature of this moment of stillness — not merely as a matter of acoustics, or for the singer, but for everybody present.

This is not merely a matter of a singer sending messages about time. While singing, a singer appears not as a sequence of signs or a segment of flesh, not as a percept or an object, but as someone *doing* something. Even in moments of stillness, the body arises to awareness as an "attitude directed towards a certain existing or possible task" (Merleau-Ponty 2002 [1945]: 115). We do not reach out to touch or measure a singer. And yet, though our hands may be folded in our laps, we do reach out to know its music. We recognize a singing body as a body, like ours. A singer appears to us not merely as an object that takes up space and has mass, but as a person with an inner life. We read this inner life in the motion of a singer's voice, hands, and face. As we shall see in chapter 6, this is what makes it possible for a student to not merely emulate her teacher's behaviors, but to construct and inhabit a musicking body of her own. First, however, chapter 5 will consider the nature of the musicking body and its virtual objects.

CHAPTER FIVE

The Musicking Body

⁓

A young boy is sitting in front of my teacher for the first time, flipping through a notebook in his lap, looking for something to sing to show what he can do. Hunched over his book, fingers rubbing the edges of the page, he tentatively sightsings a sequence of syllables from the page: "*ye-e-ri . . . a-ali. pi-yaa bi-naa, aa, aa, sa-khi.*" My teacher interrupts him by singing the phrase more forcefully, with more melodic direction. He pulls the word *yeri* vigorously from below, with both hands, as though snatching a sheet from a bed. When he gets to *piya bina*, which stabilizes around a single pitch, he holds the syllables ringingly in place with pursed fingers. After an hour and a half of singing, we take a break; the newcomer relaxes visibly and assumes the more familiar disposition of chitchat.

While the rest of us debate the merits of the previous night's concert, one advanced student keeps singing quietly, gazing at her hands, gently shaping the air in front of her face. Somebody asks her a question, and she sits up, turning quickly to him as though breaking out of a trance; her hands fall to her lap, and she gives a short answer. We leave her alone, allowing her to slip back into music.

Chapters 2, 3, and 4 investigated ways in which the moving hands and the moving voice work together in a flow of musicality. The body in this musical state sometimes feels so different than it does when chatting or reading the newspaper that beginners are often noticeably awkward when first learning and look for any excuse to wriggle out of it, as though it were an uncomfortable garment. Skilled musicians, on the other hand, are often much more at ease musicking than doing anything else. It happens often that a musician, when asked a question about raga structure, will stop talking for a moment and hum several phrases of the raga at hand, consulting the intelligence of their musicking body before jumping to conclusions. This chapter is an attempt to understand this musicking body and the various kinds of virtual objects, fluids, and materials that extend it.

What Is the Musicking Body?

It should be clear by now that we are no longer considering gesture or the voice separately, but the whole-bodily practice of singing: the swooping voice; the hands tracing shapes in the air; the navigation of temporal and modal structures; postures that align the arms, eyes, and vocal organs; practiced stances of the body and voice from which melodic action is possible.

Still, the objection may remain: how can the motion of the body and the motion of the voice be doing the same thing? Aren't the body and the voice made of utterly different substances? It is tempting to presume that they are. This separation would seem to account for the experience of an audience member seeing a beloved singer live for the first time, for whom vocalization is heard (but not seen) and gesture is seen (but not heard). It would seem to account for the fact that singers can willfully move their hands without vocalizing, or vocalize while sitting on their hands. It also allows an aesthetic critique of singers whose physical motion distracts attention from the sound of their voice (*he ought to keep his body still*, one might say, *so that we can focus on his voice*). Perhaps most powerfully, it supports an understanding of the voice as a transcendent entity flying far above the flesh-body like a ghost — free of stiff muscles, free of gravity, able to move in ways that flesh never could. The split of body and voice has a long tradition (see chapter 1) and has been reinforced by the distribution of sound recordings, the rise of scientific acoustics, the erasure of courtesanry, and the hegemony of print media.

However, this commonsense split conceals an extra, hidden move: it identifies gesture with the material of the body and sublimates vocalization to ghostly, immaterial form. Though the sound of the voice may be transcribed as a sequence of signs (such as notes or words) or acoustical data (such as amplitude or frequency) without reference to a singer, the sounding organs of the voice (the larynx, the pharynx, the teeth, etc.) are nonetheless a dynamic, organic part of the flesh-body (see, for example, the analysis of laryngeal action in the production of taans in Radhakrishnan 2011). Likewise, though we may study the dead muscles of a motionless hand on a dissecting table, the trajectories traced by living hands are not themselves made of flesh: like the melodies traced by the voice, they are weightless.

These two aspects of the body align closely with two Indic words for *body*: *sharir* (the flesh-body) and *roop* (the form of the body).[1] This apparent double vision of the body (splitting sharir from roop, flesh from form) is a sign not that the singer in question actually has two separate heads and four separate arms, but rather that there are two disciplines by which we come to know the same body differently. We weigh an arm, but not a circle;

	heard *(but not seen)*	seen *(but not heard)*
form/roop	vocal melody	gestural melody
flesh/sharir	larynx, pharynx, tongue, etc.	arm, hand, fingers, etc.

Figure 5.1. Aspects of the musicking body.

we measure the density of the larynx, but not of a svara. While the sharir is known through its relatively stable weight, density, color, and physical dimensions, the roop of a melodic form is evanescent and arises to consciousness at a particular moment: in contrast with a background, anticipated by what comes before, and retained to enrich what comes afterward. The roop of a melodic phrase enacted by a body through voice and gesture has no mass, no molecular structure. It can be actively retained, recalled, and reenacted. The body-as-sharir, on the other hand, is skin, muscle, bone. The voice-as-sharir is the complex of respiratory, resonant, and articulatory vocal organs (the lungs, the larynx, the nose, the tongue, etc.) that is the material cause of voice. An arm may carry a gestural form, as the air in a room may carry sound, but the essence of the musicking body is not flesh any more than the essence of sound is air.

Although it is perfectly reasonable, at times, to approach a singer's body as sharir (e.g., by measuring brain activity or heart rate) or roop (e.g., by transcribing the melodies of voice and gesture), the musicking body is not reducible to either. A pickled larynx is incapable of music; a curve abstracted from a swoop of the hand is not, in itself, the body. To treat voice only as *roop* and gesture only as *sharir* obscures the constant, unmistakable, disciplined action of the body in singing. To gesture spontaneously while improvising melody is to do one thing, not two. The chest fills with breath, the hands trace shapes in the air, the mouth and throat form precisely tuned resonating chambers, the cat's cradle of muscles around the voice box tenses and slackens: the body is fully alive in music. Treating a singing singer as either flesh *or* form is like treating a thrown ball as either rubber *or* moving as we try to catch it. Neither a purely realist approach (which would treat the body as objective sharir: as a bundle of skin, bones, muscle, and blood) nor a purely idealist approach (which would treat the body purely as sub- jective roop: as an imagined, formal, constructed product of pure will, ar- ticulating notes, curves, and other abstract forms) can fully account for the musicking body which spans *sharir* and *roop*.

Perhaps most importantly, the musicking body is alive, intelligent, and conscious. Its motion, its sounding, and its cognition are all brought to- gether in a single intentional field of presence. Freedom to improvise is not a result of liberation from the hands, throat, and breath — it is in the incar- nation of a musicking body trained to move freely in intimately known raga spaces, to gracefully retain and protend melodic action within metric cycles, to build and manipulate compelling melodic objects.

Posture

If you sing a melodic arch, ascending to a high note and then descending, you may notice that your chin moves up and down. This is quite common among singers. Seen strictly from the roopic point of view of sonic and spa- tial melodic forms, the essence of this action is a rise and a fall. The move- ment of the head is merely a representation of note height. In this view there is no need for recourse to the details of human kinesiology — head motion might as well be hand motion, or a design on a page.

From a shariric point of view, however, the head is quite different from the hand. Moving the head tightens and slackens the voice-producing mus- cles of the larynx (Ewan 1976). Lowering the larynx — a consequence of dropping the chin — lowers pitch (Arnold 1961; Ohala 1972). This may be a result of the slackening of the vocal cords when the laryngeal cartilages are displaced along the curve of the cervical spine (Honda et al. 1999). Vocal pitch is increased when the vocal cords are stretched by the downward pull of the strap muscles on laryngeal cartilages (Ohala 1972; Roubeau et al. 1997), and raising the chin increases this tension. The raising of the chin could likewise be seen as a by-product of nervous tension in the muscles in the neck and back. This tension is a common response in vocalists who are nervous about singing a particular passage, and few vocal actions are more stressful than singing at the top of one's range. Is the raising of the chin, then, a result of the comapping of pitch and space, the physiology of the larynx, or mere nervousness? These three explanations are not mutually exclusive; indeed, they are complementary. Consider a moment in perfor- mance, when the articulation of a phrase near the top of the vocal range, nervous tension about the successful execution of the phrase, and a sensation of up-ness arise as a single process. Melodies in this range feel as though they are located higher in space, and the head tilts upward to engage with them; melodies seem to move with greater force and speed, and the muscles tense in order to wield them artfully; when the voice becomes still at this high range, its steadiness embodies extraordinary strength and patience in light of the heightened energy and tension of the voice.

More broadly, posture is part of vocal discipline. Khyal and dhrupad singers in the twentieth century (in contrast to singers of kirtan, lavani, biraha, etc.) nearly always sit while singing, usually with the legs crossed. Some singers with sit with one foot on a thigh (singers with some yogic training sometimes call this posture by its technical name: *ardha padmasan*, or "half-lotus posture"). While playing a tanpura, some singers sit with one foot on the ground and one knee raised. Though music teachers rarely prescribe specific hand motions, many prescribe specific sitting postures for practice or performance — sitting with the spine straight, for example, with the chest open, with relaxed shoulders, and so on.[2] These postural differences make a musical difference. A singer whose neck is inclined downward, whose gaze is focused in front of their body, has a different range of vocal and gestural action available than a singer whose face is inclined upward, gazing far in front of them. These postures are not merely arbitrary ways of getting the body to hold still; a posture is a preparation for a particular range of action, both vocal (Kooijman et al. 2005) and gestural (Berthoz and Petit 2008: 67).

Adapting to a new postural regimen can also produce real pain. For example, after several months of particularly intense practice, which required many hours of sitting every day, I developed severe back pain and went to a physical therapist in Pune. To my surprise, he knew exactly what to do. He told me that this particular syndrome of musculoskeletal stress was endemic among Hindustani vocalists who sit for extended periods (he listed, in confidence, the names of several eminent singers he had treated) and prescribed a series of exercises that strengthened my upper back muscles. Note that neither the affliction nor the relief was a simple matter of good or bad posture, or of skeletal deformity or conformity. The cure for the pain was not to merely rearrange flesh structures. The cure was action: physical disciplines that recalibrated the dynamic balance of musculoskeletal forces in the back. All of this points to the plasticity of the musicking body, even at the level of flesh: muscular habits and muscular structure are mutually constitutive. As Marcel Mauss points out, various disciplines of sitting yield discernable variations in muscle and bone structure (1973 [1934]: 77). Orthopedic studies confirm that various postural habits afford distinctive muscular and vocal potentials (see McGill 1991; Angsuwarangsee and Morrison 2002; O'Sullivan et al. 2002). As we will see later in the chapter, posture is also an aspect of a singer's valual stance (Berger 2010) on the musical materials at hand.

Handshape, Grip, and Manipulating Melodic Objects

A widespread gestural-sonic link among Hindustani vocalists is the link between timbre and handshape. Closed vowels (such as the /i/ in *meet* or *teental* or the /u/ in *choose* or *poori*) tend to be affiliated with a fist or pursed fingers, and open vowels (such as the open /a/ in *father* or *Hindustaan*) with an open hand. The link here between hand and voice becomes clear when we consider that vowels are not merely sounds, but also disciplined gestures of the tongue, laryngeal cartilages, and other vocal organs (Hall 2003). The production of "closed" vowels requires the narrowing of some part of the vocal passages. This closing is likewise articulated by the hands.

A closed hand, however, is not merely a mirror of a vocal process — it is also a fundamental interface between the body and the world. A closed hand allows a body to temporarily extend itself by gripping objects. In the course of improvisation, a singer will sometimes appear to hold an established, repeated melodic pattern, as though it were a small object, in one hand. A sudden change in the melodic pattern is often affiliated with an inversion of the object, as if to flip it over in space, exposing an aspect of the virtual object that was previously hidden by position of the grip. Some performers also use their fist to grab and stretch a virtual elastic material in front of the body. As we shall see later, gripping is sometimes followed by sudden "releases" as well.

A grip may also gently tug on, twist, or tilt notes. Classical vocalist Sameer Dublay describes a particular use of this gesture by his guru, Jitendra Abhisheki, in teaching Rag Marwa, a raga with a special articulation of the komal rishabh (soft, or flat second). Shaunak Abhisheki (his son) had asked, "*Baba, ye komal rishabh kaise lagaun?* [Father, how should I sing[3] this flat second?]" Jitendra Abhisheki replied, *Aise lagao* [Sing it like this]," while pulling the quasi-fist upward, as in figure 5.2. Here the singer lifts the hand and slightly tilts it away from the body by raising the shoulder and rotating the wrist forward in the sagittal plane. While this may merely seem to indicate a komal rishabh located just above *sa*, Dublay explains that the grip is on *sa* itself: "When he used to have shadja [i.e., *sa*] proper, he used to hold it like this," and the proper articulation of the note in question is a slight modification of *sa*: "because this is the shadja [i.e., *sa*], just you have to lift it."

But what would it mean, in melodic terms, to "lift" a note? Marwa, the raga in question here, is distinguished from several other ragas with the same

Figure 5.2. "Aise lagao [Sing it like this]."

scale in part by the strong tonal weight of dhaivat (i.e., *dha*), the sixth scale degree. Even shadaj, in fact, is often avoided in favor of dhaivat's pull.[4] Phrases such as {*dha ni re*(♭) *ga dha ma*(♯) *dha*} (i.e., 6 7 ♭2 3 ♭2 3 ♯4 6) move within a pentatonic pitch space in which *dha* (6) serves as *sa* (1), *ni* (7) serves as *re* (2), and so forth (Jairazbhoy 1995: 202; Thatte 2010: 102). In other words, relative to the strong tonal weight of *dha*, the svara ordinarily named "komal rishabh" often functions as a lifted *sa* (a major third above the sixth, or gandhar-of-dhaivat) rather than as a lowered *re* (a diminished fourth, or lowered madhyam-of-dhaivat) (see Jairazbhoy 2008: 368). Figure 5.3 shows the two relationships with *dha*.

Hearing this note as lifted *sa* is to hear it as a shuddh gandhar (major third) in relation to dhaivat — which is precisely how it functions in much melodic action.[5] Though hearing melodic action in Marwa relative to dhaivat is perfectly ordinary, it poses problems in naming notes. Both "raised *sa*" and "gandhar-of-dhaivat" violate two axioms of modern sargam nomenclature: that shadaj cannot be raised, and that notes are named only relative to their interval with the shadaj sounded by the tanpura (Jairazbhoy 1995: 33). The grip pulling *sa* upward, then, seems to articulate knowledge about this note (that it functions as a raised shadaj, or a gandhar-of-dhaivat) that cannot be expressed in standard terms.

Vikas Kashalkar explains the function of these gripping actions in nearly the same terms that Dublay does: it prevents the note from going "out of

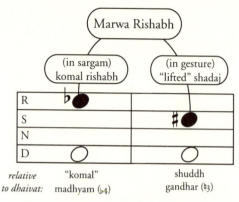

Figure 5.3. Tonal relationships of komal rishabh
(the conventional name) and "lifted" shadaj
(as revealed in Abhisheki's gesture) with
Marwa's strong dhaivat.

my control, out of my grip." But this grip may also move: figure 5.4 shows
Vikas Kashalkar holding a note in a grappolo and slowly moving it to his
left while sustaining a note. After gripping the note, he sustained it for several seconds while moving his hand horizontally. He described this action
as depicting a "hairline." These three functions associated with the grappolo seem quite different on the surface: closing (as opposed to opening,)
gripping (as opposed to releasing,) and drawing a thin horizontal line (as
opposed to vertical or rotational movement). But all three are simultaneously articulated by the handshape, the motion, and the vocalization. The
vowel (/i/) is linked to the firm grip of the note: most singers agree that
pitch is easier to control on such closed vowels. Likewise, the line is "hairline" thin by virtue of both the bunched handshape and the articulation of
the vowel: /i/ requires the tongue to rise high in the mouth, narrowing the
vocal passage.

But openness and grip seem mutually exclusive. How might an open
vowel (such as /a/) be sung when a note is to be held precisely? Should the
hand be open or closed? One way to simultaneously perform openness and
precision is shown in figure 5.5, in which the palms are exposed but the
thumb and forefinger make a precision grip. On this occasion, Vikas Kashalkar was trying to get his students to sing both an open /a/ vowel and a
precise, unwavering note for the length of a full breath. Some students held
the open vowel but were wavering in pitch; others held a steady pitch but
closed their vowel to ease the effort of sustaining the note. While it is im-

Figure 5.4. Vikas Kashalkar tracing a "hairline."

Figure 5.5. Single handshape showing both openness and precision grip.

possible to simultaneously have an open palm and a grappolo, this gesture simultaneously grips a note between the index finger and the thumb and shows an open palm. Adam Kendon (2004: 225, 281) notes that gestures of precision grip such as these, in spoken discourse, are often deployed as means of specifying topics, focusing attention on one precise point among a dynamic field of possibilities. Likewise, to grip a note in this way, as we have seen, is to hold it still, with precise intonation, as melodic motion halts for a moment and attention focuses on the note at hand.

Not all virtual objects are held so still, or with such precision — they may be held or formed with larger, looser handshapes and manipulated in various ways. Figure 5.6 shows Shaunak Abhisheki sustaining *pa* (the fifth scale degree) while placing his open palms flat in front of him. Following this clear establishment of *pa* as a temporary melodic center, he elaborates on *pa* from above and below, while turning the melodic object in his hands over and over. At first, the clockwise and counterclockwise motion of the hands could be seen as a mapping of pitch against angular displacement, as time is mapped against the angular displacement of the hands of a clock. But note that *pa* is affiliated with two different hand positions (in the third and sixth panels on the bottom row). The clockwise and counterclockwise motion affiliates consistently with ascent and descent, respectively, rather than absolute pitch.

(3 seconds)

Figure 5.6. Clockwise and counterclockwise motion.

Pulling

In addition to holding virtual melodic objects, singers sometimes grip and stretch virtual melodic materials. Leante (in Fatone et al. 2011) cites singers' accounts of the texture of the pulled material as "a rubber [band]" and "elasticity." Note that the singers describe the virtual material *itself*, not just the hands moving. This cannot be understood as a simple comapping of pitch as space. Like the "hairline" /i/ above, this pulling is a vocal/gestural action that brings pitch, amplitude, and timbre together into a single manipulative action.

This grabbing and pulling is most often coordinated with forceful vocal action, usually including long, swooping pitch glides that begin with an abrupt jump in amplitude. Figure 5.7 shows the grabbing-and-pulling patterns of two vocalists with virtually no overlap in their teaching lineages: Ulhas Kashalkar and Shafqat Ali Khan. Although each singer has a distinct kinesic articulation of these pulling gestures (Shafqat Ali tends to pull with the hands side by side, whereas Ulhas Kashalkar tends to pull with one hand in front of the other), there is remarkable consistency as well. In each case, the axis of the pull moves along the sagittal axis, from front to back.

Here the virtual material being pulled appears to be a sheet, pulled from below. In other cases, musicians pull a ropelike material from above,

Figure 5.7. Shafqat Ali Khan (above) and Ulhas Kashalkar (below) grabbing and pulling.

or (particularly among male Carnatic vocalists) stretch an elastic material horizontally in the frontal plane of the body. Other singers seem to be performing long pitch glides on the virtual string of a *been* while singing. (This is particularly evident among dhrupadiyas, perhaps because of the interweaving of *been* and vocal dhrupad traditions.) In still other cases, musicians seem to be playing rapid phrases on the fretboard of a stringed instrument while singing rapid melodic passages.

Releasing

Sometimes a grip is released without an explicit vocal affiliate, as a metric cycle ends or a new melodic logic is introduced, but sometimes the release is a melodic event in itself. Sameer Dublay recounts a particularly overt case of this in Jitendra Abhisheki's teaching, in which a *khatka* (rapid turn) on *sa* melts into a meend leading to *dha*. He first sings, then repeats the gesture while explaining the gesture: "This is the release of fingers. How to take the khatka on shadja? like this. . . . This is the shadja you are holding and . . . [*performs releasing gesture*]." Figure 5.8 juxtaposes his original melodic phrase with his later explanation and the identical gesture that accompanied them both. Here Dublayji lets the gesture speak for itself on the

"This is the shadja you are holding and   ...   "

Figure 5.8. Holding and release.

release into *dha*. The precise hold on shadja (i.e., *taar sa*, the high tonic) is maintained through the khatka around the *sa*, and then released forcefully into *dha*.

Other examples of this appear in several of the phrase-ending returns to sa by Vikas Kashalkar and his student Mukul Kulkarni that were analyzed in chapter 4. In many of these gestures, a grip is released in the final phrase leading up to the mukhra. Avartan after well-knit avartan (each becoming a melodic object through its internal formal cohesion) is constructed and released.

Virtual Objects

What exactly is being gripped, held, and thrown? Like raga spaces, they seem to be both out there in the world and inside the performed imagination of the singer. Although these objects have no objectively verifiable mass or spring constant, singers still manipulate them as though they did. The consistency of these objects is all the more remarkable when we consider that singers are not deliberately calculating the forces acting on their hands, as a computer must do for objects in simulated virtual space. Nonetheless, when I am handling a melodic object, it seems to have a consistent weight, texture, and shape; I deal with it as it is. Like a song that has not yet been written down, it is neither entirely arbitrary nor rigidly fixed — it takes on a "limited autonomy" (Berger 2010: 10). Yet should somebody interrupt my melodic action and demand to know the weight of the object in my hands, I will look down to find no object there at all. I may not even have a recollection that it ever existed. These virtual objects, then, like the musicking body, emerge only in the dynamics of musicking. Their existence does not, like the strings of a tanpura or an unmoving car, persist when motion stops. In this sense, they are like eddies in a pool: if the water stops moving, it is as if they were never there.

Chapter 4 addressed the construction of virtual objects through processes of growth and building, such as upaj, in which melodic themes come to take on the status of objects. As we have seen, individual svaras can also be gripped as objects and manipulated through holding and release. Many common gestures, in both speech and song, involve manipulation. Kendon (2004: 360) goes so far as to argue that gestural action in general may be understood as various ways of constructing and manipulating objects.

Grasping is a special way of knowing. *Pakarna* in Hindi and *grasp* in English both can be used to indicate this kind of understanding. This contrasts with the more familiar form of knowing by indicating (as when a singer points to a melodic phrase or even a single note as an entity in space, distinct from the body). Maurice Merleau-Ponty highlights the distinction between gripping and indicating by referring to a certain kind of cerebellar damage which inhibits one but not the other — the patient is, for example, perfectly capable of grasping his own nose but is unable to point at his nose with his eyes closed. He concludes from this that

> "grasping" or "touching," even for the body, is different from "pointing." . . . A point on my body can be present to me as one to be taken hold of without being given in this anticipated grasp as a point to be indicated. It is probably because knowledge of where something is can be understood in a number of ways. . . . Bodily space may be given to me in an intention to take hold without being given in an intention to know. (Merleau-Ponty 2002 [1945]: 118–119)

The handshapes of these gripping gestures are, like many others, formed even before the actual grip and its vocal affiliate occur. The beginning, in other words, anticipates the end, so that the entire grip-and-pull makes a single irreducible motion, defined by its purpose — indeed, to "disallow taking hold is sufficient to inhibit the action" (Merleau-Ponty 2002 [1945]: 118). Grip, in other words, is a particular mode of relation to a virtual object — one, we will see, among many.

Singers may also engage with virtual objects that extend inside the body. In the following interview excerpt, Vikas Kashalkar compares a particular melodic action to dropping a stone deep into a pond. The note he sings remains steady at the fifth below the tonic (*pa*), in accordance with the note-grammar of the rag. His hands, however, are the vehicle for performing the depth of the melody.

> Automatically my neck will go down. It shows that I am deep into that particular note . . . like a big stone you are throwing into the water, and it goes deep. And it, it is going and you look at it — what you see is the surface only [extends flat prone palm]. That stone is going inside. Similar to that [sings {*ni pa*} and points to top of hand] rest of the thing I assume [points below hand] I think that it is going down, touching sa, or the lowest level of the ocean or the river. . . . That suddenly comes to my mind, and so I look at it, {*ni pa*}. . . . That is the feeling that the note should go deep down into this thing. And that is the mind of the listeners and mind of the singer. That deepness is stable, but it is going deep into the hearts of the listeners or the singer also. So, that type of gesture comes into my mind.

Figure 5.9 shows the gestural affiliates of his verbal and sonic description.

This motion into depth even in the space of a single note opens the interior of the body as a field in which virtual objects can move. Some singers, especially those in the Dagar dhrupad lineage, speak of this motion in yogic

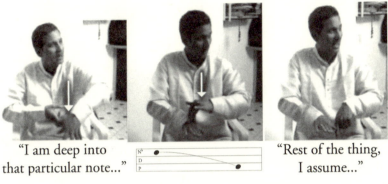

"I am deep into that particular note..."   "Rest of the thing, I assume..."

Figure 5.9. "A big stone you are throwing in the water."

terms — in terms of the movement of subtle fluids and energies, such as *kundalini*, *prana*, and *naad*. Rahim Fahim-ud-din Dagar, for example, accounts for hand gesture in terms of yogic processes: "There are nine chakras in the body. . . . We have kundalini in our spine, and that is the pillar of naad. Whatever gestures are made during singing, all of them are done according to this." His student Ashish Sankrityayan likewise claims that the motion of the body in the course of performance has "a direct relation to the internal dynamics of sound in the body of the singer" (Sankrityayan n.d.). Ritwik Sanyal, a disciple of Z. M. Dagar, describes the movements of the body as a reflection of the movement of subtle energies. In accounting for the role of the pinky finger in leading the motion of the hand, he described to me a link between the pinky and the spinning of the heart chakra, presenting the visible form of the hand as a "mirror" of invisible yogic processes. These virtual internal movements, like the materials and objects manipulated by the hands, seem to have the same limited autonomy that virtual objects do.[6]

Andolan

Many ragas feature svaras that are rendered with a gentle, swinging, microtonal oscillation. This motion is called *andolan* (wave, movement, undulation). Certain svaras in certain ragas (for example, the komal gandhar in Mian ki Malhar, or the komal rishabh in Bhairav) are consistently taken with andolan and are called *andolit svaras*. This oscillation typically doesn't reach so far up or down that it suggests other notes; it is, rather, a specialized intensification of a single svara. Unlike vibrato (i.e., *kampit*, which is also occasionally used as an ornament), the oscillation of andolan is slow

Figure 5.10. Two gestural articulations of andolan.

enough (often in the range of 1 Hz) that it can be approximated by the hand and the voice simultaneously. Depending on the singer and the situation, this swinging may be accompanied by various gestures: a rhythmic, repeated pull with the fist, a waving, circular motion of the open palm, a slow tracing of a circle in the air with the index finger, and so on. They may be performed in any bodily axis; they may be elliptical or almost circular, but all of them oscillate in coordination with vocal pitch. Nor is this circularity limited to singers: many sitarists articulate andolan with a circular motion of the index finger in the plane of the frets rather than merely sliding the string back and forth perpendicular to the neck of the instrument. Gina Fatone's term for this kind of shared feature among diverse forms is "meta-gesture" — a formal entity that is articulated via gesture variously in different situations (Fatone 2010).

Though these gestural articulations of andolan are all periodic, they reveal strikingly different orientations of the musicking body. Consider, for example, Mohan Darekar's whole-bodily orientation in the two pictures from a lesson in figure 5.10. In the picture on the left, he is instructing me in how to articulate an andolit svara. His eyes are open and his gaze is directed forward, at me, even as he is singing. In the picture on the right (a pulling andolan), his eyes are closed, and his head is pointed downward. In each of these cases, vocal pitch and hand position are tightly linked. One performing andolan points at the pitch of the note, as above, tracing a circle in the air. The only cases of this that I have on video are in lessons, when a teacher is trying to guide a student's production of andolan.

In another mode of articulating andolan, the whole hand traces the undulation of the svara (either alone or 180 degrees out of phase with the other hand), and the pitch zenith (high point) is aligned with the highest point that the finger reaches. For example, in the open-hand form, the pitch zenith (highest pitch of the undulating movement) is farthest from the body,

Figure 5.11. Open-palm articulation
of andolit gandhar in Mian Ki Malhar.

and the nadir (lowest point) is closest to the body. The pitch descends as the
hand moves upward and toward the body, and ascends as the hand moves
outward and upward. Here it is as though the hand is pushing an object
away; the point of maximum pitch height corresponds with the maximum
distance from the body.

In a third method, the andolan is articulated with a grip. The dimensions
are then reversed: the zenith is *closest* to the body, and the nadir is *farthest*
from the body. The grip is not merely as a handshape; it seems to pull on an
elastic virtual material. The motion toward the body stretches the material,
and the motion away from the body slackens it. Figure 5.12 shows these
three distinctive ways of articulating andolan.

A fourth, and rather different, way of performing andolan was demonstrated to me quite explicitly by Rahim Fahim-ud-din Dagar. He stressed
that the basis of true andolan is an inner sense of intoxication (*masti*), a
sense of being spun. He contrasted this esoteric sense (*andar ki baat*, "inner
idea") of andolan with the exoteric sense (*bahar ki baat*, "outer idea") that
is associated with merely moving individual notes up and down.

> Andar ki baat kaun samjhaa raha hai? . . . Ye bahar ki baat hai baqi jahaan ke
> jiska naam "andolit" hai. Vah bhi element hai. Vah sabse pahale apko samajna
> hai ki vah andolit ek vah tasawwur hai jo hava inke saath insaan ki yah masti
> hoti hai, ghoomta hai. Apne masti mein ghoomta hai.

> The inner idea, who is explaining this [these days]? This [merely moving the
> pitch] is the outer idea, which everywhere else [i.e., outside of the Dagar lin-
> eage] is called "andolit." This too is an element. First of all you have to under-
> stand this: andolit projects a state in which a person is intoxicated and spins
> along with the wind. In his intoxication, he spins.[7]

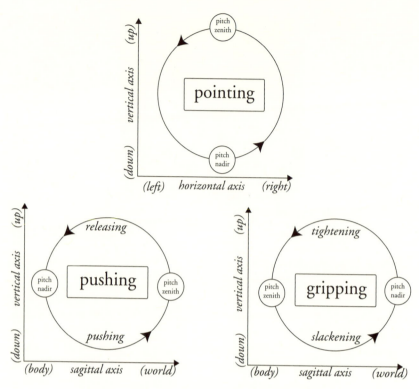

Figure 5.12. Three ways of articulating andolit gandhar.

He accompanied his description of this spinning with an evocative gesture: he spun his index finger gently in the air while allowing his entire body to sway with the motion, as though subject to an external force. This stood in dramatic contrast to the incorrect, exoteric andolan: shaking a note up and down while moving his hand forcefully up and down in a straight line (see figure 5.13). Dagar's caricature of "bahar ki" (outer) andolan is not an accurate depiction of any particular performance — he seemed instead was demonstrating an exaggerated contrast between two modes of bodily disposition. While the "outer idea" amounts to a forceful, deliberate up-and-down motion of the hand, the "inner idea" is a surrender of the whole body to a spinning motion. In other words, the pitch oscillation associated with andolan is a by-product of a more fundamental sense of the whole body spinning (spinning, in this case, in the field of the raga: recall from chapter 3 that Dagar described the entire raga space of Darbari as andolit). He describes the difference between willfully moving a svara and allowing the body to be moved.

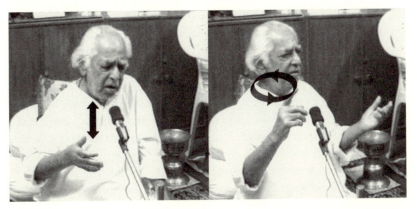

Figure 5.13. A fourth way of performing andolan: andar ki / inner andolan (right panel) as opposed to bahar ki / outer andolan (left panel).

Stances of the Musicking Body

The distinction that Dagar makes between performing from outside of the melodic action and being moved by its internal dynamics applies not just to andolan, but to any of the melodic action we have seen thus far; singers switch fluidly between them in performance and teaching. Arun Kashalkar, referring to the same distinction, once called these modes of performance "weightlifting" and "swimming," respectively, later clarifying that at a particular moment in a performance that he "is not lifting any weight," but "swimming in notes." Indeed, this distinction between standing outside a performance and standing inside it is found in speech performance as well. David McNeill points out that a person telling a story may perform gesturally from "object viewpoint" (in which the storyteller stands outside the action, indicating various objects and characters with the hands) or "character viewpoint" (in which a person telling a story gestures as though she were a character in the story, in the action) (2005: 34). For example, as I describe a leaf falling on my nephew's head, my hand may become the leaf fluttering onto my own head (putting myself in the story), or one hand may be the leaf while the other is my nephew (standing outside the story). Mark Johnson (2007: 252) describes the corresponding viewpoints of a music listener as the "observer perspective" and the "participant perspective," respectively.

There are more fine-grained modes of performance, however, than merely standing inside and outside the melody. As we have seen, a singer may point to a note as though it were hanging in the air; may grip a note to make it an extension of the body; may trace trajectories with the whole hand, as though the hand itself were the moving svara; may sway whole-bodily, as though the body were immersed in a larger musical space. When the body points, svaras become objects independent of the singer; the singer assumes the didactic pose of a teacher, demonstrating the objects' autonomous dynamics. Taking hold of these objects, however, gripping, stretching, and pulling them, the singer exerts willful force on them; the objects become an extension of the body. When the hand (or head, or arm, or chin) itself traces melodic trajectories, the melody is no longer a thing out there in the world; a part of the body itself moves as melody: both moving and moved. When the entire body is moved by music, the body submits to a musical field larger than the body, in an attitude of disciplined surrender.

These modes of performance — showing, moving, gripping, being moved — are stances (Berger 2010) that the musicking body assumes in the course of performance. In Berger's terms, stances are affective and stylistic but also, crucially, embody values. Dagar, for example, asserts that performing andolan properly is not merely a matter of notes, but a matter of a certain *tasawwur* (a projection of a kinesic state) in which one is intoxicated and spinning with the wind. In Dagar's view, this is not merely correct vocal behavior, but a proper stance in relation to music.

But where do these stances come from? And here we return, from a different angle, to the same puzzlement about the musicking body that we started from: while a beginning student moves very little while singing, apparently neither moving nor moved by music, a trained musician gracefully inhabits a musicking body, moving through repertoires of gesture and stance. Chapter 6 will investigate the ways in which a musicking body is trained to be what it is, and the ethical implications of stances and gestural dispositions passed through teaching lineages.

CHAPTER SIX

The Paramparic Body

～

I am singing at a house concert in California. It is my first performance away
from my teacher, and I try to sing as he has taught me. I deliberately choose
a raga that we spent many months working on. I try to remember all of his
admonitions about proper singing: each avartan should be well-knit; the voice
should be clear and open; the development of the raga should be gradual and
methodical; every phrase should straightforwardly evoke the raga. Restraining
myself from dashing forward into rapid taans, I will myself to relax my shoulders,
take deep breaths, and dwell in a medium-tempo melodic flow, even past the
point where my attention wanders. Even when I make a mistake and want to hide
my voice behind closed vowels, I remember his relaxed, open voice. All of these
small pieces of advice, during my training, were brought together in a single
discipline by my teacher's presence. Singing alone, I sometimes recall them
one by one. At other times, I merely remember my teacher.

One of the guests, a longtime student of Hindustani music, approaches me after
I finish. "You sing differently now," she says.

I ask her what she means.

"You never used to do this," she says, looking at her hands, tracing interlocking
ellipses with her wide open palms. The motion of her body calls my teacher to
mind: his open voice; his buoyant, curving melodic flow; his focused gaze.
Though she has never seen him, and though I have fallen far short of his ideal
tonight, she has somehow caught the presence of his music.

Chapter 5 focused on ways in which the musicking body (the body that
comes alive gesturally and vocally while musicking) serves as a vehicle for
melody. But where does this body come from? The origin and development of the flesh-body, though bewilderingly intricate, is straightforwardly

addressed in the language of developmental biology: an egg is fertilized, splits repeatedly in complex but orderly ways, and grows into an adult. But the development of the musicking body, over years of training and discipline, cannot be answered simply in terms of flesh. Despite sharing roughly the same anatomical structures, Hindustani vocalists differ markedly in their gestural, postural, and vocal dispositions.

Yet singers musically resemble their teachers in ways that are noticeable even to untrained observers.[1] Teachers, in turn, were once students; they spent hundreds of hours in front of their own teachers struggling to learn music. The word *parampara* is often used to refer to these chains of transmission. The adjectival form, *paramparik*, is commonly used to refer to compositions and musical techniques passed down in these lineages, with no single recognizable author. The term *paramparic*[2] *body* will become useful later in this chapter in addressing embodied musical dispositions that are passed down through generations of teachers and students, with no single recognizable author.

Figure 6.1 shows one such paramparic vocal-gestural pattern easily discerned across generations. Here we see Ulhas Kashalkar and two of his students performing slight variations on a single gestural form: rotating both hands in coordinated rhythm with the turns of the vocal melody, as if juggling an object from one to the other in a circular trajectory. On the surface, this resembles the two-handed circular motion depicted in figure 5.10. This vocal-gestural technique, however, is linked to a specific context of melodic texture and function. The wheeling pattern shown above, among Kashalkar's students, articulates intricate *vakra* melodic motion marked by rapid changes in direction, in which rhythmic accents dance between strong beats. Gangurde's articulation of this pattern tends to be smaller than Kashalkar's or Dadarkar's; Dadarkar's gaze, in general, tends to be higher than Gangurde's or Kashalkar's. Despite these differences, however, a distinctive, recognizable form is shared by teacher and students.

Many such shared gestural-vocal routines are obvious to connoisseurs. Students of Jitendra Abhisheki, for example, often combine a precise manual and vocal grip on a note with a characteristic, precise grip of the rings of muscle around the eyes (the *orbicularis palpebrarum*). These bodily routines (and the others sketched in this chapter) are neither vocal techniques in the exclusive service of sound nor bad habits that inhibit voice production. As gesture analyst David McNeill stresses, this kind of gestural performance does not merely indicate something else but is itself a way of being: "A gesture is not a representation, or is not only such: it is a form of being. Gestures (and words, etc., as well) are themselves thinking in one of its many forms — not only expressions of thought, but thought, i.e., cognitive

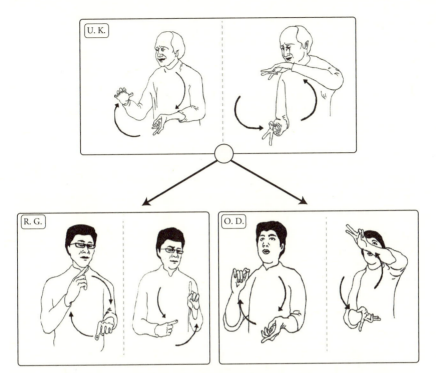

Figure 6.1. Shared vocal-gestural form. Ulhas Kashalkar (teacher) at top, Rishikesh Gangurde and Omkar Dadarkar (students) at bottom.

being, itself" (2005: 99). This "being," as embodied in gesture, voice, and posture, is not an isolated, private world; it is also a social existence. The musicking body is always already embedded in social relations, even before its first music lesson. These inherited routines, then, are learned techniques of the musicking body, disciplined ways of melodic action achieved by years of training and practice. As we will see, they are seldom a matter of deliberate imitation and, like all gestural forms, are seldom addressed in words. Yet they serve as vehicles for aesthetic and ethical values that are transmitted through generations of teachers and students.

Teaching Lineages

Dard Neuman (2004: 40–41) aptly describes the great social importance of teaching lineages in modern Hindustani music:

> One would be hard pressed to consider the world of Hindustani classical music without thinking in turn about musical lineage. Whenever a musician introduces himself, or is introduced to others, he almost always marks his

identity through his teacher and the gharana (musical house or lineage) to which they both belong. . . . [The individual musician] therefore emerges as both a person and a figure, as both an artist to whom we ascribe particular musical features and as a figure bearing the signs of a musical tradition.

Ascribing a *gharana* (*ghar*, "house") to a singer marks his musicking body as a bearer of a certain discipline and authority. This term once was used to refer to the courts and villages in which musical families would pass on specific repertoire, techniques, and musical dispositions — for example, Agra, Rampur, and Kirana (Wade 1985). These families have dispersed widely, however, and now the term refers broadly to one of a handful of prominent approaches to khyal performance. This sense of gharana as a discipline has almost entirely superseded its older sense as a house or family — as Ulhas Kashalkar once concisely put it, each gharana is "a body of principles" (Shah 2010). Thus, a singer who specializes in slow, note-by-note raga development with a wide range of vowels might be said to be singing Kirana style; a singer who develops long, dhrupad-style nom-tom alap might be said to be singing in the style of Agra gharana; a singer who relies on long phrases on the vowel /aa/ might be said to be singing according to Jaipur gharana.[3] A focus on gharana can be revealing: the repertoire of Jaipur gharana, for example, contains a great many ragas that call for vakra (crooked) melodic motion, allowing rhythmic articulation on a single vowel that would not be possible with *sapat* (straight) motion. The difficulty with using this term as a marker of style is not so much that the place-names of the original houses no longer apply to the homes of the current tradition bearers as that even the metaphysical sense of gharana, as a distinct, walled aesthetic entity, has been weakened by the distribution of recordings and the wide stylistic variation between individuals. Nearly every singer has had more than one teacher, and nearly every singer claims more than one gharana in their training.

A more flexible way of speaking about a singer's lineage is to speak of *gayaki*[4] (singing), which can refer to a gharana (e.g., Kirana gayaki), a genre (e.g., khyal gayaki), or the aesthetic approach of a single singer (e.g., Amir Khan's gayaki). Gayaki, like gharana, refers not only to techniques and practices but to values that blend aesthetics and ethics — straightforwardness, emotional purity, dignity, and so on. The contrast between these values can become quite evident at concerts, when students of a single teacher sit together and evaluate the performance from a similar point of view. Thus, while a group of students sitting on one side of a concert hall might audibly praise a singer's emotional expressiveness and sweet voice, a group of students sitting on the other side might grumble that the same performance is saccharine and insubstantial.

This chapter will explore the transmission of bodily dispositions through teaching lineages. The two lineages that are the focus of this chapter consist of the students and grandstudents of two influential (and now deceased) singers who lived and taught in Maharashtra: Gajanan Rao Joshi and Jitendra Abhisheki. Both of these singers, themselves, studied with several teachers from Agra, Jaipur, and Gwalior gharanas and integrated the different approaches of these gharanas into a single, coherent gayaki — leading Abhisheki's student Sameer Dublay to refer to him, in English, as a "melting pot." That this eclecticism was deliberate (or remembered as deliberate) is illustrated in a legend about Gajanan Rao Joshi receiving criticism about his many music gurus; he is said to have replied that he would keep on tying more threads around his wrist (ceremonially linking guru to disciple) until he ran out of room on his arm. However, though both Abhisheki and Joshi ostensibly learned from singers from these three gharanas, their own gayakis differ tremendously from each other. They synthesized different aspects of these gharanas to form two distinctive approaches to singing that each passed on their students. Each had a rather different vocal-gestural style,[5] and they produced stylistically distinct lineages. Joshi tended to sing with open palms, a wide open mouth and an accordingly open /a/ vowel. His hands often moved in broad, sweeping gestures that proceeded from the shoulder and elbow, and his raga development focused intensely on mid-tempo elaboration. He seldom gripped notes or sang taans affiliated with rapid finger motion. Abhisheki, on the other hand, produced far more gripping motions than Joshi, with a wide range of handshapes and expressive facial positions. Whereas Joshi tended to sit quite upright, with a gaze that focused far in front of him, Abhisheki's gaze and gestural space often gave the impression of introspection, focusing immediately in front of his torso. Sitting postures such as these (as we saw in chapter 5) are not merely a matter of comfort — they enable gestural and vocal motion. Joshi's open hands and mouth were mirrored by his open chest, and enabled broad, sweeping motion from the shoulder; Abhisheki's relatively closed posture created a relatively smaller gestural space, with more hand, wrist, and finger action and a wide range of gripping action affiliated with a range of relatively closed vowels. The kinds of vocal-gestural action adopted by their students, as we will see, vary widely. Nonetheless, there are clear musical resemblances within their lineages.

Parampara

Ordinarily, a student encounters traditional musical disciplines through an intensive teacher-student relationship. Such a relationship is often referred to as *guru-shishya parampara*. This is especially true when the student is not actually a blood relative of the teacher. In the strictest form of this relationship, the guru and shishya are ritually bound to one another as virtual parent and child. This relationship, however, is not simply a means of learning musical techniques or repertoire. A musical ancestry, as noted above, is an important part of a musician's identity. The structure of musical authority in these musical lineages is similar to Bhakti *sampradayas* or Sufi *silsilas* who trace their present-day spiritual authority to an originary saint and are overseen by a living torchbearer (*khalifa*). Though these spiritual and musical lineages very seldom overlap, many musicians trace their musical origins to a great founding figure who often is seen as a spiritual adept as well — for example, Swami Haridas, Gopal Naik, or Amir Khusro. Whether or not these origin narratives are supported by historical evidence, the teaching passed down over the centuries in this way is typically understood to contain esoteric knowledge not available to those outside the direct lineage. A chain of these relationships, reaching from the past to the present, is called a *parampara*.[6]

The details of the relationship between teacher and student vary widely from one situation to another. Some call their teachers "guru," others "ustad." Many teachers expect some traditional observances from their students, such as initiatory rites, ritual payment, yearly celebrations at Guru Purnima, or household service such as making tea, doing laundry, and fixing the computer. In return, some teachers house and feed their students, most spend long hours teaching, and nearly all offer instruction that goes beyond repertoire and technique. Nonetheless, the heart of this relationship consists of sitting face to face as the student attempts to reproduce the teacher's phrases in turn. As written notation is seldom used, teacher and student spend hundreds of hours sitting face to face over the course of many years, attending closely to one another. This extensive time spent together fosters a close bond, often involving a great deal of time spent together outside formal lessons. A student's training, however, often also features philosophical discourse, whispered commentary at concerts, corrections from the next room while the student is practicing, and advice regarding elocution, dress, and manners. Other teachers fulfill a role closer to that of a tutor, offering private tuition, meeting a student only a few times a month, and accepting an hourly fee. In cases where several generations of students are actually linked to the teacher by blood or marriage, and particularly in patrilineal Muslim hereditary contexts, the community of blood-related musicians in a common musical lineage is called a *khandan*.[7] In nonhereditary contexts, a family-like community (sometimes called a *gurukul*) emerges among the students studying with a single guru, and these students may even refer to each other as *guru-bhai* and *guru-bahen* (guru-brother and guru-sister). This relationship, again, resembles the special social relationship that obtains in spiritual communities — disciples of the same Sufi *pir*, for example, may refer to each other likewise as *pir-bhai* and *pir-bahen*.

These practices are also shaped by a body of folklore about individual teachers and students, often featuring tales of great mutual devotion, great sacrifices made, and long periods of grueling, nonmusical service at the beginning of a discipleship during which no explicit musical instruction takes place. This corpus of folklore serves to reinforce for students the necessity, sanctity, and authority of a close bond between teacher and student.[8] It also discursively links the teaching process to ethical values such as faith and humility (Deo 2011). By the end of the chapter, we will return to the interplay of ethics and aesthetics in the transmission of bodily dispositions. First, though, we will return to our original question: how do students come to move like their teachers when they sing?

Processes of Gestural Transmission

Teachers move their hands in lessons to articulate phrasing, melodic shape, weight, and tension. Although most teachers give copious explicit advice about vocalization, they almost never tell students how to move. The student learns by singing what the teacher sings, and though the teacher will make a correction in the case of a vocal mistake, students are generally free to gesture as they like. Although there is often evident (and generally unintentional) gestural mirroring in lessons, the gestures reproduced by students are not replicas of the teacher's. As Mukul Kulkarni puts it, the student is not to replicate the teacher's movements themselves, but the nuances of *lagao*, or melodic rendering, of which voice and movement are both vehicles:

> It is not a copy of his actions. . . . He is singing himself, and by gestures, he is also telling that this is the way it should go. So this is part of *taleem* [i.e. training with a guru]. Of course it is not intended that you learn from the gestures, but you learn it indirectly. . . . You learn that [*sings/gestures Gaud Sarang phrase*] is the way you should sing in Gaud Sarang. So your hand also starts making the same design.

Even when the student's gestures resemble those of the teacher, they are often smaller and less overt. Figure 6.2 shows an example: first Vikas Kashalkar's vocal-gestural rendition of a phrase, followed by Pavan Naik's similar but somewhat more restrained rendition of the same phrase a moment later.

Figure 6.2. Student reproducing
teacher's gesture.

In the few cases in which I've seen a teacher give explicit instruction
about gesture, a student is simply told to do less of it. In accord with the
traditions of gesture discourse outlined in chapter 1, teachers will often
chastise their students for making faces or showing visible strain (see Scott
1997: 456–458). Otherwise, the methods of gestural transmission are oblique:
information about melodic motion is foregrounded (e.g., the *ni–pa* curve
in figure 5.9), a demonstration of a particular melodic nuance is given gestural expression (e.g., the lifted *sa* in figure 5.2), or a teacher deliberately and
clearly traces out a shape in the air as a means of teaching (e.g., Darekarji's
andolan in figure 5.10). I have even seen a case of a teacher shaking a student
by the shoulders to get him to produce deep gamak (which the student was
then able to sing even while holding still). But in none of these cases are
teachers telling students how to move.

Similarities in gestural performance seem to arise indirectly, through a
shared understanding of disciplines of melodic motion. This, in itself, is not
so unusual: speech gesture dialects (for example, the varying gestural traditions of Naples and Northamptonshire described in Kendon 2004: 328) are
also transmitted without explicit instruction or straightforward imitation.
Sometimes in the course of a lesson, a student will be unable to reproduce
a phrase sung by the teacher; the teacher then sometimes repeats the sonic
content of the phrase for the student using slightly different gestures to
model an aspect of melody that the student does not yet see (as in, for example, figure 3.7). The teacher may also accentuate similarities and differences between different subphrases by placing them in contrasting locations
in space. The teacher repeatedly provides the same sonic content, but uses
space to suggest various alternate ways of conceiving the music. These are

Figure 6.3. Vikas Kashalkar tacitly guiding
Mukul Kulkarni's phrase ending.

among the most intense moments in the course of a lesson because they require a student to unlearn a habitual way of conceiving of a melodic fragment and to reconceive it according to the teacher's demonstration. Even if a student has the sequence of notes right, the particular way of shaping these notes into a phrase may be mistaken and is often corrected through gestural demonstration.[9]

Teachers also sometimes guide a student's melody by gesturing along with them as they sing. In these moments of intense melodic sympathy, the student is watching the teacher closely for guidance and taking cues. For example, figures 4.5 and 4.10 showed how both Vikas Kashalkar and his student, Mukul Kulkarni, sometimes treat the design of a single avartan as an object to be set aside before the mukhra. Figure 6.3 shows Vikas Kashalkar in concert, gesturing without singing while Mukul takes a brief solo. Specifically, he silently urges Mukul back to *sa* before the arrival of the mukhra.[10] By gesturally enacting his student's melody, Kashalkar presents a kinetic model for how the musicking should proceed.

On one occasion, a fellow student of my teacher told me that he could show the types of taan patterns we had been taught in a series of gestures. He demonstrated them to me systematically: a pattern with varying stresses such as {*srrr, rggg, gmm, mpp*} was performed with the hands facing each other loosely, with a twist of the wrists at each point of rhythmic stresses; a vakra pattern such as {*sgrmgpmdp*} was performed with open palms tracing interlocking loops. Although this gestural taxonomy did not, in fact, account exhaustively for our teacher's gestural repertoire, the power of our shared gestural discipline became clear to me when we were practicing together and he urged me on in improvisation by making these melodic shapes with his hands. As I was preparing for each taan in turn, he would indicate one of these patterns with his hands, and I clearly understood what to sing. These gestures do not explicitly represent note sequences, as letters indicate sounds. But in the shared melodic discipline that we had both learned, these gestural cues clearly implied melodic shapes that I was able to trace vocally and gesturally at will. Gesture analyst David McNeill (2005: 159) calls the sympathy embodied in this shared space of gestural potential the "joint inhabitance of the same state of cognitive being." But inhabiting this shared cognitive state is also inhabiting a shared kinetic discipline — like passing a soccer ball to a teammate who, after months of playing together, knows exactly where and how the ball will come. How did we both end up with this shared melodic-kinetic discipline?

Inheritance

One common way to account for musical continuity within a teaching lineage is by analogy with inheritance (Mukherjee 1989: 5; Dan Neuman 1990: 58; Ashok Roy 2004: 12; Qureshi 2007). With so much possibility for improvisation within a khyal performance, musical lineages provide direction through a focus on musical scope. For a singer, a musical lineage, reinforced by training and practice, serves both as a way of narrating the past and as an always-available musical discipline in the present. Young singers are generally expected to commit to such a discipline for many years before developing an individual style. Vocalist Arun Kashalkar describes this process by analogy with developing a handwriting style: everybody's handwriting is different, but in learning to write, a child must commit to a single method of writing each letter and must do it a thousand times. Once you follow a discipline for some time, he said, "a light comes to you. . . . Then, the whole world looks different, and you have no interest in other gayakis." His brother, Vikas Kashalkar, emphasized that a discipline like this is necessary in order for one's own ideas to emerge: "Have *some* system. System doesn't mean frame, the outer frame. System means method. Follow the method, and expand the frame, and *then* have your own ideas."

Resemblances between generations range from conscious, deliberate imitation (e.g., B. R. Deodhar's convincing childhood impersonations of Abdul Karim Khan's gestures [Deshpande 1989: 169]) to the unconscious absorption of habits from teachers (e.g., Faiyyaz Khan's unintentional adoption of the gestures of thumri singers [Deodhar 1993: 201]). It should be noted here that intentionally imitating a teacher is considered at best an elementary stage of learning. While Arun Kashalkar doesn't dispute that he resembles Gajanan Rao Joshi, he emphasizes that the resemblance is unintentional:

> That day [of the concert], somebody was mentioning, I had either the gestures or the singing style, whatever, mostly like Gajananbuwa. . . . It might be coming naturally, because I was with him for a long time. With that association it might come. I'm not doing it purposefully.

Such claims to inheritance of a musical tradition are not only claims about a personal experience of learning, but also claims about a position in a social matrix. In addition to a particular teacher, nearly every singer identifies with other musical "ancestors" — even, in some cases, legendary musicians from hundreds of years ago. A claim of inheriting music is thus also a claim of inheriting status (Dan Neuman 1990). But this is not merely a matter of rhetoric: no amount of boasting about lineage is a replacement for a performance of musical excellence via a trained musicking body. A Hindustani vocalist who fidgets on the stage like a child while singing prearranged taans in rigid sync with the tal is not just failing to behave in an arbitrarily determined high-status way; that singer simply is not musicking as a master does. An *ustadi* (ustad-like, masterful) singer traces melodic patterns fluently with hand and voice, moves skillfully through raga spaces, navigates temporal structures, constructs and manipulates melodic objects. Such a singer is ustadi by virtue of the whole-bodily gestural-vocal-postural disciplines she has received through a lineage. In this sense, the training of a musicking body is both individual and social, both objective and subjective — much like, in Pierre Bourdieu's subtle reworking of Aristotelian ethics, *hexis*:

> Bodily hexis . . . [is] a pattern of postures that is both individual and systematic, because linked to a whole system of techniques involving the body and tools, and charged with a host of social meanings and values: . . . children are particularly attentive to the gestures and postures which, in their eyes, express everything that goes to make an accomplished adult — a way of walking, a tilt of the head, facial expressions, ways of sitting and of using implements, always associated with a tone of voice, a style of speech, and (how could it be otherwise?) a certain subjective experience. (Bourdieu 1977: 87)

How could a singer learn such complex bodily-vocal dispositions without deliberate imitation? There is ample clinical evidence to show that the "contagion" of posture, gesture, and subtle facial expression (and their affiliated affective states) can occur without any conscious effort on the part of the recipient (Hatfield, Cacioppo, and Rapson 1994; Brennan 2004; Tamietto and de Gelder 2009). More important, it is easy to apprehend observed motion directly as purposive action. It is quite ordinary, for example, for a student to understand that a teacher is tracing a melodic loop (rather than merely moving her hand in the air) or gripping a note (rather than merely moving her fingers into a bunch). This "action understanding" (the empathetic apprehension of the purpose of another's action as though it were one's own) constitutes a different kind of knowing than merely observing the others' hand moving in objective space (Thioux et al. 2008). A tantalizing neurological explanation to account for the link between observation, imitation, and understanding rests on the discovery of so-called mirror neurons in macaque monkeys (Rizzolatti and Craighero 2004; Gazzola and Keysers 2009). Mirror neurons seem to behave like both motor and sensory neurons, firing in the same way both when an action is observed and when the action is executed. More specifically, most mirror neuron activity seems to correlate not with the observation of a precise sequence of behaviors (e.g., pinching three fingers together, raising the hand, and then inverting it), but with the observation of intentional actions with clear goals (e.g., picking an object up and turning it over) (Thioux et al. 2008). Mirror neuron activity has been widely celebrated as a likely neural basis for action understanding, though there is good reason to remain skeptical about this explanation.[11] In any case, learning an action by identifying with the person one is observing seems to be a fundamental capability that underlies face-to-face learning. Michael Tomasello (1993: 496) points out that the ability "to see a situation the way the other sees it . . . in which the learner is attempting to learn not *from* another, but *through* another" seems to be available to most children even before their first birthday.

Although the absorption of individual gestures is mostly unconscious, students are selective about whose dispositions they absorb. Hindustani vocal students do not go around haphazardly absorbing whatever they see. As Mukul Kulkarni puts it, when "the disciple starts moving hands as his guru," it is a result of "the devotion he has put into learning." The ambiguity in Mukul's phrasing here strongly accords with Tomasello's model of action understanding: moving hands "*as* the guru" implies both an observed likeness and a process of identity. A close affective connection between teacher and student thus seems to be crucial. Sameer Dublay emphasizes that the full reception of Jitendra Abhisheki's gestural knowledge was possible only within the context of a dedicated, long-term guru-shishya relationship. Here he is commenting on the "tilted grip" of komal rishabh/lifted *sa* (shown in figure 5.2), emphasizing that the interpretation of this gestures requires having spent time in the teacher's company.

You only know these gestures if you live with him . . . For the sake of gesture, if you see this [*demonstrates gesture*], it might not convey anything. But for us who were learning from him, it immediately brought to mind the exact position of komal rishabh and helped us to reach that level. Now this interpretation is something which you know if you stay with that person.

Here, the analogy with inheritance begins to break down. Face-to-face learning is a capacity for encountering music through the body and voice of a beloved teacher, rather than merely a process of passive reception. In addition to the mere fact of having a teacher, and even the sheer length of time that teacher and student spend together, the mutual devotion that bonds the two together seems to be crucial in the transmission of the musicking body. Mohan Darekar emphasizes that this respect for the guru is a necessary foundation for adopting their bodily disposition:

You pick up a person's gesture and posture if you like them. . . . That impression, which you like, you start doing that. If you go under that impression, naturally you will do it. . . . If you like this person, then you naturally you pick up these things, not purposefully. And because of that, you learn more.

The relationship between teacher and student is marked through various bodily disciplines. As students approach their guru for a lesson, it is conventional for each to bend down and ritually touch their teacher's feet before beginning. While students may sit casually in chairs along with their teacher, it is generally considered rude to sit on a chair while the teacher sits on the floor. Many musicians keep a small photo of their guru with them while touring; in some cases, a musician will set up a small shrine to a guru centered around a photograph.[12] Homes of musicians often feature at least one framed photograph of their teacher, sometimes marked reverentially with saffron powder or draped with garlands, as would be a photo of a spiritual teacher or a beloved divinity. For example, Jitendra Abhisheki's son, Shaunak Abhisheki, lives and teaches in the same house his father did, and his father is a palpable presence — but not only as intangible memory. A photograph of his father, draped with cloth and a garland of flowers, is displayed prominently in the music room. Before Shaunak teaches a lesson, he touches the ground in front of the chair, as he might if Abhishekiji were sitting there in the flesh. The other students of the elder Abhisheki likewise hang garlanded photos of him in their practice rooms. Nor is this a matter of dry ritual — as one of his students was recalling his teaching methods to me, he suddenly broke down in tears of grief for his late teacher.

These practices and rituals reveal that intense devotion to a teacher is a matter of both intentional commitment and spontaneous affection. A fulsome understanding of the construction of the musicking body, likewise, must consider volition as well as inheritance. In most narratives of musical greatness, merely inheriting a style is insufficient. A student chooses a teacher, and remains loyal even when his dedication is tested through hardship. In addition to this deliberate, often heroic devotion to a teacher, a serious musician must, after years of training, become distinct from their teacher even as they carry on a musical tradition (see Napier 2006 and Hurie 2009). At this point, students may freely borrow features from other lineages as well, or try something new. Arun Kashalkar balanced a conversation centered on his gurus with a caveat about personal style:

> I keep myself away from the exact singing of my gurus. I always want something of my own. Nowhere you can just tell me that I am just imitating a particular person. I do remember my gurus while singing, no doubt about it. . . . But finally, I will just attach them with my own things and try to find out a different vista.

Nor is this predilection for a different vista merely a personal preference. It is echoed by other singers as necessary for the development of one's own skills. According to Sameer Dublay, Jitendra Abhisheki was clear in his insistence that his students sing in their own way:

> Completely blind following takes you nowhere. The students with whom I learned . . . we have our individual singing styles, with predominantly Abhisheki effect in it. We all have our individualities intact. No one sings like one another. We are students of the same guru, but having distinct identities of our own. He used to shout at us! — "Don't sing like me. Sing in your own voice!" That has helped us. Each one of us has his own style, his own way of presentation, with distinct elements of Abhisheki in each one of us.

This variety-within-discipline, as we might now expect, extends to gestural-vocal practice. One such pattern specific to Jitendra Abhisheki's teaching lineage is a spread-fingered open hand, kept virtually stationary, during the vocal articulation of dense, fast taans (extended melodic phrases on single vowels), in which the range of the passage is relatively small (3-5 scale degrees), and the notes are articulated with deep, rapid oscillation. Figure 6.4 shows various incarnations of this gestural form in his students.

As is clear from figure 6.4, there are many possible specific articulations of this gestural-vocal mode. Whereas Jitendra Abhisheki tended to have a very tense handshape, with the fingers spread to their maximum extent, all of his students have looser handshapes, and Vijay Koparkar often uses both hands in this situation. But in all of these cases, there is a salient kinetic

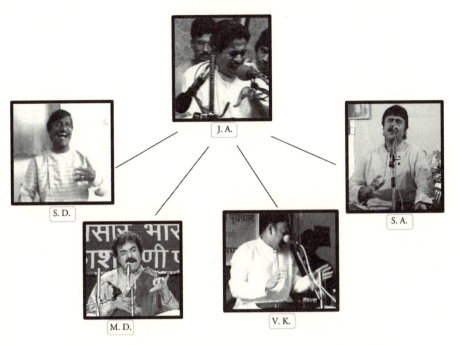

Figure 6.4. Variations in stationary spread-fingered taan handshape.

gestalt perceivable, in which the steady, seamless texture of the taan is matched by a relatively steady hand and a spread-fingered handshape.

Just as students may incarnate a particular gestural-vocal feature differently, each student of a given teacher pieces together a unique gestural repertoire from that teacher. For example, Jitendra Abhisheki passed on several gestural-vocal forms, each of which, as far as I can determine, was only picked up by a single student. The first is a moving palms-together form affiliated with delicate slides, which seems to have been adopted only by his son, Shaunak Abhisheki. The second is a cupped grip for sustained notes with precise intonation, which seems to have been adopted only by Sudhakar Deoley.

Gestural repertoires are not passed on in a wholesale, deterministic fashion; rather, they appear in various combinations in different students, suited to their own musical sensibilities. Sameer Dublay notes that this was a special feature of Jitendra Abhisheki's style:

Abhishekiji's whole being was a message of this pluralist approach. His entire learning process was plural. He learned from different sources . . . and created his own source. And again, dissemination of information was . . . person-based. He gave me something which he didn't give to Hemant, he didn't give to Shaunak. He gave something to Shaunak that he didn't give to anyone else.

Mohan Darekar (2004: 125–126) recalls Jitendra Abhisheki saying to him:

> Do not think "This is from this singer or that gharana and I am imitating this style or using that pattern." Whatever you have got, is yours, and how you combine or merge these building blocks . . . how you want to sing, you decide and experience the result as one wholeness that is yours. . . . Your skill decides which elements to choose and how to link them.[13]

Students of Gajanan Rao Joshi report that he, too, gave different instruction to each student. In one facile account of the different disciplines given to the Kashalkar brothers, Joshi divided his teaching by gharana: Ulhas Kashalkar received predominantly Jaipur gharana gayaki, Vikas Kashalkar received predominantly Gwalior gharana gayaki, and Arun Kashalkar received predominantly Agra gharana gayaki. Each brother retains the ability to sing in each of these three gharana styles, and indeed Ulhas Kashalkar, in turn, reports passing on gharana-based instruction to his disciples depending on their own "temperament" (Banerjee 2009). All three brothers fundamentally agree with their guru's dictum that though a singer may span several gharana gayakis in one performance, each raga should be rendered according to the discipline of a single gayaki. Indeed, Kumar Mukherjee (2006: 81) reports that Gajanan Rao Joshi had drastically different dispositions when singing various pieces according to these various gayakis in the same concert: "It seemed as if the artiste had changed clothes inbetween." Like claims of inheritance, these assignments of individual styles to particular gharanas are not merely innocent objective descriptions. They imply a classificatory matrix (Brinner 1995) that serves to prescribe particular aesthetic frameworks, different stances for the evaluation and legitimation of these various styles. As we shall see later, these aesthetic ideals often overlap with ethical ideals and are central to the construction and inhabitation of paramparic bodies.

Although Jitendra Abhisheki and Gajanan Rao Joshi were unusual in the degree to which they integrated disparate styles into a coherent gayaki, many singers in the twentieth century have also learned from more than one teacher, piecing together a way of singing out of the gayakis of their teachers. Mohan Darekar, though he has studied with both Jitendra Abhisheki and Vikas Kashalkar, has little in common with the latter in terms of gesture. Indeed, he acknowledges the much deeper influence of Jitendra Abhisheki on his singing, as he came to him as a boy and stayed with him for many years, while he approached Kashalkar late in life, as a mature singer, for advice and guidance. These were two different kinds of relationship. Whereas Kashalkar is his "guide," Abhisheki is his guru. Darekar goes on to cite many other influences, of varying importance: he grew up listening to Amir Khan, Bade Ghulam Ali Khan, and Pandit Jasraj; he studied dhrupad-style alap with Said-ud-din Dagar for many years; he studies the recordings of Ghulam Mustafa Khan for inspiration in taan patterns. In the last five years, he has undergone formal, intensive training with Rajan and Sajan Misra. Darekar describes the relationship of these elements:

> Imitation is very important at the beginning. After that, mixture of the other things, your Guruji's style, things you learn from others, and your own expressions, blending together, a mixture . . . You have to determine "how much I can do, what is suitable for me." Otherwise . . . nobody can help you.
>
> Inside you should realize yourself — you should know your personality.

Nor is Darekar unusual in this respect; exposure to a wide range of teachers and recordings has largely become the norm. In the middle of his training, Vikas Kashalkar told Gajanan Rao Joshi that he had come to admire Bhimsen Joshi's singing by listening to recordings. His guru's response was instructive:

> Okay, fine. If you like, you adopt [Bhimsen Joshi's] singing. . . . Whatever you like, you can do. But if you want to enrich your singing, you could add the good portion from his singing, and have our [style], too. . . . You have some similarity of sound, or voice, so you adopt that. But have this Gwalior gharana . . .

Kashalkar went on to derive a general principle from this:

> This type of leading student on his *own* path is the best method. . . . So whenever my student Mukul [Kulkarni] sings like me, I get upset. Don't imitate my voice, don't imitate my singing. You take the ideas, and add your own. Nobody should say he is a replica. (Vikas Kashalkar, interview with Ingrid Le Gargasson, Pune, 2008)

A few weeks later, in a lesson, Mukul Kulkarni was gently chided for just this "replication" of his guru. In singing a note with very delicate intonation, he held the back of his hand up to his mouth to hear his own voice better — an idiosyncrasy of Kashalkar's that both he and Mukul have noted to me. Teacher and student burst into laughter, and Mukul dropped his hand and resumed singing.

The problems with mechanically imitating one's teacher are most evident in accounts of students who unthinkingly assimilate their teacher's obvious shortcomings: vocal defects, postural idiosyncrasies, and so on. Stories of these serve, in musical folklore, as warnings to young students about blind mimicry (Deshpande 1976: 19). But apart from these obvious defects, students also must make decisions about musical discipline that, while not simply undesirable, may be inappropriate for them as individual singers. Pavan Naik, a student of Vikas Kashalkar, reports that the instruction to find his own path was quite explicitly linked to a difference in body:

> Guruji says . . . "Don't forget yourself. Main thing is your identity." Because by birth I have a different body. "Don't follow blindly." Guruji always says that. First *naql* [imitation] then *aql* [intelligence]. . . . *Khuda ko pahechana* [Recognize yourself]. . . . Guruji is ready to give me all things, but some of them are not suitable for me. . . . You have to know yourself. What is Pavan Naik, then Guruji's own style, then inbetween that, you have to follow the things which suit you. . . . My *pinda* [body] is different [from Guruji's]. . . . If you don't want something, then you don't take. You have to take only good things.

The assertion that his *pinda* (body) is different from his guru's may seem trivial, but taken in a musical context in which the student is expected to embody the guru's music, it is quite significant. This transmission, at the level of the musicking body, is not merely a matter of putting on the guru's body like a ready-made suit. Nor can a student simply wish their way into an arbitrary singing style. Even under the most liberal circumstances, a young singer has only a handful of teachers available for intensive taleem. This is especially the case within hereditary musical families, in which students may be prohibited in principle from learning from, or even listening to, musicians from outside the gharana. The extensive training required for the disciplining of a paramparic body takes years. Some great singers have attended music schools, and some have not; no great singers have done without this intensive period of training with a model teacher. Serious students must develop a musicking body suitable for their own predisposition out of the limited set of materials given in their training with various teachers.

The Paramparic Body

The reception of musical knowledge in guru-shishya parampara, then, spans the whole volitional spectrum from passive, unconscious absorption of habits to active choices. As Harris Berger (2010: 103) puts it in describing traditions of stance in general, "We see agents drawing on practices from the ocean of surrounding social life and reproducing, reinterpreting, and remaking the stances of others." In the case of Hindustani music training, the stances most readily available to a student are those cultivated by their guru and their fellow students. This dialectic between inheritance and choice within a tight-knit family is captured well by what Katharine Young calls the "family body":

Bodies are passed down in families, not as assemblages of biological traits enjoined on the bodies of children by parents but as intentional fabrications devised by children out of the bodies of parents. . . . Within families, memory is passed down, not only as oral lore or material artifacts but also as something that is neither mentifact nor artifact: corporeal dispositions. . . . Family bodies, like family stories, provide their heirs positions, situated perspectives, on parents' ways of being in the world, out of which children can devise their own "presentations of self." (2002b: 25–26)

In Young's work, the formation of a family body is seldom fully conscious or easily articulated in words. Like adapting a guru's musicking body to one's own, this process is both conscious and unconscious, both conservative and innovative. Most important, the process of transmission she describes has not so much to do with mimicking behaviors as with adopting "situated perspectives": stances, modes of action understanding. To adapt this term to musical transmission through lineages of teachers, I will use the term *paramparic body*.

An Indic term that does some of the same work as paramparic body is *sanskar*, a term used both for nature and nurture, to describe an inborn disposition, an early family influence, or even a retained habitus from a past incarnation. This applies especially well to singers who have been brought up in a musical family and have come to inhabit a paramparic body that is also a family body. Sanskar can also refer to the musical disciplines to which a student consciously submits when they choose a teacher later in life, as in this description of Sharatchandra Arolkar's training:

[He] got the Gwalior style taleem under the tutelage of Aacharya Krishnrao Pandit of Gwalior, then under his cousin Pt. Eknath Pandit and finally under the Been player Pt. Krishnarao Mulay. The sweet combination of *sanskaras* from these three Gurus was imbibed by Pt. Arolkarji in his musical personality and he brightened it by using his own intuition. (Bhagwat 2009: 1)

Mohan Darekar describes a smooth continuity between audible and inaudible features of a teachers' paramparic body that students learn from: "You are learning from him, you are looking at his everything, and singing, and expressions, and style of singing, everything. Style of walking, dress . . . everything you adopt, or think of." As Daniel Neuman (1990: 48) puts it in his ethnographic study of music teachers and students in Delhi, "The guru communicates something of his being, and this must remain true and immutable." Sameer Dublay, another student of Jitendra Abhisheki, emphasizes that the tacit transmission of being is a central part of musical instruction:[14]

Teaching bandish [compositions] was just one very tiny part of his entire being. And he used to say, "If you want to really, really learn music, just *be* with me." And he really had that ability to . . . communicate many things without saying a word.

Dublay went on to describe this being as *mudra*, a rich word with a range of meanings, from imprint to posture to handshape to bearing. The expression "shuddh bani, shuddh mudra" often refers to merely a still, beautiful countenance while singing, but Dublay clarified that he meant mudra in its broadest sense — "a complete presence": "There is an aphorism: 'Pure voice, pure mudra.' [Jitendra Abhisheki] was unsurpassed in keeping his mudra pure. So his mudra was such that when he sat down to sing, it seemed as though some entirely different person was sitting there."[15]

Tomie Hahn (2007: 149–150) describes a similar transformation in her *Nihon Buyo* teacher, whose presence as a performer differed so radically from her quotidian presence that she had to remind herself that it was the same person. Apart from "being," other quotidian usages of "mudra" deal with distinctive material impressions (seal, sign, imprint, stamp). This usage finds resonance with the common English phrasing in which one musician "bears the stamp" of another, as various colors of sealing-wax may bear a common stamp impression. Likewise, various bodies may bear a common *mudra*. The impression borne by these bodies, as we will see, is both aesthetic and ethical.

Ethical Practice and the Paramparic Body

The great variety of paramparic bodies (and thus the great variety of ways of musically being) may lead us to relegate them to the realm of pure aesthetics: of taste, of arbitrary preference. Yet we have seen that vocal, postural, and gestural dispositions are also described in terms with undeniable ethical valence: humble versus arrogant, devotional versus erotic, open versus concealed. A beloved teacher's musical disposition is exemplary (and therefore paramparic) not only because it is beautiful, but also because it is virtuous. A paramparic body carries both aesthetic and ethical value.

Musical performance, of course, is not the only kind of bodily action that blends the good and the beautiful. "Good posture," for example, serves both as evaluation and prescription, spanning kinesiology, aesthetics and ethics. Pierre Bourdieu (1977: 94) points out that everyday bodily practices such as table manners and walking gaits are "capable of instilling a whole cosmology, an ethic, a metaphysic, a political philosophy, through injunctions as insignificant as 'stand up straight' or 'don't hold your knife in your left hand.'" However, as is evident from his examples, Bourdieu's approach tends to focus on unconscious, coercive constraints on the body from above. He rather understates its dialectical counterpart: the deliberate choice of bodily discipline in accord with what one *wants* to be. Consider, for example, the rigorous physical exercises prescribed by wrestling guru Shanti Prakash Atreya that change the aspirant's "whole attitude toward life," make his "character and personality shine," and allow him to live a "fuller and more meaningful life" (Atreya quoted in Alter 1992). Another example is provided by Richard Wolf (2000), who describes a rich, and apparently quite intentional, tradition of cultivating a moral self through Muharram performance (both drumming and *maatam*, or ritual chest-beating). Charles Hirschkind (2006) describes various aural and kinesthetic practices that Egyptian Muslims use to deliberately cultivate piety. For example, *ishirah* (the "opening of the heart" that allows God to remove sins and implant faith) is linked to a specific gestural routine: "opening up the arms, raising and relaxing the chest, turning the face upward." The ethical implications of bodily actions such as these, though deliberate, are not explicitly taught in words; they are "learned with the body, in all of its kinesthetic and synaesthetic dimensions" (Hirschkind 2006: 76). The paramparic body, likewise, is ethically disciplined not at the level of explicit moral reasoning (e.g., deducing a correct course of action from axioms about natural rights) or conventional emotion (e.g., a public expression of disgust at a political scandal), but at the level of affective stances (e.g., humility, calm, openness) that are known and practiced through habits of posture, gesture, and voice. It is in this sense that paramparic bodies are ethical: a student is disciplined not only to perform beautifully, but also to perform virtuously.

Depending on the teacher, the particular ethos that is imparted may vary widely, and as noted earlier, the values of different traditions are often fiercely at odds. Indeed, debates about the relative merits of two musicians often hinge on ethical values. Consider the disagreement between V. H. Deshpande and Babanrao Haldankar over Agra gharana singers. Deshpande (1976: 42) writes that the Agra singer "never even for a moment departs from the rigid observance of the rules" and that Agra singers' founding figures "exaggerated the importance of discipline and order." Haldankar (2001: 68–73), positioning himself explicitly against Deshpande's view, argues that the great power of Agra singers derives not from rule-bound rigidity but from "total involvement" and *boj* (i.e., weightiness, dignity), both of which are manifest in a specific technique of voice production, long breaths, and a preference for extended, weighty melodic phrases. Here, as in other debates, music criticism is saturated with ethical overtones but is full of contention over the specific values that apply. This does not mean that every revered musical figure is (or could be) a moral exemplar in, say, business dealings, family matters, or politics. There is no easy system of translation between gestural-vocal disposition and moral fiber. Accordingly, in the following discussion I am not arguing for an overarching moral system in which any particular approach to music is universally redemptive, either in legend or in fact. I merely hope to point toward a few of the many ways in which paramparic bodies exceed aesthetics, and serve as vehicles for ethical traditions.

One crucial field of ethical responsibility borne by a singer is a responsibility to the audience. The view that musicians can dramatically affect the ethos of an audience is implicit in the moral debates about music from Plato to Al-Ghazzali to the twentieth-century attempts to snuff out courtesan performance on the grounds that they are morally corrupting. But this view may also be used to support claims to ethically beneficial performances, as in dhrupadiya Ashish Sankritayayan's (2006) claim that when singers achieve "complete identity with the voice, the music and the sound, then the same inner state is created in the listener." V. H. Deshpande (1973: 23) insists that the key determining feature of Hindustani vocal traditions is "restraint," in contrast to "superficial emotional excitement" and "arousing passions." On many occasions, I have seen teachers insist that a student take a deep breath and become calm before beginning to sing. Some singers start their lessons by uttering "bismillah" ("in the name of God") or a similar formula; others have more elaborate rituals of prayer or devotion. The responsibility of the singer to cultivate a certain attitude in himself for the sake of the audience is evident in Mukul Kulkarni's assertions (in chapter 4) that as a singer must maintain consistency in gestural-vocal rhythmic flow because "you take people with yourself," and that you should give a feeling of melodic wholeness "to yourself as well as to the audience." Vikas Kashalkar explicitly criticizes singers who switch abruptly from idea to idea, from gait to gait; instead, he says, a singer should have the patience to develop a performance gradually. Indeed, advocates of orderly methods of raga development sometimes attribute the degeneration of patience among audiences to just such an excess of "fireworks" — dramatic, surprising vocal-gestural action — on concert stages (Deshpande 1973: 58–60). These propositions are both aesthetic and ethical: inasmuch as a musicking body serves as a model for musical attention, it bears responsibility for the musical world that is inhabited by both the singer and the audience.

As we saw in chapter 1, the very discipline and control of gesture also bears great ethical weight. Conspicuous spontaneous motion in the course of performance is often marked as showy, arrogant, and even erotic, in contrast to devout, restrained stillness. For women, certain modes of eye and hand movement may evoke echoes of courtesan performances; a properly reformed female body, according to the dominant post-Independence concert ethos, is relatively introspective and still. For women and men, this deliberate stillness is not merely a lack of gesture — it is a cultivated bodily disposition, sometimes even linked discursively to the stillness of yogic practice.

Two other contrasting stances of the musicking body, described at the end of chapter 5, carry ethical values. In one stance, the body makes music move; in the other, the body is moved by music. Here, willfulness, harshness, and arrogance is contrasted with surrender, humility, and gentleness. Shaunak Abhisheki once told me that his father, Jitendra Abhisheki, modified his Agra training by singing gentle curves instead of angular patterns (as though, in his words, "rounding the edges of a triangle"). Using his hands, Shaunak contrasted the "harsh," abrupt changes of direction with the "gentle," flowing curves cultivated by his father. This gentleness matters, in part, because of the ethos it evokes in the audience. But gentleness (in contrast to harshness) is also a sign of humility: as Abhisheki says, "A gentle approach shows that the raga is bigger than you." Vikas Kashalkar once admonished me for forcing my notes into place, saying that my melodic action should amount to "praying upward" (singing an ascending phrase up to high *sa*, raising his open palms and facing his gaze up, in the manner of the ishirah gesture described by Hirschkind) and "a feeling of surrender" (descending to *sa*, inclining his open hands toward the ground, as though offering a virtual object). This accords closely with Rahim Fahim-ud-din Dagar's contrast between two ways of singing andolan (in chapter 3) — in the outer approach, one exerts effort to move specific notes up and down; in the inner approach, the whole raga is undulating, and the singer "is intoxicated [*masti mein*, "in intoxication"] and spins along with the wind." This account of spinning [*ghoomna*] in ecstasy [*masti*] evokes the stylized *raqs* (spinning) of Chisti Sufi practice (Qureshi 2006: 122; Clayton 2001: 17). The ethical power resulting from bodily immersion in raga space recalls Ali Jihad Racy's (2003: 120–123) account of ecstatic practices among Arab musicians. The musical efficacy of these musicians is often attributed to *saltanah*, a special inspirational state in which a musician derives musical power, paradoxically enough, by surrendering to the melodic mode at hand. Though different in their particularities, all of these formulations present a kinestheic-devotional frame in which an individual musicking body is immersed in a spacious, fluid presence which is larger than the body, and to which the body surrenders.

Open palms are linked to another ethically charged bodily technique: *khula awaz* (open voice). Khula awaz is marked both by relative timbral openness (i.e., richness in overtones) and by relative openness of the lips, tongue, and jaw. The most extreme khula sound is produced with a wide-open jaw and lips, with the back of the tongue lying low, out of the way of the voice. A range of vocal positions, however, can be considered khula. For example, Amir Khan's voice is sometimes described as *antar se khula* (open on the inside: with nasal resonance and lowered tongue) but *bahar se band* (closed on the outside: lips only slightly open). Within the Gajanan Rao Joshi lineage, khula refers to the moderately open vocal configuration that produces an open /a/ vowel, with relaxed lips, tongue, and jaw. This is often contrasted to *band awaz* (closed voice); the English term *false voice* is used too, not only for falsetto but also for a weak, constricted, or breathy tone. *Khula* itself has a rich set of ethical connotations beyond phonetics; in addition to "open," it can mean "clear," "direct," "uninhibited," and "undisguised." The ethical implications of khula awaz seem to derive partially from the physiology of voice production: singing with open voice requires one to keep the path of the voice unobstructed. Raising the back of the tongue or closing the jaw is the vocal equivalent of standing with one's hands in one's pockets: it conceals the upper overtones, softens the voice, and can hide poor intonation; indeed, beginning singers often resort to closing their voice when they are unsure of what they are singing. Khula awaz, on the other hand, is unobstructed and unconcealed; any defects of the voice are plainly audible. Khula awaz is nearly always linked to a hand shape in which the hand is held open, with the fingers extended and the palm exposed (see chapter 5). In the context of Vikas Kashalkar's gurukul, an open voice is connected to a certain open musical disposition as well: musical elaboration should be straightforward, simple, and clear. While a soft, closed voice is widely accepted in film and pop songs (and this may be part of why it is marked as it is), many devotional[16] and classical singers seem to prefer khula awaz on principle. The voice should not be hidden behind the tongue or the jaw; likewise, there is nothing concealed in the hand. Sudokshina Chatterjee, in an interview conducted by Laura Leante, reports that she was told explicitly about this link: "Ustad Bade Ghulam Ali Khan Sahab used to say you have a open sound if you have a open hand. My teacher also says you should open your hand. Then you will have an open sound" (in Fatone et al. 2011).

Mukul Kulkarni reported that this was the most striking change he encountered when he began his studies with Vikas Kashalkar: "The first thing he did was, he worked hard on the opening of my voice, which was not very powerful, not very khula." Hardly a day went by in the first year of my training with Kashalkar when he did not show me an open palm to remind me to open my voice as I sang. And Kashalkar himself, in his early apprentice-

Figure 6.5. Pavan Naik singing with
open hand and open voice.

Gajanan Rao Joshi

Vikas Kashalkar

Pavan Naik

Figure 6.6. Khula avaz /
khula hath (open voice
/open hand) lineage.

ship with Gajanan Rao Joshi, had to work hard to open his own voice. Among the most dedicated adherents to this disposition is Pavan Naik, another student of Vikas Kashalkar. Figure 6.5 is a photograph of Pavan singing an aakar taan on the vowel /aa/, with both open hand and an open voice. This resemblance across generations was not lost on Vikas Kashalkar. In the video clip from which the picture in figure 6.5 was taken, he smiled at me immediately afterward and said, "Gajanan Rao Joshi used to sing this way." Figure 6.6 shows this open-handed, open-mouthed disposition in Gajanan Rao Joshi, in Vikas Kashalkar, and in Pavan.

On one occasion, I was showing Pavan a video of Gajananrao Joshi performing. Joshi had died before Pavan had a chance to meet him, and this was the first time he had seen a video of him. Very soon after the video began, Pavan remarked, "He looks like me here" (pointing to his open jaw) "and here" (pointing to his flat palm). After watching several more minutes of the video of his grand-guru, Pavan looked at me in amazement and said, "I am the next birth of Gajananrao Joshi," moving his hand along with the video. A few minutes later, as the performance gained intensity, Pavan smiled and said, "Yes, it's confirmed, I'm the next birth."

But it would miss Pavan's point to interpret his claim of being the "next birth" of Gajananrao Joshi as a claim about the transmigration of an autonomous, immaterial soul into a separate flesh-body. (As Pavan was well aware, he was born several years before Joshi died.) The sense in which Gajananrao Joshi has been reborn in Pavan bridges body and soul: the incarnation occurs continuously in the musicking body. Pavan's recognition of his own gestural disposition in his grand-guru's musicking was akin to that of a person recognizing his smile in a photograph of a distant ancestor.

But to describe this resemblance merely in terms of passive inheritance obscures the role of volition in this process. Pavan has not simply absorbed this body through his teacher — he has also chosen it. Indeed, he has consciously taken it further than his own teacher does. Even in the early stages of performance, he avoids closed vowels and their attendant gripping gestures. He also has deliberately chosen not to adopt other features of his teacher's paramparic body. For example, inspired by his drama training, he has chosen an unusually upright orientation of his torso while performing, and pointedly makes eye contact with the audience from the beginning. Furthermore, he reports that his original training in khula awaz occurred very early in life, when his teacher repeatedly cautioned him not to sing with closed vowels, like "a girl singing." Kashalkarji, while also nurturing this open voice, taught Pavan to sing gently as well. This training was specialized for Pavan, though — Mukul Kulkarni, in talking about his early training, reports that Kashalkar had to work to get him to sing with more power, as "this gayaki requires a very powerful, very open voice." Mukul and Pavan are visibly in the same musical lineage: they both make wide use of khula awaz, clear phrasing, similar taan shapes, and open-handed, flowing gestures. But the processes by which they arrived at their particular paramparic bodies, owing to their rather different prior training and tendencies, are rather different, and even opposite in some ways.

Through discipline and devoted attention, through vocalization, posture, and gesture, singers incarnate lineages of embodied musicking through their paramparic bodies. Although singers show a striking gestural resemblance to their teachers, different students resemble their teachers in different but musically consequential ways. Students learn to construct and inhabit a paramparic body, full of ethical and aesthetic potential, through sustained, devoted attention to their teachers over many years. These bodies are neither blindly inherited nor arbitrarily chosen, but crafted.

Beyond Individual Bodies

Analyzing a paramparic body (whether formally or informally) highlights the social dynamics by which bodies are trained, but it also tends to ossify the dynamics of a moving body into a static disposition. The allure of transmission and continuity threatens to pull us back into a metaphoric frame in which resemblance between generations is a matter of wholesale, unintentional inheritance: a matter of passing a treasured object through generations. Claims about ethical contagion, like claims about musical continuity with a great musical ancestor, are also claims to musical status. Legends of musicians with extraordinary powers of ethical transmission (such as the ability to tame savage animals or reform sinners through song) stand alongside legends of musicians with supernatural power over the physical world (such as the ability to summon fire or rain through an exquisite rendition of a raga).

There is also a danger here. To say that the ethos of one generation is inherited mechanically by the next, that the moral life of our forebears is simply and automatically "in our blood," is to posit a world of discrete, self-evident cultures that determine the ethos of their constituents. But we have already seen that mere exposure is not enough to deeply inculcate a musical ethos. As I have tried to demonstrate, the processes of paramparic transmission require students to discern what is to be accepted, what is to be rejected, and from which exemplary sources. As Carrie Noland (2009: 7–8) puts it,

> Despite the very real force of social conditioning, subjects continue to invent surprising new ways of altering the inscribed behaviors they are called on to perform. Individual bodies generate "tactics" that successfully belie the "durable" body *hexis* to which they have been subjected, the disciplining that, if we were to follow a long Marxist tradition, should make humans into gesturing machines.

Bourdieu's grim vision, in which generation after generation involuntarily replicates the mudra of their forebears, applies only partially to the world of Hindustani music, in which mature performance is a matter not only of *hexis* but of *energeia*: action, agency, and creativity. Every singer, though grounded in a tradition of whole-bodily musicking, moves and sings differently. As we have seen students choose what to accept and what to reject, choose how to constitute their own musicking bodies, choose how to be musically.

Thus, my sketches of a few gestural-postural-vocal resemblances only hint at the wide range of aesthetic and ethical sensibilities that coexist side by side among Hindustani vocalists — sometimes even in the same body. Though the construction of a paramparic body requires agency and insight, these bodies are not purely arbitrary; they are built in particular times and places. The Indian music reform movement was bolstered by a sense that it was also ethical reform. Music instruction in modern music schools, in addition to inculcating motor skills, also produced a particular kind of subject with a particular ethos: a way of listening, being, feeling, and musicking (Bakhle 2005: 63–64; Purohit 1988: 870–872, 880; Devidayal 2009). To adapt Rebecca Bryant's (2005) elegant phrasing, a student who wishes to learn from a teacher not only learns a particular discipline of vocal and gestural motion but also learns how to be the type of person who could sing that way. A closer look at the ethical valences of various paramparic bodies cultivated in various lineages may illuminate various models of how a modern subject is to musically be — rather *more* various, perhaps, than is suggested by thinking in terms of a single music reform movement, a single modernity, or a single nationalism.

On the other hand, Hindustani musicians are not alone in conceiving of melody as movement, or in moving as they sing. Nor is India the only place where ethical and bodily traditions are tightly intertwined. No body, after all, moves in a vacuum; no body learns to be itself by itself. Every body, whether speaking, singing, or silent, has a parampara.

Appendix A

❧

Planes of the Body

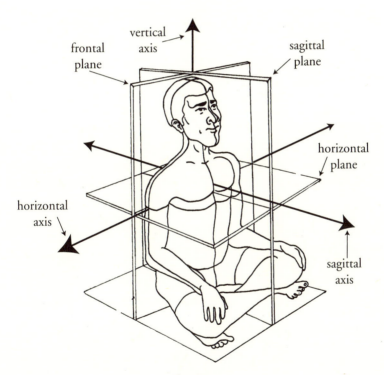

Figure A.1.

Appendix B

❧

Teaching Lineages of Jitendra Abhisheki and Gajanan Rao Joshi

Each line shows a pedagogical relation; the vertically higher placed of two singers linked in this way is the teacher. Solid lines indicate primary teacher-student relationships; dotted lines indicate relatively short-term or casual relationships.

For the sake of diagrammatic clarity, many excellent singers not interviewed or analyzed in this book are not listed here. Padma Talwalkar and Jayashree Patnekar, for example, were senior students of Gajanan Rao Joshi; Hemant Pendse was a gifted student of Jitendra Abhisheki; Ram Marathe was an important teacher of Ulhas Kashalkar, etc. Gulubhai Jasdanwala was likewise a disciple of Jaipur singers Alladiya Khan and Manji Khan (Bhurji Khan's father and brother, respectively).

Conversely, several excellent singers who are mentioned in this book, such as Veena Sahasrabuddhe and Rahim Fahim Ud-Din Dagar, but who are not in these lineages, are not listed here.

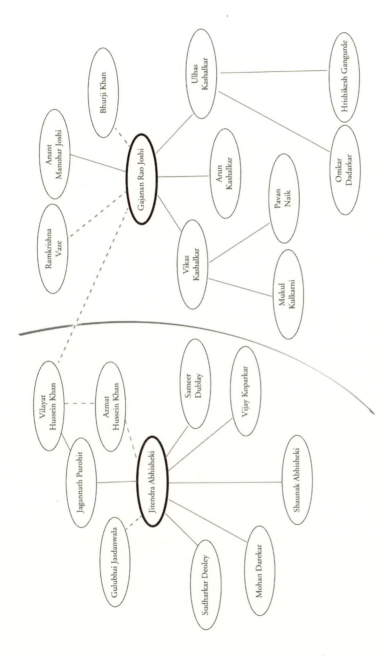

Figure B.1. Highly simplified diagram of the principal musical lineages of Jitendra Abhisheki and Gajanan Rao Joshi.

Appendix C

❧

A Note on Methods

VIDEO ANALYSIS

Although video data may seem to be a simple, transparent, objective record of physical facts, the translation of live performance into video — at any resolution or frame rate — is always a partial depiction, highlighting some things and obscuring others. Video does not capture the moment-to-moment state of every inch of the body; instead it records the light impinging on a digital retina from a single point of view. For example, my archive contains approximately one hundred hours of lessons, concerts, and interviews; nearly all of this material depicts the front of singers' bodies. Doing so focuses attention on the movement of the hands and face rather than the line of the back or the back of the neck. Furthermore, only the very surfaces of the body are visible. The complex muscular action underlying vocalization and gesture remains concealed beneath the sheath of skin. Video is a wonderful tool, but it is always incomplete.

Some studies of the moving body attempt to overcome these limitations by measuring the precise positions of particular joints (cf. van Noorden 2010), and this works very well for studies that are primarily concerned with the objective position of body in three-dimensional space. My analyses, however, deal in general with movement relative to the rest of the body, rather than movement in absolute space. One reason for this is that the technical requirements of measuring absolute space — affixing transmitters to a singer's joints and setting up at least three sensors — would have been an awkward intrusion, both socially and kinesthetically. Although I have not seen cases of singers altering their gestures in the face of complicated camera equipment (to do so, even with deliberate intention, is very difficult), I had hoped to make singers feel more comfortable by using simple, nonintrusive means of recording performances — my handheld camera was far less conspicuous than the elaborate video and audio recording equipment found at most public concerts. More importantly, as chapters 3 and 5 will explain, the spaces at issue in gesture typically have to do with the body's own spatial layout, based on relationships between its parts. The space of this phenomenal body (Merleau-Ponty 2002: 221) is the central concerns of these analyses, not absolute position in a body-independent coordinate system. The human visual system processes more than just sight: it is oriented toward action, for detecting that a virtual object is being stretched, that a singer is reaching for something, or that a singer has come to some degree of rest between gestures. Though the human eye may not be able to precisely measure position, velocity, and acceleration in standard units, it does an excellent job of identifying and interpreting what the body is *doing*. An array of numerical data generated from gesture sensors shows none of this without a human interpreter. As my analyses and interviews are aimed at understanding the virtual world inhabited and acted upon by musicking bodies, rather than the objective world of Euclidean three-dimensional space, the ensemble of video recordings and human visual processing is the appropriate tool for the job.

I also had to choose my shots. Some of this video, especially from lessons, includes both teachers and students in the frame, in order to examine the real-time dynamics of gestural transmission. The majority of the camera work, however, frames a single body. In contrast with conventional concert filming techniques, this shot excludes the accompanying musicians (harmoniumists, violinists, sarangiyas, tabliyas, tanpura players, supporting vocalists). For the purposes of gestural analysis, I treat the singer's performance as independent of these musicians — indeed, it is a matter of wide agreement that the singer gives musical cues to these musicians, but only rarely takes cues from them (Napier 2007). My analytic focus on the individual musicking body as a site for the transmission of music is accommodated by these camera angles.

INTERVIEWS

I used two methods for structuring interviews. The first was asking singers questions about their musical heritage and their experience of performance, positioning myself both as a researcher and as a student of music. Thus, the responses I received shifted fluidly between reports of musical experience (offered by a practitioner to a researcher) and personal advice to me (offered by a musical elder to a student). This method evoked a good deal of quasi-hagiographic folklore about legendary musicians and beloved gurus and, indeed, put me in the position of interviewing my own guru about the musical tradition he has been working so hard to impart to me. Positioning myself in this way forced me to sacrifice critical distance regarding musical valuation, as I have deep personal respect for the singers I interviewed and inescapable prejudices about the musical style that I have inherited. (In fact, however, most singers are quite tolerant of other traditions, even those — like my teacher — who maintain a strict discipline among their students about the parameters of performance and openly profess admiration for singers from dramatically different traditions. For my own part, while committed to Gwalior Gayaki as a matter of personal discipline, I also admire the rather different singing styles of Amir Khan, Kesarbai Kerkar, and Salamat and Nazakat Ali Khan.) Were this book primarily oriented toward determining the relative merits of singing styles, this would have been an unacceptable compromise. However, even the most didactic personal advice was useful, not only in gathering introspective accounts of embodied musicking, but also in better understanding the personal relationships that nurture and sustain Hindustani vocal music. My purpose in conducting these interviews was not to evaluate musical worth but to enrich my understanding of the lived experience of performance and transmission with reports from a range of singers. These accounts of cherished musical traditions shed light on the teacher-student bond that serves as the foundation for the transmission of musical/gestural dispositions.

I was initially confused by the degree to which singers would downplay the significance of their own gestures, which many claimed were merely automatic, natural, or unintentional. The difficulty in finding words to talk about gestural performance is likely conditioned, in part, by traditional systems of musical ethics that value stillness over motion (addressed in chapters 1 and 6). But it also may be a consequence of the apparent transparency of one's own gestures. Anthropologist Adam Kendon notes that gesture is almost never remembered as an autonomous utterance apart from what was spoken: "So transparent are [gestures] that they are hardly even noticed. It was the ability that audio-visual recording technology provided for us that made it possible to 'look back' at gesture, to contemplate it as an 'object,' that created for many a sense of puzzlement" (2004: 358–360). I thus made it a point to show singers recordings of themselves singing, and the puzzlement that these videos produced (both for me and the singers watching themselves) was a major source of inspiration for this work. The singers were often surprised and fascinated by their own intricate movement on the screen — in most cases, they did not even realize that they had been moving. At that point, their dismissal of gesture turned into a desire to try to account for it, often in poetic terms that informed my attempts to develop a phenomenology of performance and lineage.

The bulk of my fieldwork, however, consisted of sitting and singing with other vocalists. Both lessons with senior singers and practice sessions with my fellow students yielded a rich archive of demonstrations, corrections, misunderstandings, and poetic description. The richest accounts of what the body does in the course of musicking, unsurprisingly, came up in the course of musicking.

Notes

Introduction

1. The term *music* likewise has a long extrasonic tradition in Islamic and European scholarship. In the Boethian *musica mundana /musica humana /musica instrumentalis* scheme, for example, only the last is, strictly speaking, audible. The classic Aristotelian dismissal of the music of the spheres on the basis of its inaudibility (1984 [350 BCE]: II.9 [290b30–291a6]: 479) is founded, tautologically, on the necessary audibility of music. But a parallel tradition of speculative music theory that reaches beyond sound has nonetheless persisted (see Shihab-ud-din Subrawadri in Godwin 1986 [12th c.] and Ilnitchi 2002: 44).

2. *Improvisation* is, admittedly, a word that means too much. Among other things, it seems to pit creative spontaneity against traditional repertoire, an unsustainable opposition in Hindustani music. Here I follow Widdess and Nooshin (2006) in using it loosely to refer to the generation of music in the course of performance by the performer. Later chapters will introduce a number of more precise Indic terms to refer to improvisation.

3. There is a slight difference between my use of *musicking* in this context and Christopher Small's influential reworking of the English verb *to musick* (1998). Small's expanded sense of musicking includes what Daniel Cavicchi (2011) calls "audiencing": attending concerts, listening to sound recordings, and other means of directing oneself toward the musical performances of other people. There certainly is much to say about the bodily engagement of listeners with music. In this book, however, for the sake of clarity, musicking refers strictly to singing and playing instruments — whether alone, in teaching, or in concert, with a special focus on the bodily action this involves.

4. Sometimes two singers perform together: Nazakat and Salamat Ali Khan, Mohammad Rashid and Mohammad Sayeed Khan, Rajan and Sajan Misra, etc. In these cases, singers typically alternate between singing through-composed sections in unison, and taking turns improvising. It is rare that two singers will sing overlapping improvised parts except briefly and incidentally.

5. My use of *flesh* may remind some readers of Merleau-Ponty's sophisticated development of the term *chair*, translated as "flesh" in English (1969), but there is

no connection. My use of *flesh-body* is more closely akin to Merleau-Ponty's *corps objectif* and to Husserl's *Körper*.

6. *Man* and *dimagh*, like *soul* and *spirit*, have entered modern vernaculars from different languages (*man* is Sanskritic, while *dimagh* is Arabic; *soul* is Germanic, while *spirit* is Latinate). Also like *soul* and *spirit*, they are both among the resources used by speakers of modern vernaculars to describe distinct facets of the self.

7. The -ic adjectival suffix in English is phonetically and grammatically equivalent to the -ik adjectival suffix in Indic languages (*dharmic, karmic, tantric*, etc.). As *paramparic* serves here as an Indic loan word in English, I have preferred the conventional English suffix.

1. A History of Moving and Singing in India

1. Although gesture tends to be mapped onto the prevailing Muslim/Hindu binary as "Muslim," particularly in films, it is not the case that Muslims are, either in depiction or in fact, particularly voracious gesturers. Amir Khan, for example, the "yogi-like" singer described later in the chapter, was a Muslim.

2. Although closed eyes function as a sign of piety here, it is important to note that closing the eyes was among the faults found in formulaic lists in medieval music treatises.

3. One important exception to this trend was the great dancer Balasaraswati, who occasionally made a point of singing while dancing.

4. Though this shift was profound, it also appears to have occurred over the course of decades. An intermediate stage between the old order of singing courtesans and the new order of the respectable female concert singer was marked by an intermediate, English-language term for the new kind of female singer: the "songstress." Songstresses typically performed thumri while seated, and the recitals took place at the houses of wealthy patrons (Pradhan 2004: 341). Although songstresses typically did not stand and dance, many still performed *ada* — stylized gestures that mimed the words of the song being sung. Quinn interprets ada and other similar seated dance forms as an intermediate step in the elimination of dance from musical performance (1982: 92).

5. An exception is the recitation of drum syllables by Kathak dancers, and the relatively new practice, among students of Chitresh Das, of softly singing a naghma (fixed melodic loop) to oneself while dancing as a way of rigorously staying attuned to the progress of tala cycles.

6. There is at least one important exception to this: the work of Gudiya Sansthan, an organization that organizes concerts for women from courtesan communities, allowing them to perform gesturally rich song and dance traditions in public without shame or the implication of prostitution. The fact that such an organization must raise money and marshall resources to arrange public concerts for these women, however, is a sign of just how unusual such concerts are.

7. As we will see in chapter 5, phonologists have made great strides in understanding how the voice is linked to extralaryngeal physiology in the past decades.

8. This process was not limited to India; early Egyptian singers, for example, found that recording rendered their gestures unnecessary (Racy 1977).

9. Consider, for example, the intimate Doordarshan documentary on Amir Khan, in which he is seen going about his day silently, as the steady gaze of the camera follows him smoothly from intimate private spaces to public spaces: at turns sleeping, cuddling his child, and drinking tea in a crowded Bombay street. The initial shots of him singing, by contrast, are extreme close-ups of his face, in which there is virtually no visible motion.

10. Surviving films clearly indicate, however, that Amir Khan did indeed move his hands while singing.

2. Gesture and Melodic Motion

1. These two conceptions of melody of Hindustani musicians (the first as a sequence of notes, the second as continuous flow) accord closely with Charles Seeger's (1958) distinction between "chain" and "stream" models, respectively. Seeger's understanding of these models, however, is almost exclusively focused on sound, and especially on pitch.

2. This also assumes that the pitches used are all shuddh (natural.) The dots underneath notes denote lower octaves.

3. This mechanical account of gesture may have in tune with his purpose in publishing this article in a British journal: to provide a satisfying explanation of Indian music for Europeans with "scientific minds" (Roy 1934: 320).

4. This is an interesting parallel with the St. Gall and Laon dialects of adiastematic cursive neumes.

5. It is tempting to speculate that this is a consequence of the layout of the harmonium. But even singers who play the harmonium occasionally reverse the mapping, so that left becomes high and right becomes low.

6. In this, Kurth was not so different from other German Romantics in preferring organic to atomistic forms (consider, for example, Ernst's contemporary, physicist Ernst Mach, who rejected the very idea of atoms). One does not need to go as far as Kurth does to find his ideas of melody useful.

7. This bears a striking resemblance to the technical terms drawing from the motion of waterfalls that are used by Kaluli singers to describe melodic motion (Feld 1981).

8. Sometimes, for the sake of teaching, a moving svara may be analyzed into fragments, as when an ornate rendering of pancham in yaman may be laid out as {*pa dha pa pa*}. But ordinarily this svara is merely conceived and sung as *pa*.

9. The program of cultural revival that motivated Dom Mocquereau's chirographic theory of gesture at Solesmes (Bergeron 1998: 116) bears many similarities to Ernst Kurth's theory of melodic kinesis. Both were reacting against a music-theoretic world that focused on notes (figured as excessively rational), and both saw themselves as champions of an alternative, deep-seated, humanizing way of knowing music. My approach is somewhat different in emphasis, in that I see

melody-as-motion and melody-as-notes as mutually necessary, complementary ways of knowing.

10. Here I focus on the world of human melodic exchange, but as musical thinkers such as Iannis Xenakis (in Iliescu 2005), Ted Levin (2006), Steven Feld (1982), and Inayat Khan (1996) remind us, nonhuman melody informs human melodic imagination as well.

3. Ragas as Spaces for Melodic Motion

1. There is a wide literature that discusses raga. For readers of Hindi or Marathi, Bhatkhande's works are thorough and authoritative. In English, see Jairazbhoy 1971; Bagchee 1998; Bor et al. 2002; Powers and Widdess 2001; and www.parrikar .org.

2. Though I focus on motion here, a raga — notoriously hard to describe in words — is also sometimes likened to a certain quality of light, a person (Sanyal and Widdess 2004: 169–172), a season (Bor et al. 2002), or a time of day. This is most obvious when ragas are explicitly spatialized in visual imagery, as in Raga-mala paintings (Ebeling 1973), which depict ragas as characters or deities in dramatic situations. Although music theorists have mostly abandoned these systems in favor of approaches that focus on ragas' characteristic note sequences, the sense that a raga has extrasonic characteristics endures, both in the minds of musicians and in popular representations that account for the power of ragas spatially. For example, a well-known comic book representation (*Amar Chitra Katha*) of a legendary singer (Tan Sen, the greatest musician of Akbar's court) singing Raga Dipak depicts yellow and orange zigzags emanating from him as he fills the air with the raga's heat (Rizvi and Lien 1998: 29); in *Baiju Bawra* (1952), a devoted singer is visited by raga-persons as a reward for his sadhana.

3. This is not to say that note sequences are irrelevant here; there are some phrases in each case which clearly indicate one raga and not the other.

4. This mention of khyal where before he had been using the word *baat* may have been a wry pun, referring both to its literal meaning as "thought" and to the genre *khyal*, typically considered to be lighter and less substantial than dhrupad. Dagar knew, after all, that I had been studying khyal, and dhrupad singers attribute khyal's relative lightness to just this kind of ignorance about the subtleties of raga (Gundecha and Gundecha 2001).

5. As far as I can tell, there is no etymological link between *pakad* and *catchment*, though their shared sense of "thing to catch hold of" is remarkable.

6. There are, in fact, several variant approaches to Ramkali. Some musicians say that it differs from Bhairav in terms of phrase structure as well as pitch set and insist that while Bhairav emphasizes madhyam, Ramkali emphasizes pan-cham. Others say that this emphasis on pancham is merely a consequence of the pancham-centric action of the Ramkali shifts. Many singers also avoid komal nishad, restricting themselves to shuddh nishad even during phrases with tivra madhyam. Girija Devi's rendering is virtually indistinguishable from Bhairav,

except for her introduction of tivra madhyam and komal nishad, so here I have, for simplicity, emphasized her implicit version of Ramkali's grammar.

7. The distinctness of these subspaces marked further, in a particular performance by Girija Devi, by the use of two different syllable sets in singing alap. Nom-tom vocables — syllables with no lexical reference — are used only for the Ramkali shifts, whereas "Hari Om," an invocation to the divinity Hari, is used for the quasi-Bhairav parts.

8. As with the Ramkali case, there are exceptions. Sometimes other gestural forms are associated with {*ma re pa*} (such as a gathering of space during the *ma–re* segment, which is pinched into a grip on pancham during the early part of an alap, when intonation is most important). In some cases, {*ma re pa*}, articulated in the sagittal plane, seems to map pitch onto the vertical axis. In other cases, however, the hand swoops in the horizontal plane, or in a diagonal plane angled between the two. In any case, this region of the raga is curved, and its precise orientation depends on to melodic context.

9. The terms *space* and *subspace*, in addition to their geometric connotations, also may evoke the algebra of vector spaces. The loose analogy works to a certain extent: a raga space, like a vector space, is defined by relations between its elements rather than by pregiven boundaries. A raga space can furthermore be seen to be closed over certain melodic operations the way that a vector space is closed over certain arithmetic operations (e.g., there is no path of motion in yaman that will land one on a komal dhaivat). However, like any analogy, this one has limits: if raga spaces were actually as strictly delineated as vector spaces, a singer would be unable to stop singing one raga and start singing another!

4. Melodic Motion in Time

1. This is slightly different in emphasis from Husserl's account of melodic perception (1964 [1928]: 60), which stresses the connections between successive moments of awareness of discrete notes. The melodic motion at issue in Hindustani music, while analyzable as discrete steps, also consists of continuous, curvaceous motion that is not reducible to sequences.

2. Sam may be marked in many ways: with a slap of the thigh; with a strong gesture down, with open hands, as if offering a virtual object; with a grabbing motion, as if picking up a virtual object; with a quick jerking movement away from the center of the gesture space as though tossing something aside; with a quick twist of the wrist. Audience members often mark sam by making one of these gestures along with the singer.

3. For descriptions of how the living present is informed by the past and future in stand-up comedy, nineteenth-century symphonic music, and other performance traditions, see Harris Berger's *Stance* (2010: 48–50).

4. In some cases, a singer will continue to develop a melodic pattern developed in the last avartan even after singing the mukhra. Certainly, in most cases, the gradual progression of the performance from low to high, mellow to intense,

and sparse to dense requires a retention of the general feel of what has been sung, even if recent melodic patterns have been discarded.

5. This is reflected in the course of lessons as well. During slow, unmetered melodic exploration, a teacher will often stop a student who misses a crucial note, but during later, faster elaboration, the overall flow of a phrase is more important than the exact sequence of notes.

6. Not all singers, however, share this preference. For some, sudden, unpredictable melodic action is valued as expressive and spontaneous. In this latter frame, the carefully structured development described here (and widely associated with Gwalior gharana) is considered excessively plain and straightforward, even boring.

7. This association of circular gestures with verbal descriptions of wholeness seems to obtain broadly across languages; see Calbris 1990.

8. *Bahlava* is a slippery term, used in several ways. In Qawwali performance, it often refers to the slow alap that precedes a song. Singers trained in Gwalior gayaki tend to use it instead for medium-tempo raga development.

5. The Musicking Body

1. While *sharir*, unmodified, typically refers to the flesh-body (for example, sharirik, "physical," is often contrasted with adhyatmik, "spiritual"), it may also, in compounds, refer to various other bodies as well — e.g., the suksma sharir (subtle body) or the karana sharir (causal body). Inasmuch as these bodies include will and consciousness, they may offer further useful ways of describing the musicking body. All I mean to highlight here is the tendency to think of the musicking body as split into pure flesh (i.e., sharir in its usual, unmodified sense) and pure form (i.e., roop in its usual sense.) In Husserl's terms, *sharir* corresponds roughly to *Körper* (the body as material object), but, crucially, *roop* does not correspond neatly to *Leib* (the lived body). Roop is sometimes used by musicians to indicate particular melodic movements. *Sva-roop* is a term used for both musical and bodily forms — for the essential shapes of ragas and for particular manifestations of a divinity (as, for example, the two sva-roops of Krsna as a child and as a young man).

2. Many of these prescriptions draw on the blend of vedantic, yogic, and ayurvedic physiology that undergirds the description of singing in the *Sangitarat-nakara* (see chapter 2).

3. I have chosen a fairly dry translation ("sing") of the semantically rich verb *lagaana* ("to affix, to connect with, to establish," etc.). *Lagaana* can refer to both instrumental and vocal sounding. The related verbal noun *lagao* is used to describe the precise pronunciation of a svara or phrase, implying a certain amount of musical nuance aside from what a named sequence of notes might convey.

4. Some musicians even tune one tanpura string to dhaivat (instead of nishad) when rendering Marwa: see, for example, Ali Akbar Khan's recording of Marwa on *Signature Series Volume 3*. One legend about Kumar Gandharva describes him entering so deeply into the dhaivat-centric pentatonic space of Marwa that he claimed to have "lost the shadaj" in the course of performance.

5. In phrases such as {*dha ni sa re sa ni re sa*}, the *re* may appear momentarily as a flatted fourth relative to dhaivat, but the pull of *sa* embraces its still-retained echo as a komal rishabh. It also is significant that a gandhar-of-dhaivat — in accordance with its gestural articulation as the slightest bit higher than *sa* — would seem to correspond to a lower pitch than a typical komal rishabh (assuming a 5/4 gandhar of a 5/6 dhaivat, this would give a 25/24 ratio between a lifted *sa* and the *sa* of the tanpura.)

6. It should be noted that an introspective account of the dynamics of internal subtle energies is also a claim to a special kind of musical power and status. As the dynamics involved are, in principle, invisible (unlike the manipulation of a virtual objects), these are doubly hard to evaluate.

7. Conventionally, in Quranic exegesis, *tasawwur* refers to the poetic evocation of images. Though linked to an Arabic root (sad-waw-ra) indicating resemblance, it is not exclusively visual; it also can refer to the evocation of sound, taste, touch, and psychological states (Hirschkind 2006: 155). Using the word *image* in translation here would suggest that what is projected in this case — spinning along with the wind — is exclusively visual. But Dagar is emphasizing that the tasawwur of andolit is primarily kinesthetic: one sings from the point of view of one spinning with the wind, rather than from the point of view of one watching someone else spin. As this distinction is precisely what is at issue in Dagar's utterance, I have preferred to translate *tasawwur* as "state" rather than "image."

6. The Paramparic Body

1. The development of lineage-based vocal-gestural styles is similar in many ways to the development of recognizable regional speech gesture dialects (Kendon 2004: 349). But dialects of speech-affiliated gesture (of regions) and music-affiliated gesture (of teaching lineages) are largely independent. Even if a singer has a very strong regional gesture dialect, he takes on a very different gestural disposition while singing. For example, I gesture like a middle-class New Englander while speaking but resemble my teacher — and not other singers — while singing. Musical gesture patterns come alive specifically in the moment of musicking and are learned only after hundreds of hours of sitting in front of one's teacher.

2. The Hindi -ik and English -ic adjectival forms are phonetically and semantically equivalent. I have preferred the latter when using the word *paramparic* in English prose.

3. Though this is among the most commonly cited markers of Jaipur gayaki, Rajshekar Mansur (son of Jaipur gharana stalwart Mallikarjun Mansur) points out that Jaipur vocalists use a range of vowels in addition to /a/ (Mansur n.d.).

4. Gayaki's rough equivalent among instrumentalists is *baj*.

5. Both of these singers passed away before I began this study; my descriptions here are based on surviving video/audio recordings and descriptions from their students.

6. The idea of guru-shishya parampara, though it implicitly evokes unbroken connections to ancient practice, is difficult to decisively map before the twentieth century. It is clear that in courtly, hereditary contexts, and especially before Independence, a teacher of raga music in the North would often be called *ustad* (master), and his student would be a *shagird* (apprentice) (Dan Neuman 1990). By the mid-twentieth century, the word *guru*, with all of its implications of Hindu sacrality, had become dominant throughout South Asia. (See Bakhle 2005: 138 for more on this.) The functions of a guru and an ustad, however, are nearly identical—though the term *ustad* is nowadays reserved for Muslim musicians.

7. For more about the interplay of lineage, musical style, and social status, see Dan Neuman 1977, Dard Neuman 2004, and Deo 2011.

8. The conservatism of traditional teaching lineages has been tempered somewhat in the past century by the rise of textbooks, sound recordings, and music schools, all of which provide a student with recourse to an authority other than his or her guru. The wide variation that previously seems to have obtained among the diverse musical lineages linked to various courts and temples has been smoothed out in large part by a movement toward standardization. Treatises and textbooks on music, such as V. N. Bhatkhande's *Hindustani Sangit Paddhati* and S. Bhagyalekshmi's *Ragas in Carnatic Music*, have served to standardize the melodic prescriptions of raga. Music conferences in the early part of the twentieth century attempted to settle disputes over intonation, repertoire, and other musicological questions. Sound recording, radio, and television have aided in the construction of a canon of recorded performances that are heard, studied, and emulated by musicians throughout India, regardless of lineage.

9. These moments are reminiscent of moments of gestural "mismatch" in math students that immediately precede a cognitive breakthrough (Goldin-Meadow 2005: 47).

10. This is akin to the way in which a *Nihon Buyo* dance teacher might guide a student's body with her own hands once the student has grasped the basic steps of a routine. In the case of Nihon Buyo, however, the teacher may actually touch the student's body (Hahn 2007: 105).

11. The extent to which the mirror neuron action observed directly in monkeys applies to humans is still unclear. Indeed, even if mirror neurons were shown to be the neural correlate of motor learning, motor learning by itself does not seem to fully account for action understanding in humans (Hicock 2009).

12. For more on a range of photographic practice as social practice, including guru-disciple relations, see Pinney 1998: 177–178 and passim.

13. This mode of writing, in which one paraphrases one's teacher's remembered words at great length, is common in biographies of great singers written by their disciples. Though by ethnographic standards this practice may be dismissed as a kind of ventriloquism, it has much in common with a student's dynamic embodiment of a teacher's voice in the moment of musicking.

14. It also called to mind advice that Jon K. Barlow once gave me about how to approach learning music from masters. Referring to several master musicians (the

Carnatic vocalist T. Viswanathan, his piano teacher John Kirkpatrick, and the Ghanaian drummer Abraham Adzenyah) he emphasized that such people, by teaching music, teach a way of life.

15. "Ek sutra hai bataate hain: 'suddha baani, suddha mudra.' To ye mudra sudh hone ki unki ek charam simaa thi. Ki unki mudra jo thi vo gaane baithe, to aise lagate the koi alag hi inasaan baithe hain." This is an interesting variation of Hakim Mohammad Karam Imam's use of the phrase "Shuddh Bani, Shuddh Mudra" in his *Ma'dan al-Musiqi*. There he describes the singer Bandi Jan, who showed "shudh mudra in its perfect form. When this singer sat and sang, one thought it was not she, but the lady sitting next to her who was singing" (in Imam 1959 [1856]: 10). *Simaa* literally translates as "the ultimate limit."

16. For example, Kabir singer Prahlad Tipanya encourages his accompanying singers to sing with khula awaz — not like film singers. Shafqat Ali Khan, who sings both classical and Sufi devotional songs, notes that khula awaz seems to mark them as "Sufi" even when applied to film songs with secular themes (Ali 2008: 3).

Guide to Transliteration,
Glossary of Terms, and List of Names

~

Hindi and Urdu pose many puzzles for transliteration. There is no perfect way to move between Devanagri, Urdu, and Latin script. Urdu script, for example, often uses the same letter for the various nasal sounds *n*, *ñ*, *ṇ*, and *ṅ*; Devanagari script often uses a single letter for the stops *k* and *q*. There is also a range of conventions about when to write and pronounce the inherent short *a* vowel at the ends of syllables. Furthermore, depending on who is speaking, and in what context, fine phonemic distinctions between *n* and *ṇ*, *kh* and *ḵẖ*, or *ś* and *ṣ* may not appear in ordinary speech. The intention here is not to present an exhaustive, one-to-one system of transliteration, but simply to provide a guide for pronunciation, and to eliminate any ambiguity in the meaning of the words used in this book, so that, for example, *bahār* (spring) is not confused with *bāhar* (outside).

Vernacular Hindi-Urdu spellings and pronunciations have generally been preferred over Arabic, Persian, and Sanskrit ones. Thus, *riṣabh* is given instead of the Sanskrit *ṛṣabh*, and *tabla* instead of the Arabic *ṭabl*, etc. No special Latin characters are used to transliterate Arabic letters such as ʿayin and ṣād, or Sanskrit letters such as the vowels *ṛ* and *ṝ*, which are sometimes preserved in scholarly writing, but which are pronounced in the same way as common letters in spoken Hindi-Urdu. The one exception is the retroflex labial approximant /ḷ/, transliterated as *ḷ*, which is found in many of the Maharashtrian names transliterated below.

The table shows the sounds indicated by each of the Latin characters used in the glossary. Urdu letters are given in initial or independent forms. Despite the awkward appearance, I hope the sound that is intended in each case will be unambiguous. "Dental" indicates a sound produced with the tongue against the teeth; "retroflex" indicates a sound produced with the tongue farther back in the mouth, against the alveolar ridge. "Aspirated"

153

indicates a sound produced with a clear expulsion of breath; "unaspirated" indicates that the breath is retained.

The Latin characters that are used in the glossary to indicate pronunciation are given in the left-hand column; an English equivalent (if any) is given in the next column; the third column contains notes on pronunciation. The far rightmost columns give the applicable Urdu and Hindi characters; the next column to the left gives an example of a Hindi-Urdu word spelled according to this system.

a	ahead		tabla	अ	آ
ā	father		sitār	आ	آ
ai	shell		taiyār	ऐ	اَی
au	cough		aurat	औ	اَو
b	back		bandiś	ब	ب
bh	clubhouse		lagbhag	भ	بھ
c	chip	unaspirated	campā	च	چ
ch	match head		chotā	छ	چھ
d	diablo	dental, like Spanish 'd'	dargāh	द	د
dh	band house	as above, but aspirated	bodhi	ध	دھ
ḍ	guard	retroflex	ḍanḍā	ड	ڈ
ḍh	bird house	as above, but aspirated	ḍhābā	ढ	ڈھ
e	pale	pure /e/ vowel; no dipthong	bhed	ए	اے
f	fun		fārsī	फ़	ف
g	gut		rāg	ग	گ
gh	jug head		ghar	घ	گھ
ġh		voiced velar fricative /ɣ/ like French 'r'	ġhulām	ग़	غ
h	hover		Hindustān	ह	ہ
i	tin		Sindh	इ	اِ

ī	spl<u>ee</u>n		Gujarātī	ई	ای
j	<u>j</u>ungle		jangal	ज	ج
jh	he<u>dge h</u>og		jhaptāl	झ	جھ
k	<u>c</u>ool	unaspirated	karma	क	ک
kh	bac<u>k h</u>oe		rākhī	ख	کھ
k͟h	Ba<u>ch</u>		k͟hyāl	ख़	خ
l	<u>l</u>emon		gulāb	ल	ل
ḷ		in Marathi: retroflex labial approximant /ʋ/	Kashāḷkar	ळ	ل
m	<u>m</u>elon		Mahārāṣṭra	म	م
n	<u>n</u>oon	dental	Guru Nānak	न	ن
ṅ	ri<u>ng</u>		raṅgolī	ङ	ن
ñ	o<u>ni</u>on		Rañjanī	ञ	ن
ṇ	cor<u>n</u>er	retroflex /ɳ/	Gaṇeś	ण	ڻ
o	h<u>o</u>tel	pure /o/ vowel; no dipthong	ṭopī	ओ	او
p	<u>P</u>unjabi	unaspirated	Panjābī	प	پ
ph	pum<u>p h</u>ouse		phūlwālā	फ	پھ
q	<u>q</u>ur'an	uvular plosive /q/, far back in throat	qismat	क़	ق
r	tor<u>t</u>illa	tapped like Spanish /r/	riyāz	र	ر
ṛ		flapped retroflex /ɽ/ something like 'bor<u>d</u>er'	pakaṛ	ड़	ڑ
ṛh		as above, but aspirated /ɽʰ/ something like 'guard <u>her</u>'	baṛhāī	ढ़	ڑھ
s	<u>s</u>ing		sarod	स	س
ś	<u>sh</u>ine		madhuśālā	श	ش
ṣ	hu<u>sh</u>	sometimes retroflex /ʂ/ often pronounced like ś	riṣabh	ष	ش
t	splin<u>t</u>	dental, like Spanish 't'	tānpūrā	त	ت
th	splin<u>t h</u>and	as above, but aspirated	thānā	थ	تھ

t̤	cou<u>rt</u>	retroflex	t̤appā	ट	ت
t̤h	cou<u>rt h</u>ouse	as above, but aspirated	t̤hīk	ठ	ﺘﻪ
u	l<u>oo</u>k		<u>u</u>ttam	उ	ٱ
ū	<u>oo</u>ze		ūpar	ऊ	او
v	lo<u>v</u>e or <u>w</u>et	a range of sounds from /v/ to /ʊ/ to /w/	V̱ārāṇasī	व	و
y	<u>y</u>ard		<u>y</u>ār	य	ى
z	ba<u>z</u>aar		bā<u>z</u>ar	ज़	ز

GLOSSARY OF TERMS

action understanding — apprehending physical movement as an action (intentional, goal-oriented, conscious) undertaken by a subject, rather than mere mechanical behavior exhibited by an object.

alap (ālāp) — slow, unmetered melodic exposition of a rāga preceding the bandish; more broadly, any melodic improvisation.

amad (āmad) — a melodic line leading to the mukhṛa at the end of an āvartan.

andolan (āndolan) — oscillation.

andolit svara (āndolit svara) — a note that is consistently produced with andolan.

avartan (āvartan) — one cycle of tāla.

bada khyal (baṛā k̤hyāl) — a relatively slow, expansive piece within a suite of k̤hyāls in a single rāga.

bahlava (bahlāvā) — medium-tempo elaboration of the words and melody of a khyāl, often including extensive rhythmic play.

bandish (bandiś) — a vocal composition, consisting of words and text, to be elaborated through rhythmic and melodic expansion.

barhat (barhāt) — a gradual process of melodic elaboration, usually progressing upward, focusing phrases around note after note in turn.

beat — one of several recurring, isochronous points at which one is compelled to tap a foot, take a step, clap the hands etc. Note that mātras are often longer or shorter than beats (see mātra).

been (bīn) — large stick zither used in rendering extensive dhrupad ālāp.

bhaav (bhāv) — mood, soul, disposition, being.

bhajan (bhajan) — a devotional song, usually with a repeated refrain and several verses.

calan (calan) — melodic movements characteristic of a given rāga.

Carnatic (karṇāṭak) music — the rāga music of South India.

catchment — a recurring gestural discourse segment (McNeill 2005).

chota khyal (choṭā khyāl) — a relatively fast, energetic piece within a suite of khyāls in a single rāga.

devadasi (devadāsī) — women, particularly in South India, who are ritually wedded to a temple deity and usually trained in music and dance.

dhaivat (dhaivat) or **dha** — the sixth scale degree.

dhrupad (dhrupad) — genre of Hindustani raga music featuring extended ālāp and rigorous, systematic elaboration on compositions.

dimagh (dimāgh) — the faculty of analysis and discernment typically located in the head.

dosha (doṣa) — in general, any sort of moral failing or defect; in music treatises, one of a canonical list of vocal flaws.

drut khyal (drut khyāl) — see choṭā khyāl

fado (fādo) — Portuguese song, popular in Goa.

family body — a bodily disposition constructed from the dispositions of family members (Young 2002).

flesh-body — the body as a material object: muscle, bone, blood, etc.

gandhar (gāndhār) or **ga** — the third scale degree

gayaki (gāyakī) — singing style.

gestural affiliate — the gestural action coperformed with a given vocal action.

gesture space — the region around the body in which gesture is performed.

gharana (gharānā) — one of several lineages of musical practice in Hindustani music, with characteristic aesthetic values, technique, and repertoire.

growth point — in the work of gesture analyst David McNeill: an atom of cognition, corresponding to a meaningful distinction that precedes both gesture and speech.

guru (guru) — in Indian music, a mentor who takes responsibility for the musical development of his or her student.

gurukul (gurukul) — the "family" of a guru's students, whether blood relatives or not.

Hindustani (hindustānī) music — North Indian rāga music.

isochronous — evenly spaced in time.

jagah (jagah) — Hindi: space/place, including key regions within raga spaces.

khalifa (ḳhalīfā) — the highest living authority of a Sufi brotherhood or a musical lineage.

khandan (ḳhāndān) — in music, a musical lineage, usually related by blood or marriage.

khula avaz (khulā āvāz) — a manner of singing in which the voice is unobstructed by the tongue or lips, usually with an open ā vowel.

khyal (ḳhyāl) — the major genre of North Indian classical vocal music, featuring a great deal of improvisation and stylistic variation.

kundalini (kuṇḍalinī) — a subtle, ordinarily latent energy associated with the human body, described in Tantric literature and sometimes used by musicians to describe interior musical processes.

lagao (lagāo) — rendering.

lavani (lāvaṇī) — song and dance form usually performed by women, often with erotic texts, in Mahārāṣṭra and South India.

maand (mānd) — genre of Rajasthani folk song.

madhyam (madhyam) or **ma** — the fourth scale degree.

man (man) — the faculty of aesthetic apprehension and feeling typically located in the chest.

masti (mastī) — ecstatic intoxication.

matra (mātra) — unit of metrical measurement within a tāla.

melograph — machine used to produce pitch/time graphs from sonic inputs.

melographic — conception of melody as a pitch/time graph.

mudra (mudrā) — in Indian classical dance, one of dozens of stylized handshapes. In Hindustani classical music, the "stamp" of a teacher's being, impressed upon his or her students.

mukhra (mukhṛā) — a fragment of a bandish to which an improvising musician returns periodically.

musicking body — the moving body in the course of making music.

neume — in Byzantine, Gregorian, and many other chant traditions, a characteristic, named vocal gesture sung on a single vowel, or a cursive written sign that indicates such a gesture. In music-theoretic terms developed by Jon K. Barlow, a neume is a dynamic form that unfolds in time: the motion of a hand playing a slide guitar, the buildup and release of ions across a membrane, the trajectory of a bicycle through a crowded market.

nishad (niṣād) or **ni** — the seventh scale degree.

nom-tom (nom-tom) — a method of alap in which nonlexical syllables (*ri, re, ra, nom*) are used as vehicles for melody.

nyaas (nyās) — a melodic resting point; a nyās svar is a svara on which it is generally appropriate to take rest in the context of a given rāga.

pakad (pakaṛ) — a "catch phrase" that gives an instant impression of a raga.

pancham (pañcam) or **pa** — the fifth scale degree.

parampara (paramparā) — a succession of teachers and students.

paramparic (pāramparik) — something passed along in a parampara.

paramparic body — the patterns and dispositions of the musicking body, developed from gestural-vocal-postural dispositions made available through teaching lineages.

prana (prāṇ) — vital breath.

pravaha (pravāha) — flow.

preparatory phase — the phase of a gesture preceding its significant portion, e.g., raising the hand to chest level before giving a thumbs-up sign.

purnavad (purṇavād) — an aesthetic-ethical approach that values organic wholes above independent parts; holism.

quasi-Bhairav (kvāzī-bhairav) — melodic movement in Ramkali that is similar to Bhairav.

raga (rāga [in Sanskrit and academic contexts], rāg [ordinary registers of Hindi and Hindustāni music], rāgam [in Carnatic contexts]) — a melodic mode used in Indian music, including characteristic patterns of melodic motion and weight, a pitch set, and, in many cases, extra-musical associations with seasons, festivals, divinities, times of day, etc. See chapter 3 for a systematic exploration.

raga alapana (rāga ālāpana) — in Carnatic music, the unmetered exposition of a rāga.

ragam-tanam-pallavi (rāgam-tānam-pallavī) — the major method of extended raga development in Carnatic music, consisting of unaccompanied, spontaneous rāga exposition, followed by a presentation and elaboration of a canonical composition (pallavī) with melodic and rhythmic accompaniment.

ramkali shift (rāmkalī śift) the insertion of tivra madhyam and/or komal nishad in Rāg Rāmkali.

rishabh (riṣabh) or *re* — the second scale degree.

roop (rūp) — form, especially beautiful form, especially the visible form of the body.

roopic — formal (having to do with roop), as opposed to material (having to do with sharir).

sam (sam) — the recurring point in a tāla cycle where the previous cycle culminates and the first mātra of a new cycle begins.

sangeet (saṅgīt) — In ancient Sanskrit treatises: the unified art of singing, dancing, and playing instruments. In medieval and modern treatises: music.

Sangitaratnakara (saṅgītaratnākara) — influential music-theoretic text written in the thirteenth century by Sāraṅgadeva, royal accountant at the Devgiri court of Singhana.

sanskar (sanskār) — an deep-rooted habit of thought or action inculcated at an early age or even inborn, sometimes attributed to past incarnations.

sargam (sārgam) — conventional names for notes in Indian music, relative to a fixed tonic: ṣaraj (*sā*), riṣabh (*re*), gāndhār (*ga*), madhyam (*ma*), pañcam (*pa*), dhaivat (*dha*), niṣād (*ni*).

shadaj / shadja (ṣaraj) or sā — the first scale degree.

sharir (śarīr) — the material flesh-body: muscle, bone, skin, etc. Sometimes used as a technical term to refer to nonfleshy bodies (e.g., the karaṇa śarīr, or causal body).

shariric (śārīrik) — of the material flesh-body.

shishya (śiṣya) — a disciple of a guru.

staff — in music notation, an arrangement of horizontal lines, indicating different vertical levels of pitch, on which noteheads are placed.

subspace — a space within a space.

sur (sur) — as used by music theorists, a precise, measured frequency. As used by musicians, a properly rendered sound.

svara (svara) — among music theorists, a theoretical pitch located relative to a given tonic (named according to sārgam); among musicians, a dynamic instantiation of a theoretical pitch.

svar-jnan (svar-jñān) — the melodic knowledge that allows one to name a svara when it is heard, or to sing a svara whose name is given (Bhatkhande 1964).

tala (tāla) — one of several traditional metrical cycles consisting of a fixed number of matras, organized into subsections; in Hindustani music, a tala is also marked by a fixed sequence of drum strokes.

tamasha (tamāśā) — a genre of musical theater popular in rural Mahārastra.

tan (tān) — a melisma consisting of a series of rapid, more or less isochronous svaras.

tanpura (tānpūrā) — the long-necked lute that typically provides an atmospheric drone on sā to accompany vocal performance.

tasawwur (tasawwur) — evoking or projecting an image, a sound, or a state.

tawaif (tavāyaf) — a woman from a North Indian commnunity of trained dancer-singers; used informally, the term often connotes loose morals or prostitution.

tayyar (taiyār) — having undergone sufficient training and practice to perform as a soloist.

thumri (ṭhumrī) — a semiclassical song genre often including ambiguously erotic and devotional song texts.

tonic — a foundational note relative to which other notes are heard and to which melodies tend to return at important structural points. In Hindustani music, as the tānpura tends to sound ṣaraj (*sa*), it quite often (but not always) serves as the tonic.

translational — moving in a straight line.

Tukaram (Tukārām) — seventeenth-century Maharashtrian singer-saint.

upaj (upaj) — a process of melodic improvisation in which a given melodic segment is developed on in successive phrases.

ustad (ustād) — a master of music, particularly in families of musicians.

ustadi (ustādi) — An authoritative, masterful manner of performance or comportment — literally, ustād-like.

vakra (vakra) — crooked, wending, curvaceous movement. In music, melodic action that changes direction periodically.

vilambit khyal (vilambit khyāl) — see baṛā khyāl.

vistar (vistār) — the slow unfolding of a rāga by showing the dynamics of each svara in turn (often "svar vistar").

vocal affiliate — the vocal action coperformed with a given gestural action.

vyaktitva (vyāktitvā) — manifest personality, bearing, as a manifestation of an inner state.

Jitendra Abhisheki "Abhisheki-buwa": Jitendra Abhiṣekī

Shaunak Abhisheki: Śaunak Abhiṣekī

Ombkar Dadarkar: Omkār Dādarkar

Rahim Fahim-ud-din Dagar: Rahīm Fahīm-ud-dīn Ḍāgar

Mohan Darekar: Mohan Darekar

Sudhakar Deoley: Sudhākar Deoḷe

Girija Devi: Girijā Devī

Sameer Dublay: Samīr Dubḷe

Hrishikesh Gangurde: Hriṣikeś Gāngurḍe

Anant Manohar Joshi "Antu-buwa": Anant Manohar Jośī

Gajanan Rao Joshi "Gajanan-buwa": Gajānan Rāv Jośī

Arun Kashalkar: Aruṇ Kaśāḷkar

Ulhas Kashalkar: Ulhās Kaśāḷkar

Vikas Kashalkar: Vikas Kaśāḷkar

Bade Ghulam Ali Khan: Baṛe Ghulām Alī Khān

Bhurji Khan: Bhurjī Khān

Shafqat Ali Khan: Śafqat Ali Khān

Vilayat Hussein Khan: Vilāyat Husain Khān

Vijay Koparkar: Vijay Koparkar

Mukul Kulkarni: Mukul Kulkarṇī

Pavan Naik: Pavan Nāīk

Veena Sahasrabuddhe: Vīṇā Sahasrabuddhe

Ritwik Sanyal: Ritwik Sanyāl

Bibliography

Ali, Shabana. 2008. "The Surefire Success Formula." *Radio and Music*, accessed March 13, 2011, at www.radioandmusic.com.

Alter, Joseph S. 1992. *The Wrestler's Body: Identity and Ideology in North India*. Berkeley: University of California Press.

———. 2004. *Yoga in Modern India: The Body between Science and Philosophy*. Princeton, NJ: Princeton University Press.

Angsuwarangsee, T., and M. Morrison. 2002. "Extrinsic Laryngeal Muscular Tension in Patients with Voice Disorders." *Journal of Voice* 16: 333–343.

Aristotle. 1984 [350 BCE]. *On the Heavens*, translated by J. L. Stocks, in *The Complete Works of Aristotle: The Revised Oxford Translation*, edited by J. Barnes. Princeton, NJ: Princeton University Press.

Arnold, Godfrey E. 1961. "Physiology and Pathology of the Cricothyroid Muscle." *Laryngoscope* 71: 687–753.

Bagchee, Sandeep. 1998. *Nad: Understanding Raga Music*. New Delhi: BPI.

Bailur, Chitra. 1955. "Music and Personality." *Lakshya Sangeet* (2)3: 40–42.

Baily, John. 2006. "John Blacking and the Human/Instrument Interface: Two Plucked Lutes from Afghanistan." In *The Musical Human*, edited by Suzel Reily. Burlington, VT: Ashgate.

Bakhle, Janaki. 2005. *Two Men and Music*. New York: Oxford University Press.

Bamberger, Jeanne. 1991. *The Mind behind the Musical Ear: How Children Develop Musical Intelligence*. Cambridge, MA: Harvard University Press.

Bandura, Albert, et al. 1961. "Transmission of Aggression through Imitation of Aggressive Models." *Journal of Abnormal and Social Psychology* 63: 575–582.

Banerjee, Meena. 2009. "Pure, Smooth, and Patient: Pandit Ulhas Kashalkar." *The Hindu*, April 10.

Barker, A. 1989. *Greek Musical Writings*, vol. 2: *Harmonic and Acoustic Theory*. Cambridge: Cambridge University Press.

Barlow, Jon K. 1998–2000. Unpublished class notes, Wesleyan University.

Becker, Judith. 2004. *Deep Listeners: Music, Emotion, and Trancing*. Bloomington: Indiana University Press.

Becking, G. 1958 [1928]. *Der Musikalische Rhythmus als Erkenntnisquelle*. Stuttgart: Ichthys.

Berger, Harris. 1999. *Metal, Rock, and Jazz: Perception and the Phenomenology of Musical Experience*. Hanover, NH: Wesleyan University Press.

———. 2010. *Stance: Ideas about Emotion, Style, and Meaning for the Study of Expressive Culture*. Middletown, CT: Wesleyan University Press.

Berger, Harris, and Giovanna P. Del Negro. 2004. *Identity and Everyday Life: Essays in the Study of Folklore, Music, and Popular Culture*. Middletown, CT: Wesleyan University Press.

Bergeron, Katherine. 1998. *Decadent Enchantments: The Revival of Gregorian Chant at Solesmes*. Berkeley: University of California Press.

Berthoz, Alain, and Jean-Luc Petit. 2008. *The Physiology and Phenomenology of Action*. New York: Oxford University Press.

Bhagwat, Neela. 2009. "Gwalior Gharana and Style [*Gayaki*]." Unpublished manuscript.

Bharatamuni. 1998. *Natyasastra*. Translated by N. P. Unni. 4 vols. New Delhi: Nag.

Bhatkhande, Vishnu Narayan. 1964. *Bhatkhande Sangitshastra: Hindustani Sangit Paddhati*. 3rd Hindi ed. Hathras, India: Sangeet Karyalaya.

Blacking, John. 1959. "Patterns of Nsenga Kalimba Music." *African Music* 2(4): 26–43.

———. 1977. "Towards an Anthropology of the Body." In *The Anthropology of the Body*, edited by John Blacking, 1–28. Association of Social Anthropologists Monograph Series, No. 15. London: Academic Press.

Blackmore, John. 1985. "An Historical Note on Ernst Mach." *British Journal for the Philosophy of Science* 36(3): 299–305.

Booth, Gregory. 1987. "The North Indian Oral Tradition: Lessons for Music Education." *International Journal of Music Education* 9(1): 7–9.

———. 2005. "Pandits in the Movies: Contesting the Identity of Hindustani Classical Music and Musicians in the Hindi Popular Cinema." *Asian Music* 36(1): 60–86.

Bor, Joep, et al. 2002. *The Raga Guide: A Survey of 74 Hindustani Ragas*. Monmouth, UK: Wyastone Estate Limited.

Bourdieu, Pierre. 1977. *Outline of a Theory of Practice*. New York: Cambridge University Press.

Bowman, Wayne, and Kimberly Powell. 2007. "The Body in a State of Music." In *International Handbook of Research in Arts Education*, edited by Liora Bresler, 1087–1106. Dordrecht: Springer.

Brennan, Teresa. 2004. *The Transmission of Affect*. Ithaca, NY: Cornell University Press.

Brinner, Benjamin. 1995. "Cultural Matrices and the Shaping of Innovation in Central Javanese Performing Arts." *Ethnomusicology* 39(3): 433–456.

Brown, Katherine Butler. 2003. "Hindustani Music in the Time of Aurangzeb." PhD diss., SOAS, University of London.

———. 2010. "The Origins and Early Development of Khayal." In *Hindustani Music: Thirteenth to Twentieth Centuries*, edited by Joep Bor. Delhi: Manohar Books.

Bryant, Rebecca. 2005. "The Soul Danced into the Body: Nation and Improvisation in Istanbul." *American Ethnologist* 32(2): 222–238.

Calbris, Genevieve. 1990. *The Semiotics of French Gestures*. Bloomington: Indiana University Press.

Cardine, Eugene. 1982. *Gregorian Semiology*. Translated by Robert M. Fowells. Solesmes, France: Abbaye Saint-Pierre de Solesmes.

Cavicchi, Daniel. 2011. *Listening and Longing: Music Lovers in the Age of Barnum*. Middletown, CT: Wesleyan University Press.

Chandra, Sarvesh. 1979. "The Gharana System of Teaching in Hindustani Music: A Critical Analysis." *Journal of the Indian Musicological Society* 10: 31–33.

Chatterjee, Partha. 1993. *The Nation and Its Fragments: Colonial and Post-Colonial Histories*. Princeton, NJ: Princeton University Press.

Chaudhary, Pravas Jivan. 1959. "Vedanta as Transcendental Phenomenology." *Philosophy and Phenomenological Research* 20(2): 252–263.

Chordia, Parag, and Alex Rae. 2007. "Modeling and Visualizing Tonality in North Indian Classical Music." In "Neural Information Processing Systems: Workshop on Music, Brain, and Cognition."

Clayton, Martin. 2001. *Time in Indian Music: Rhythm, Metre, and Form in North Indian Rag Performance*. New York: Oxford University Press.

———. 2007. "Time, Gesture and Attention in a Khyal Performance." *Asian Music* 38(2): 71–96.

Coomaraswamy, Ananda K. (1936). *The Mirror of Gesture, Being the Abhinaya Darpana of Nandikesvara*. New York: E. Weyhe.

Coorlawala, Uttara Asha. 1992. "Ruth St. Denis and India's Dance Renaissance." *Dance Chronicle* 15(2): 123–152.

Crocker, Richard. 2000. *An Introduction to Gregorian Chant*. New Haven, CT: Yale University Press.

Csordas, Thomas. 1990. "Embodiment as a Paradigm for Anthropology." *Ethos* 18(1): 5–47.

Cusick, Suzanne. 1994. "Feminist Theory, Music Theory, and the Mind/Body Problem." *Perspectives of New Music* 32(1): 8–27.

Darekar, Mohankumar. 2004. *Pandit Jitendra Abhisheki: A Life Dedicated to Music*. Pune: Mudra Press.

De Certeau, Michel. 1984. *The Practice of Everyday Life*. Translated by Steven Rendall. Berkeley: University of California Press.

Deo, Aditi. 2011. "Alternative Windows into Tradition: Non-Hereditary Practices in Hindustani Khyal Music." PhD diss., Indiana University.

Deodhar, B. R. 1993. *Pillars of Hindustani Music*. Bombay: Popular Prakashan.

Deshpande, Vamanrao H. 1973. *Indian Musical Traditions: An Aesthetic Study of the Gharanas in Hindustani Music*. Bombay: Popular Prakashan.

———. 1976. *The National Center for the Arts Presents Mogubai Kurdikar with Kishori Amonkar*. Bombay, September 16.

———. 1989. *Between Two Tanpuras*. Bombay: Popular Prakashan.

Devidayal, Namita. 2009. *The Music Room: A Memoir*. New York: Thomas Dunne.

DeWitt, Mark. 2003. "The Diatonic Button Accordion in Ethnic Context: Idiom and Style in Cajun Dance Music." *Popular Music and Society* 26(3): 305–330.

Dhar, Sheila. 2001. *The Cooking of Music*. New Delhi: Permanent Black.

Ebeling, Klaus. 1973. *Ragamala Painting*. Basel: Ravi Kumar.

Eitan, Z., and Roni Granot. 2006. "How Music Moves: Musical Parameters and Listeners' Images of Motion." *Music Perception* 23(3): 221–247.

Ellis, Alexander. 1885. "On the Musical Scales of Various Nations." *Journal of the Society of Arts* 33.

Ewan, W. G. 1976. "Laryngeal Behavior in Speech." PhD diss., University of California at Berkeley.

Faqirullah. 1996 [1666]. *Manakutuhala and Raga Darpana*. Edited and translated by Shahab Sarmadee. New Delhi: Indira Gandhi National Centre for the Performing Arts.

Fatone, Gina. 2010. "'You'll Break Your Heart Trying to Play It Like You Sing It': Intermodal Imagery and the Transmission of Scottish Classical Bagpiping." *Ethnomusicology* 54(3): 395–424.

Fatone, Gina, Martin Clayton, Laura Leante, and Matt Rahaim. 2011. "Imagery, Melody, and Gesture in Cross-Cultural Perspective." In *New Perspectives on Music and Gesture*. Aldershot: Ashgate.

Fauconnier, Mark, and Mark Turner. 2003. *The Way We Think: Conceptual Blending and the Mind's Hidden Complexities*. New York: Basic Books.

Feld, Steven. 1981. "Flow Like a Waterfall: The Metaphors of Kaluli Music Theory." *Yearbook for Traditional Music* 13(1981): 22–47.

———. 1982. *Sound and Sentiment*. Philadelphia: University of Pennsylvania Press.

———. 1986. "Orality and Consciousness." In *The Oral and the Literate in Music*, edited by Y. Tokumaru and O. Yamaguti. Tokyo: Academia Music.

Ganeshan, Gautam Tejas. 2010. Unpublished flyer for "Pure Music" workshop, San Francisco.

Garagi, Balawant. 1991. *Balawanta Folk Theater of India*. Kolkata: Rupa and Co.

Gazzola, V., and C. Keysers. 2009. "The Observation and Execution of Actions Share Motor and Somatosensory Voxels in All Tested Subjects." *Cerebral Cortex* 19: 1239–1255.

Gentilucci and Volta. 2007. "The Motor System and the Relationship between Speech and Gesture." *Gesture* 7(2): 159–177.

Godøy, Rolf Inge, and Marc Leman. 2010. *Musical Gestures: Sound, Movement, and Meaning*. New York: Routledge.

Goldin-Meadow, Susan. 2005. *Hearing Gesture: How Our Hands Help Us Think*. Cambridge, MA: Harvard University Press.

Gritten, Anthony, and Elaine King, eds. 2006. *Music and Gesture*. Aldershot, UK: Ashgate.

———. 2011. *New Perspectives on Music and Gesture*. Aldershot, UK: Ashgate.

Gundecha, Umakant, and Ramakant Gundecha. 2001. "Notation: Where Has It Led Us?" *Sangeet Natak* 36(1): 41–43.

Hahn, Tomie. 2007. *Sensational Knowledge: Embodying Culture through Japanese Dance*. Middletown, CT: Wesleyan University Press.

Haldankar, Babanrao. 2001. *Aesthetics of Agra and Jaipur Traditions*. Pune: Popular Prakashan.

Hall, Nancy. 2003. "Gestures and Segments: Vowel Intrusion as Overlap." Phd diss., University of Massachusetts, Amherst.

Halliburton, Murphy. 2002. "Rethinking Anthropological Studies of the Body: Manas and Bodham in Kerala." *American Anthropologist* 104(4): 1123–1134.

Hatfield, E., J. L. Cacioppo, and R. L. Rapson. 1993. "Emotional Contagion." *Current Directions in Psychological Sciences* 2: 96–99.

———. 1994. *Emotional Contagion*. Cambridge: Cambridge University Press.

Hatten, R. S. 2004. *Interpreting Musical Gestures, Topics, and Tropes: Mozart, Beethoven, Schubert*. Bloomington: Indiana University Press.

Hicock, Gregory. 2009. "Eight Problems for the Mirror Neuron Theory of Action Understanding in Monkeys and Humans." *Journal of Cognitive Neuroscience* 21(7): 1229–1243.

Hirschkind, Charles. 2006. *The Ethical Soundscape: Cassette Sermons and Islamic Counterpublics*. New York: Columbia University Press.

Honda, K., H. Hirai, S. Masaki, and Y. Shimada. 1999. "Role of Vertical Larynx Movement and Cervical Lordosis in Fo Control." *Language and Speech* 42: 401–411.

Howard, Wayne. 1982. "Music and Accentuation in Vedic Literature." *World of Music* 24(3): 23–34.

Hucke, Helmut. 1980. "Towards a New Historical View of Gregorian Chant." *Journal of the American Musicological Society* 33(3): 437–467.

Husserl, Edmund. 1962. *Ideas: General Introduction to Pure Phenomenology*. Translated by W. Boyce Gibson. New York: Collier.

———. 1964 [1928]. *The Phenomenology of Internal Time-Consciousness*. Bloomington: Indiana University Press.

Ihde, Don. 2007. *Listening and Voice: Phenomenologies of Sound*. Albany: State University of New York Press.

Iliescu, Mihu. 2005. "Glissandi and Traces: A Study of the Relationship between Musical and Extra-Musical Fields." In *Definitive Proceedings of the International Symposium Iannis Xenakis*, edited by Makis Solomos et al. Athens: International Symposium Iannis Xenakis.

Ilnitchi, Gabriela. 2002. "'Musica Mundana,' Aristotelian Natural Philosophy and Ptolemaic Astronomy." *Early Music History* 21: 37–74.

Imam, Hakim Mohammad Khan. 1959 [1856]. "Ma'dan al-Musiqi." Translated by Govind Vidyarthi. *Sangit Natak Akademi Bulletin* 14: 6–14.

ITC-SRA. N.d. "Tribute to a Master: Bade Ghulam Ali Khan." Accessed March 10, 2009, at www.itcsra.org/tribute.asp?tribute=4.

Jairazbhoy, Nazir Ali. 1971. *The Ragas of North Indian Music: Their Structure and Evolution*. Middletown, CT: Wesleyan University Press.

——. 1995. *The Rags of North Indian Music: Their Structure and Evolution*. Bombay: Popular Prakashan.

——. 2008. "What Happened to Indian Music Theory? Indo-Occidentalism?" *Ethnomusicology* 52(3): 349–377.

Jairazbhoy, Nazir Ali, and A. W. Stone. 1963. "Intonation in Present-Day North Indian Classical Music." *Bulletin of the School of Oriental and African Studies* 26.

Johnson, Mark. 2007. *The Meaning of the Body: Aesthetics of Human Understanding*. Chicago: University of Chicago Press.

Kahn, Louis. 2003. *Essential Texts*. New York: W. W. Norton.

Kapur, A., P. Davidson, P. R. Cook, P. F. Driessen, and W. A. Schloss. 2005. "Preservation and Extension of Traditional Techniques: Digitizing North Indian Performance." *Journal of New Music Research* 34(3): 227–236.

Kapur, A., G. Percival, M. Lagrange, and G. Tzanetakis. 2007. "Pedagogical Transcription for Multimodal Sitar Performance." *Proceedings of the International Conference on Music Information Retrieval, Vienna, Austria*, 351–352.

Katsman, Roman. 2007. "Gestures accompanying Torah Learning/Recital among Yemenite Jews." *Gesture* 7(1): 1–19.

Katz, Max. 2010. " Hindustani Music History and the Politics of Theory." PhD diss., UC Santa Barbara.

Kendon, Adam. 2004. *Gesture: Visible Action as Utterance*. Cambridge: Cambridge University Press.

Khan, Inayat. 1996. *The Mysticism of Sound and Music*. Boulder: Shambhala.

Khan, Sakhawat Hussain. 1976 [1952]. "Gayan Camera: Notation" (Singing Camera: Notation). In *Swarna Jayanti Smarika (Golden Jubilee Souvenir)*, edited by P. Dadheech. Lucknow: Bhatkhande Hindustani Sangeet Mahavidyalaya.

Kippen, James. 2006. *Gurudev's Drumming Legacy: Music, Theory and Nationalism in the Mrdang aur tabla vadanpaddhati of Gurudev Patwardhan*. Aldershot: Ashgate.

Kobayashi, Eriko. 2003. "Hindustani Classical Music Reform Movement and the Writing of History, 1900s to 1940s." PhD diss., UT Austin.

Kooijman, P. G., et al. 2005. "Muscular Tension and Body Posture in Relation to Voice Handicap and Voice Quality in Teachers with Persistent Voice Complaints." *Folia Phoniatrica et Logopaedica* 57(3): 134–147.

Krishnan, Hari. 2008. "Inscribing Practice: Reconfigurations and Textualizations of Devadasi Repertoire in Nineteenth and Early Twentieth-Century South India." In *Performing Pasts: Reinventing the Arts in South India*, edited by India Peterson and Davesh Soneji. New York: Oxford University Press.

Kurth, Ernst. 1922. *Grundlagen des linearen Kontrapunkts*. Bern: Verlag Krompholz and Co.

Lakoff, George, and Mark Johnson. 1980. *Metaphors We Live By*. Chicago: University of Chicago Press.

Lange, Roderyk. 1977. "Some Notes on the Anthropology of Dance." In *The Anthropology of the Body*, edited by John Blacking. Association of Social Anthropologists Monograph Series, No. 15. London: Academic Press.

Leante, Laura. 2009. "The Lotus and the King: Imagery, Gesture, and Meaning in a Hindustani Rag." *Ethnomusicology Forum* 18(2): 185–206.

Le Guin, Elizabeth. 2006. *Boccherini's Body: An Essay in Carnal Musicology.* Berkeley: University of California Press.

Levin, Ted. 2006. *Where Rivers and Mountains Sing: Sound, Music, and Nomadism in Tuva and Beyond.* Bloomington: Indiana University Press.

Levy, Kenneth. 1987. "On the Origin of Neumes." *Early Music History* 7: 59–90.

Levy, Mark. 1982. *Intonation in North Indian Music: A Select Comparison of Theories with Contemporary Practice.* New Delhi: Biblia Impex.

Locke, John. 1990 [1690]. *An Essay Concerning Human Understanding.* Edited by Peter H. Nidditch and G. A. J. Rogers. Oxford: Clarendon Press.

MacIszewski, Amelia. 2001. "Multiple Voices, Multiple Selves: Song Style and North Indian Women's Identity." *Asian Music* 32(2): 1–40.

Magriel, Nicholas. 1997. "The Barhat Tree." *Asian Music* 28(2): 109–133.

Mansur, Rajshekar. N.d. Interview with Irfan Zuberi. Accessed Nov. 1, 2011, at india.tilos.hu/english_int_masur1.html.

Marcus, Scott. 2006. "Now Ladies Also Sing: Gender Politics in Post-1990 Biraha, a North Indian Folk Music." Unpublished paper delivered at the 51st SEM Conference, Honolulu.

Martinez, José Luiz. 2001. *Semiosis in Hindustani Music.* Delhi: Motilal Banarsidass.

Massumi, Brian. 2002. *Parables for the Virtual.* Durham, NC: Duke University Press.

Mauss, Marcel. 1973 [1934]. Techniques of the Body. In *Economy and Society* 2(1): 70–88.

McGill, S. M. 1991. "Kinetic Potential of the Lumbar Trunk Musculature about Three Orthogonal Orthopaedic Axes in Extreme Postures." *Spine* 16(7): 809–815.

McGregor, R. S. 1997. *The Oxford Hindi-English Dictionary.* New York: Oxford University Press.

McIntosh, Solveig. 2005. *Hidden Faces of Indian Song.* Burlington, VT: Ashgate.

McNeill, David. 1992. *Hand and Mind.* Chicago: University of Chicago Press.

———. 2005. *Gesture and Thought.* Chicago: University of Chicago Press.

Meduri, Avanthi. 2008. "Temple Stage as Historical Allegory in Bharatanatyam: Rukmini Devi as Dancer-Historian." In *Performing Pasts: Reinventing the Arts in Modern South India.* New York: Oxford University Press.

Merleau-Ponty, Maurice. 1969. *The Visible and the Invisible.* Evanston, IL: Northwestern University Press.

———. 2002 [1945]. *Phenomenology of Perception.* New York: Routledge.

Mersmann, H. 1922/23. "Versuch einer Phänomenologie der Musik." *Zeitschrift für Musikwissenschaft* 5: 226–269.

Milner, David, and Melvyn Goodale. 2006. *The Visual Brain in Action.* New York: Oxford University Press.

Mokkapati, Vijayshree. 1997. "Modal Action: An Indo-European Perspective on Gregorian Chant." Phd diss., Wesleyan University.

Moran, Nikki. 2007. "Measuring Musical Interaction: Analysing Communication in Embodied Musical Behaviour." PhD diss., Open University, Milton Keynes.

———. 2011. "Music, Bodies and Relationships: An Ethnographic Contribution to Embodied Cognition Studies." *Psychology of Music*, published online 9 May 2011

Mukherjee, Bimal. 1989. *Indian Classical Music: Changing Profiles*. Calcutta: West Bengal State Music Academy.

Mukherjee, Kumar Prasad. 2006. *The Lost World of Hindustani Music*. New Delhi: Penguin.

Mundy, Rachel. 2009. "Birdsong and the Image of Evolution." *Society and Animals* 17(3): 206–223.

Nadkarni, Mohan. 1999. *The Great Masters: Profiles in Hindustani Classical Vocal Music*. New Delhi: Somaiya.

Napier, J. 2006. "A Subtle Novelty: Repetition, Transmission and the Valorisation of Innovation within North Indian Classical Music." *Critical Studies in Improvisation* 1(3). Accessed January 24, 2012, at www.criticalimprov.com/article/view/55/105.

———. 2007. "The Distribution of Authority in the Performance of North Indian Vocal Music." *Ethnomusicology Forum* 16(2): 271–301.

Navras. 2004. Interview with Veena Sahasrabuddhe, September 2004. http://www.it.iitb.ac.in/~hvs/Veena/navras_interview.html.

Neuman, Daniel. 1977. "The Social Organization of a Music Tradition: Hereditary Specialists in North India." *Ethnomusicology* 21(2): 233–245.

———. 1990. *The Life of Music in North India*. Chicago: University of Chicago Press.

Neuman, Dard. 2004. "A House of Music: The Hindustani Musician and the Crafting of Traditions." PhD diss., Columbia University.

Nicomachus the Pythagorean. 1993 [ca. 100 CE]. *The Manual of Harmonics*. Translated by Flora Levin. Grand Rapids, MI: Phanes Press.

Noland, Carrie. 2008. *Migrations of Gesture*. Minneapolis: University of Minnesota Press.

———, ed. 2009. *Agency and Embodiment: Performing Gestures/Producing Culture*. Cambridge, MA: Harvard University Press.

Nunez, Rafael, and Eve Sweetser. 2006. "With the Future Behind Them: Convergent Evidence from Aymara Language and Gesture in the Crosslinguistic Comparison of Spatial Construals of Time." *Cognitive Science* 30(3): 1–49.

Ohala, John J. 1972. "How Is Pitch Lowered?" Paper delivered at the 83rd meeting of the Acoustical Society of America, Buffalo, NY.

———. 1994. "The Frequency Codes Underlies the Sound Symbolic Use of Voice Pitch." In *Sound Symbolism*, edited by L. Hinton, J. Nichols, and J. J. Ohala, 325–347. Cambridge: Cambridge University Press.

O'Shea, Janet. 1998. "'Traditional' Indian Dance and the Making of Interpretive Communities." *Asian Theatre Journal* 15(1): 45–63.

O'Sullivan, Peter, et al. 2002. "The Effect of Different Standing and Sitting Postures on Trunk Muscle Activity in a Pain-Free Population." *Spine* 27(11): 1238–1244.

Parrikar, Rajan. 2001. "Bhimpalasi Inc." *Rajan Parrikar Music Archive: Musical Traditions of India*. Accessed March 22, 2011, at www.parrikar.org/raga-central/bhimpalasi.

Pingle, Bhavanrav. 1962 [1894]. *History of Indian Music with Particular Reference to Theory and Practice*. Calcutta: Susil Gupta.

Pinney, Christopher. 1998. *Camera Indica: The Social Life of Indian Photographs*. Chicago: University of Chicago Press.

Pollock, Sheldon, ed. 2011. *Forms of Knowledge in Early Modern Asia*. Durham, NC: Duke University Press.

Powers, Harold S., and Richard Widdess. 2001. "India, Sub-Continent of, III.2 Raga." In *The New Grove Dictionary of Music*, edited by S. Sadie. London: Macmillan.

Pradhan, Aneesh. 2004. "Perspectives on Performance Practice: Hindustani Music in Nineteenth and Twentieth Century Bombay (Mumbai.)" *South Asia: Journal of South Asia Studies* 27(3): 339–358.

Purohit, Vinayak. 1988. *Arts of Transitional India: Twentieth Century*. Bombay: Popular Prakashan.

Quinn, Jennifer Post. 1982. "Marathi and Konkani Speaking Women in Hindustani Music, 1880–1940." PhD diss., University of Minnesota.

Qureshi, Regula Burckhardt. 2006. "Female Agency and Patrilineal Constraints: Situating Courtesans in Twentieth-Century India." In *The Courtesan's Arts: Cross-Cultural Perspectives*, edited by Martha Feldman and Bonnie Gordon. New York: Oxford University Press.

——. 2007. *Master Musicians of India*. New York: Routledge.

Racy, Ali Jihad. 1977. "The Impact of Commercial Recording on the Musical Life of Egypt, 1904–1932." *Essays in Arts and Sciences* 6(1): 58–94.

——. 2003. *Making Music in the Arab World: The Culture and Artistry of Tarab*. Cambridge: Cambridge University Press.

Radhakrishnan, Nandhakumar. 2011. "Laryngeal Dynamics of Pedagogical Taan Gestures in Indian Classical Singing." *Journal of Voice* 25(3): 139–147.

Rahaim, Matthew. 2011. "That Ban(e) of Indian Music: Hearing Politics in the Harmonium." *Journal of Asian Studies* 70(3): 657–682.

Ranade, Ashok. 2000. "Thoughts, Values, and Culture: The Performing Arts." In *Intersections: Socio-Cultural Trends in Maharashtra*, edited by Meera Kosambi. New Delhi: Orient Longman.

——. 2011. *Some Hindustani Musicians: They Lit the Way!* New Delhi: Promilla and Co.

Randall, Annie. 2009. *Dusty!: Queen of the Postmods*. New York: Oxford University Press.

Ranvig, Harriotte Hurie. 2009. *Taking It to the Third Level: A Model for Identifying Aspects of Personal Style in the Khayal Genre*. PhD diss., Wesleyan University.

Rizvi, Dolly. 1998. *Tansen*. Amar Chitra Katha Series. Mumbai: India Book House.

Rizzolatti, G., and L. Craighero. 2004. The Mirror-Neuron System. *Annual Review of Neuroscience* 27: 169–192.

Roubeau, B., et al. 1997. "Electromyographic Activity of Strap and Cricothyroid Muscles in Pitch Change." *Acta Oto-Laryngologica* 117(3): 459–464.

Roy, Ashok. 2004. *Music Makers: Living Legends of Indian Classical Music.* Kolkata: Rupa and Co.

Roy, Rabindra Lal. 1934. "Hindustani Ragas." *Musical Quarterly* 20(3): 320–333.

Roychaudhuri. 2000. *The Dictionary of Hindustani Classical Music.* Motilal Banarsidas.

Sankrityayan, Ashish. N.d. "The Fundamental Concepts of Dhrupad." Unpublished ms.

———. 2006. "To Identify with the Sound." Interview with Johan Laserna. Accessed January 2012 at www.dhrupad.info/Toidentifywiththesound.pdf.

Sanyal, R., and R. Widdess. 2004. *Dhrupad: Tradition and Performance in Indian Music.* Aldershot, UK: Ashgate.

Sarangadev. 1991 [13th c.] *Sangitaratnakara.* Translated by R. K. Shringy and P. L. Sharma. New Delhi: Munshiram Manoharlal.

Sarukkai, Sundar. 2002. "Inside/Outside: Merleau-Ponty/Yoga." *Philosophy East and West* 52(4): 459–478.

Schimmel, Annemarie. 1994. *Deciphering the Signs of God: A Phenomenological Approach to Islam.* Albany: State University of New York Press.

Schutz, Alfred. 1976. "Fragments on the Phenomenology of Music." In *In Search of Musical Method*, edited by F. J. Smith, 23–71. London: Gordon and Breach Science.

Scott, Stanley. 1997. "Power and Delight: Vocal Training in North Indian Classical Music." PhD diss., Wesleyan University.

Seeger, Charles. 1958. "Prescriptive and Descriptive Music-Writing." *Musical Quarterly* 44(2): 184–195.

Shah, Vidya. 2010. "Mallikarjun Mansur Was Really My Ideal." *Times of India*, September 24.

Shannon, Jonathan. 2004. "The Aesthetics of Spiritual Practice and the Creation of Moral and Musical Subjectivities in Aleppo, Syria." *Ethnology* 43(4): 381–391.

———. 2006. *Among the Jasmine Trees: Music and Modernity in Contemporary Syria.* Middletown, CT: Wesleyan University Press.

Sinha, Debabrata. 1985. "Human Embodiment: The Theme and the Encounter in Vedantic Phenomenology." *Philosophy East and West* 35(3): 239–247. Slawek, Steven. 1996. "Engrossed Minds, Embodied Moods and Liberated Spirits in Two Musical Traditions of India." *Bansuri* 13: 31–41.

Smart, Mary Ann. 2005. *Mimomania: Music and Gesture in Nineteenth-Century Opera.* Berkeley: University of California Press.

Soneji, Davesh. 2012. *Unfinished Gestures: Devadasis, Memory, and Modernity in South India.* South Asia across the Disciplines. Chicago: University of Chicago Press.

Srinivasan, Doris. 2006. "Royalty's Courtesans and God's Mortal Wives: Keepers of Culture in Precolonial India." In *The Courtesan's Arts: Cross-Cultural Perspectives*, edited by Martha Feldman and Bonnie Gordon. New York: Oxford University Press.

Sruti magazine. 1989. "S. Ramanathan." No. 55 (April).

Stone, Ruth. 1982. *Let the Inside Be Sweet*. Bloomington: Indiana University Press.

Subramanian, Lakshmi. 2006. *From the Tanjore Court to the Madras Music Academy: A Social History of Music in South India*. New Delhi: Oxford University Press.

Sudnow, David. 1995. *Ways of the Hand*. Cambridge, MA: MIT Press.

Suhrawardi, Shihabuddin. 1986 [12th c.]. "Music and the Imaginal World." In *Music, Mysticism, and Magic: A Sourcebook*, edited by Jocelyn Godwin. New York: Arkana.

Sweetser, Eve. 2004. "What We Mean by Meaning: Conceptual Integration in Gesture Analysis and Transcription." *Gesture* 4(2): 197–219.

Sweetser, Eve, and Marisa Sizemore. 2008. "Personal and Interpersonal Gesture Spaces: Functional Contrasts in Language and Gesture." In *Language in the Context of Use: Discourse and Cognitive Approaches to Language*, edited by Andrea Tyler, Yiyoung Kim, and Mari Takada. Berlin: Mouton de Gruyter.

Tagg, Philip. 2004. "Gestural Interconversion and Connotative Precision: Université de Montréal." Accessed December 27, 2007, at mmsmp.com/tagg/articles/filminternato412.html.

Tagore, Rabindranath. 2004 [1912]. *My Reminiscences*. Whitefish, India: Kessinger.

Tamietto, M., and B. de Gelder. 2009. "Emotional Contagion for Unseen Bodily Expressions: Evidence from Facial EMG." In *Proceedings of the Eighth International Institute of Electrical and Electronic Engineers Conference on Automatic Face and Gesture Recognition*. Amsterdam: IIEE.

Taruskin, Richard. 2010. *The Oxford History of Western Music*, vol. 1. New York: Oxford University Press.

Taub, Sarah. 2001. *Language from the Body: Iconicity and Metaphor in American Sign Language*. New York: Cambridge University Press.

Thatte, Arawind. 2010. *Sangeet Vimarsha: A Bouquet of Thoughts about the North Indian Classical Music*. Pune: Swanandi Prakashan.

Thioux, Marc, et al. 2008. "Action Understanding: How, What and Why." *Current Biology* 18(10): R431–434.

Titon, Jeff Todd. 2008. "Knowing Fieldwork." In *Shadows in the Field: New Perspectives for Fieldwork in Ethnomusicology*. New York: Oxford University Press.

Tomasello, Michael, et al. 1993. "Cultural Learning." *Behavioral and Brain Sciences* 16: 495–552.

Tzanetakis, George, et al. 2007. "Computational Ethnomusicology." *Journal of Interdisciplinary Music Studies* 1(2): 1–24, art. #071201.

Van Der Meer, Wim. 1977. "Hindustani Music in the Twentieth Century: A Study of the Dynamic Nature of Classical Vocal Music in North India." PhD diss., University of Utrecht.

Viswanathan, T., and Matthew Allen. 2004. *Music in South India: The Karnatak Concert Tradition and Beyond*. New York: Oxford University Press.

Wade, Bonnie. 1985. *Khyal: Creativity within North India's Classical Music Tradition*. New York: Cambridge University Press.

——. 1998. *Imaging Sound: An Ethnomusicological Study of Music, Art, and Culture in Mughal India*. Chicago: University of Chicago Press.

Weidman, Amanda. 2003. "Guru and Gramophone: Fantasies of Fidelity and Modern Technologies of the Real." *Public Culture* 15(3): 453–476.

——. 2006. *Singing the Classical, Voicing the Modern: The Postcolonial Politics of Music in South India*. Durham, NC: Duke University Press.

Widdess, Richard, and Laudan Nooshin. 2006. "Improvisation in Iranian and Indian Music." *Journal of the Indian Musicological Society* 36–37: 104–119.

Wilber, Ken. 1995. *Sex, Ecology, Spirituality: The Spirit of Evolution*. Boulder: Shambhala Press.

Wolf, Richard. 2000. "Embodiment and Ambivalence: Emotion in South Asian Muharram Drumming." *Yearbook for Traditional Music* 32: 81–116.

——. 2009. *Theorizing the Local: Music, Practice, and Experience in South Asia and Beyond*. New York: Oxford University Press.

Wulff, Helena. 2006. "Experiencing the Ballet Body: Pleasure, Pain, Power." In *The Musical Human*, edited by S. A. Reily. Burlington, VT: Ashgate.

Young, Katherine. 2002a. "The Dream Body in Somatic Psychology: The Kinaesthetics of Gesture." *Gesture* 2(1): 45–70.

——. 2002b. "The Memory of the Flesh: The Family Body in Somatic Psychology." *Body and Society* 8(3): 25–47.

Zbikowski, Lawrence. 2005. *Conceptualizing Music: Cognitive Structure, Theory, and Analysis*. New York: Oxford University Press.

Zuckerkandl, Victor. 1969. *Sound and Symbol*. Princeton, NJ: Princeton University Press.

Index

Page numbers in italics refer to illustrations; page numbers in bold refer to glossary entries.

breath, 18, 43, 51, 71, 73–75, 76, 89, 94, 107, 127, 128
British colonialism, 23, 27, 28
Bryant, Rebecca, 134

calan, 35, 57, **157**
cancal ragas, 58
Cardine, Eugene, 49
Carnatic music, 6, **157**
catchments, 62–63, 146n5, **157**
Cavicchi, Daniel, 143n3
Certeau, Michel de, 68
chanting, 49
Chasme Baddur (1981), 25–26
Chatterjee, Partha, 28
Chatterjee, Sudokshina, 130
Chordia, Parag, 56
chota khyal, **157**
circularity, 45, *46*, 82, *82*, 95, *96*. *See also* looping movements
class: distaste for courtesanry, 23–24; gestural displays of status, 17–19; gesture associated with low-status occupations, 30; professional public performances and, 24; Sri Raga as high status raga, 60
Clayton, Martin, 7, 12, 73, 83–84
courtesanry: courtesan advocacy, 144n6 (chap. 1); female performance and, 22–24, 26, 128–29; moral reform campaign against, 23–24, 26, 88, 128, 144n4; in *Sant Tukaram*, 21–22, *23*; voice/body separation and, 88
Csordas, Thomas, 11
Cusick, Suzanne, 10

dadra, 24
Dagar, Bahauddin, 59
Dagar, Rahim Fahim-ud-Din, ix, 59–61, 101, 103–6, 129, 146n4, 149n7
Dagar, Said-ud-din, 123
Dagar, Z. M., 101
dance: anti-nautch campaign, 23; performing body in, 11; separation of song and dance, 25; singing while dancing, 24–25, 144n3, 144n5; in thumri performance, 24
Darekar, Mohan, 102, 114, 119, 122–23, 125
Das, Chitresh, 144n5
Dbangs Yig (Tibetan chant notation), 49
Delhi, 4, 125
Deodhar, B. R., 31–32, 60–61, 116
Deole, Sudhakar, 42, *43*
depth, 73, 100–101, *101*
Deshpande, Vamanrao H., 30, 127–28

devadasis, 23–24, **157**
Devi, Girija, 63–64, *64*, 79, 146n6, 147n7
DeWitt, Mark, 11
Dhanammal, Vina, 25
Dhar, Sheila, 35, 45, 56, 80
dhrupad, 2, 25, 91, 100–101, 128, 146n4, **157**
dimagh, 13, **157**
dosha, 16, **157**
drut khyal, *5*, **157**
Dublay, Sameer, 2, 92–94, 98, *98*, 111, 118, 120, 125–26

Eitan, Z., 47
embodiment (as paradigmatic focus), 11
ethics: bodily hexis, 117, 133; dignity, 127; ethical affect, 11, 15, 58, 126–27; humility, 129; legendary ethical powers, 21, 133; moral reform, 22–32; openness, 130; paramparic body and, 126–27; restraint, 128; steady flow, 85, 128; stillness, 22–26, 85, 128–29; teaching lineages and, 11, 17, 109, 110, 113, 133–34; wrestling and, 127
ethnography of bodily practices, 11

facial gestures: chin motion, *43*; closed eyes, 3, 22, 35, 144n2; facial grip, 109; lineage-based dialects of, 108; in lists of singers' faults, 19; sandasta (singing with teeth clenched), 18
fados, 6, **157**
false voice, 130
family body, 124–25, **157**
Fatone, Gina, 12, 102
Feld, Steven, 146n10
film, 21–22, 144n1, 151n16
flesh-body, 8–9, 88–90, *89*, 143n5, 148n1, **157**. *See also* sharir

gamak, 61, 114
gambhir ragas, 58
Gandharva, Kumar, 148n4
gayaki (singing style), 110–11, 116–17, 120–22, **157**
gender, 22–25, 128–29, 144n4
gestural affiliate, **157**
gesture: action understanding of, 118; catchments, 62–63; conventional disapproval of, 16–17; as embodied music, 7–8; as enactment of kinetic forms, 12; gestural consistency in mukhras, 76–77; gestural transmission, 2, 102, 113–16, 124–26, 131–32, 150n10; gesture/voice unity, 51–52; interior experience and,

looping patterns, 44–45; on melodic shape, 44; on melodic trajectory, 35; on pravaha, 85

Kashalkar, Ulhas, *97*, 108, 110, 122, 137

Kashalkar, Vikas: as Gajanan Rao Joshi student, 5, 122–23; on gayaki disciplines, 116; on melodic phrasing, 73; on melodic trajectory, 35; phrasing gestures of, 83; on Raga Mian ki Malhar, 60; on tala cycles in vilambit khyal, 76–78, *77*; as teacher, 53, 113–14, *114*, *115*, 124; "water flowing down steps" melodic image, 48

Kendon, Adam, 39, 51, 95, 99, 140

Kerala, 13

khalifa, 112, **158**

Khan, Abdul Karim, 116

Khan, Ali Akbar, 148n4

Khan, Alladiya, 137

Khan, Amir, 30–31, 80, 123, 130, 144n1, 145n9–10 (chap. 1)

Khan, Bade Ghulam Ali, 31, 123, 130

Khan, Bhurji, 137

Khan, Bundu, 31–32

Khan, Faiyyaz, 116–17

Khan, Faiyyaz and Niaz Ahmed, 35

Khan, Ghulam Mustafa, 123

Khan, Iqbal Ahmad, 70

Khan, Manji, 137

Khan, Mirza, 19

Khan, Mohammad Sayeed, 143n4

Khan, Nazakat, 143n4

Khan, Rahimat, 84–85

Khan, Sakhawat Hussein, 48

Khan, Shafqat Ali: duet singing by, 143n4; gestural rests performed by, 74, *74*; gesture-pitch affiliation in, 38–39, *39*, 41, 54, *54*, 64, 66–67; hand slide of, 64; on khula awaz, 151n16; phrasal organization of, 83; on pravaha (flow), 84; pulling gestures of, *97*

Khan, Vilayat Hussein, 59

Khan, Wahid, 80

khandan, 112–13, **158**

Khansahab, Bade Ghulam Ali, 60–61

khula avaz (open voice), 129–133, *131*, 151n16, **158**

khyal: overview, 4, **158**; disciplines of improvisation in, 2, *5*, 24; disciplines of posture in, 91; lightness of, in comparison with dhrupad, 146n4; performance structure, 4, *5*; as preferred reformer genre, 24; as soloist-dominated genre, 4–5; vilambit khyal example, 76–77

kinetic model of melodic motion, 12, 47–48, 145n9 (chap. 2)

King, Elaine, 11

Kirana gharana, 35, *80*, 110

Kirkpatrick, John, 150n14

kirtan, 22, 91

komal notes, xiii

Koparkar, Vijay, 73

Kulkarni, Mukul: on gestural transmission, 113, 118; on gesture/voice unity, 51; on looping patterns, 48; on melodic trajectory, 35–36, 39; open voice technique of, 130, 132; on pravaha (flow), 85; on raga space, 58; on rain imagery, 61; releasing gestures of, 99; on the unity of gesture and voice, 10; on upaj, 82–83, *83*; as Vikas Kashalkar student, 115

kundalini, 13, **158**

Kurdikar, Mogubai, 30

Kurth, Ernst: German Romanticism and, 145n6; gesture/voice unity and, 51–52; "melody is motion" formula of, 50; theory of melodic kinesis, 12, 47–48, 145n9 (chap. 2)

lagao (melodic rendering), 35–36, 92, 113, 148n3, **158**

laghana, 35

Lange, Roderyk, 11

language: development of scientific linguistics, 27; mind-body problem, 144n6 (Intro.); redundant gestures in, 6; speech gesture dialects, 3, 114; technical music terms, xvii; terms for melodic motion, 47; terms for ontological faculties, 13; transliteration of Hindi and Urdu, 153–56

"Lapak Jhapak Tu Aare Badarva," 86

Latour, Bruno, 17

lavani, 24, 91, **158**

Leante, Laura, 12, 60, 97, 130

leaping motions, 35, 56

learning. *See* teaching/learning

Le Guin, Elizabeth, 11

Leman, Marc, 11

Levin, Ted, 146n10

lift, 92–94, *94*, 148n5

lineages: as conservative forces, 150n8; gayaki, 110–11, 116–17, 120–22, *157*; gestural inheritance in, 17, 116–120, 132–33; gharanas compared with, 6, 110; idiosyncratic vs. common gestural patterns in, 65, 97, 120–22; khyal performance structure and,

68; on raga space, 57, 62; on the separation of voice and body, 27

neumes: in chant notation, 49, 145; as dynamic forms in time, 50, 51, 71, **158**

Noland, Carrie, 133

nom-tom, 110, 147n7, **158**

Nooshin, Laudan, 143n2

notation, 28, 33–34, 49. *See also* sargam notation system

note-based model of melody: Bhatkhande as influential theorist, 29; Ernst Kurth's rejection of, 48; inside/outside raga experience and, 58–59; raga space and, 57; raga theory and, 53–56; Seeger chain/stream model, 145n1; visualization of notes and, 50. *See also* sargam notation system

nyaas, 79, **158**

pakad, 62–63, 146n5, **159**

Pandit, Eknath, 125

Pandit, Krishnrao, 125

parampara, 3, 11, 108, 111–13, **159**. *See also* guru-shishya parampara

paramparic, **159**

paramparic body: defined, 8–9, 108, **159**; ethical practice and, 126–27, 132–33; musical lineages and, 14–15, 133; musical training and, 124–26; volition and, 124, 131–32

Parrikar, Rajan, 56

Patnekar, Jayashree, 137

Pendse, Hemant, 137

performance: construction of raga space in, 65–66, 148n4; dance performance, 11; gharana consistency in, 122; inner/outer andolan, 103–5; khyal performance structure, 4, 5; performing inside/outside a raga, 58–59; practice as performance, 8; professional pubic performances and, 24; stances of the musicking body, 105–6

phenomenal body, 139

phenomenology, 12

phonology, 26–27

phrasing: overview, 72–74; in alap, 74–76; density of melodic action and, 80; in vilambit khyal, 76–77

Pingle, Bhavanrav, 30

pointing, 6, 50, 99–100, 102–3, 105–6

posture: overview, 90; as bodily practice, 126–27; female tanpura posture, 24–25; Hindustani posture traditions, 2, 19, 30–31; Joshi and Abhisheki styles compared,

111; musicking body and, 88; music reform and, 20, 23; vocal range and, 90–91

Pradhan, Aneesh, 24

prana, 18, 101, **159**

pravaha, 84–85, **159**

preparatory phase, **159**

protention, 46, 79

psychoacoustics, 27

pulling: overview, 97–98, *97*; description of, 87, 92; nishad/gandhar glide pulling gesture, 54–55; *svara* motion and, 49, 92–93

Pune, 5

purnavad, *82*, **159**

quasi-Bhairav, 63–64, 146n6, 147n7, 159, **159**

Quinn, Jennifer Post, 144n4

Qureshi, Regula Burckhardt, 24

Racy, Ali Jihad, 129

Radhakrishnan, Nandhakumar, 88

raga: overview, 55–60, **159**; cancal/gambhir pairs of, 58; inside/outside experience of, 58–59; instrument-based gestures in, 7; inter-performer gestural communication, 11–12; as melodic and metrical framework, 4, 14, 53–54; melodic classification of, 29; spatial vs. grammatical musicianship, 68–69; visual depiction of, 146n2. *See also* raga space

raga alapana, **159**

ragam-tanam-pallavi, 2, **159**

ragas

Adana, 78

Ahir Bhairav, 63

Bagesri, 66–67

Bahar, 58

Basant, 58

Basant Mukhari, 63

Bhairav: andolan in, 101–2; gestural subspaces for, 64–65, *65*; as Ramkali relative, 63–64, 146n6, 147n7, 159; scale degrees in, 49

Bhimplas: gesture affiliation with vocal phrases in, 41; gesture-pitch affiliation in, 44–45; hand slide in, 54, *54*, 64, 66–67; mukhras in, 78; partial and full rests in, 74, *74*; phrasal organization of, 83; spatial images for, 56

Bhupali, 58

Bihag, 55, 56, *56*

Brindavani Sarang, 68

taan handshapes, 30–32, 80, 115–16, 120–21, 121

tabla, 4, 7, 11–12, 24, 71–72, 85–86

Tagore, Rabindranath, 26–27, 30

tala: overview, 71–72, 72, **160**; hand gestures and, 25; as melodic and metrical framework, 4, 14; tala cycles in vilambit khyal, 76, 83–84; tal clapping gestures, 71–72, 147n2

Talwalkar, Padma, 137

tamasha, 26, **160**

tan, **160**

tanpura, 24–25, 85, 91, 93, 99, 139, 148n4, **160**

Tansen (1943), 21

tantric philosophy, 18–19

tasawwur, 106, 149n7, **160**

tawaif, **160**

tayyar, **161**

teaching/learning: description of lesson, 87, 112; development of the musicking body, 107–8; gayaki, 110–11, 116–17, 120–22, **157**; gestural transmission, 2, 113–16, 124–26, 131–32, 150n10; imitation, 30, 84, 109, 116–120, 123–24, 150n13; lineage-based gesture dialects, 14–15, 108–9, *109*; posture regimens, 91–92; practice as performance, 8; practice of melodic sequences, 148n5; spatial vs. grammatical musicianship, 68–69; sustained svaras as sign of readiness, 85–86; teacher gesturing, 51; teacher/student mutual devotion, 118–120. *See also* gayaki; gharanas; lineages

temporal awareness, 46, 83–84

thigh-slapping, 25, 26

thumri, 2, 24, 144n4, **161**

Tipanya, Prahlad, 151n16

Titon, Jeff Todd, 12

tivra notes, xiii

Tomasello, Michael, 118

tonality: discrete pitch (svar-jnan) and, 29; gestural pitch mapping, 37–38, 46, 95, 145n3; lifted pitches, 92–94, *94*, 148n5; psychoacoustics and, 27; Ramkali shift, 63–64, *63–64*, 79, *79*, 146n6, 147n7, **159**

transcription, xiii–xv, *xiv*, 28, 33. *See also* sargam notation system

Tukaram, **161**

undulating/andolit movement, 49, 59, 101–2

upaj, 80, 82–83, *83*, **161**

ustad, 112, 117, 150n6, **161**

vakra motion, 44–45, *45*, 59, 85, 108, 110, **161**

vedanta, 13

velanti, 36–37, *36–37*

Venkatamakhi, 29

vibrato, 101–2

video analysis, 138

vilambit khyal, *5*, 76–77, 83–84

violin, 4

virtual objects: overview, 99–100; avartan bharna (filling the avartan) and, 81; in common gestures, 3; hand gestures and, 6, 92, 95, 97–98; melodic phrasing and, 73; vocal production and, 6

vistar, 80, **161**

Viswanathan, T., 25, 150n14

voice production: action of vocal organs, 26–27, 72; head posture and, 90–91; khula avaz (open voice), 129–133, *131*; musicking body as voice/body unity, 8–10, 14, 51–52; separation of voice and body, 26–28, 88; timbre/handshape relationship and, 92–95; voice as transcendent entity, 88. *See also* breath

water imagery, 47–48, 60–61, 145n7

Weidman, Amanda, 25, 27–28, 30

Western art music, 20–21, 29–30

Widdess, Richard, 143n2

Wilber, Ken, 9

Wolf, Richard, 127

Wulff, Helena, 11

Xenakis, Iannis, 146n10

yogic practices, 13, 30–31, 91, 100–101, 129, 144n1

Young, Katharine, 124–25

Zuckerkandl, Victor, 50

MUSIC / CULTURE
A series from Wesleyan University Press
Edited by Harris M. Berger and Annie J. Randall

Originating editors: George Lipsitz, Susan McClary, and Robert Walser

Listening to Salsa:
Gender, Latin Popular Music,
and Puerto Rican Cultures
by Frances Aparicio

Jazz Consciousness:
Music, Race, and Humanity
by Paul Austerlitz

Metal, Rock, and Jazz:
Perception and the Phenomenology
of Musical Experience
by Harris M. Berger

Identity and Everyday Life:
Essays in the Study of Folklore, Music,
and Popular Culture
by Harris M. Berger and
Giovanna P. Del Negro

Stance:
Ideas about Emotion, Style, and Meaning
for the Study of Expressive Culture
by Harris M. Berger

Monument Eternal:
The Music of Alice Coltrane
by Franya J. Berkman

Bright Balkan Morning:
Romani Lives and the Power of Music
in Greek Macedonia
by Dick Blau and Charles and Angeliki Keil

Musical Childhoods and
the Cultures of Youth
edited by Susan Boynton and Roe-Min Kok

Music and Cinema
edited by James Buhler, Caryl Flinn,
and David Neumeyer

Music and Cyberliberties
by Patrick Burkart

Listening and Longing:
Music Lovers in the Age of Barnum
by Daniel Cavicchi

My Music
by Susan D. Crafts, Daniel Cavicchi,
Charles Keil, and the
Music in Daily Life Project

Born in the USA:
Bruce Springsteen and the American Tradition
by Jim Cullen

Presence and Pleasure:
The Funk Grooves of James Brown
and Parliament
by Anne Danielsen

Echo and Reverb:
Fabricating Space in Popular Music Recording,
1900–1960
by Peter Doyle

Recollecting from the Past:
Musical Practice and Spirit Possession
on the East Coast of Madagascar
by Ron Emoff

Locating East Asia in Western Art Music
edited by Yayoi Uno Everett
and Frederick Lau

Music, Politics, and Violence
edited by Susan Fast and Kip Pegley

Black Rhythms of Peru:
Reviving African Musical Heritage
in the Black Pacific
by Heidi Feldman

"You Better Work!"
Underground Dance Music
in New York City
by Kai Fikentscher

The Hidden Musicians
Music-Making in an English Town
by Ruth Finnegan

The Other Side of Nowhere:
Jazz, Improvisation, and Communities
in Dialogue
edited by Daniel Fischlin and Ajay Heble

Empire of Dirt:
The Aesthetics and Rituals of
British "Indie" Music
by Wendy Fonarow

The 'Hood Comes First:
Race, Space, and Place in Rap and Hip-Hop
by Murray Forman

Wired for Sound:
Engineering and Technologies
in Sonic Cultures
edited by Paul D. Greene
and Thomas Porcello

Sensational Knowledge:
Embodying Culture through
Japanese Dance
by Tomie Hahn

Voices in Bali:
Energies and Perceptions in
Vocal Music and Dance Theater
by Edward Herbst

Traveling Spirit Masters:
Moroccan Gnawa Trance and
Music in the Global Marketplace
by Deborah Kapchan

Symphonic Metamorphoses:
Subjectivity and Alienation in Mahler's
Re-Cycled Songs
by Raymond Knapp

Umm Kulthūm:
Artistic Agency and the Shaping
of an Arab Legend, 1967–2007
by Laura Lohman

A Thousand Honey Creeks Later:
My Life in Music from Basie to
Motown — and Beyond
by Preston Love

Music and Technoculture
edited by René T. A. Lysloff
and Leslie C. Gay, Jr.

Songs, Dreamings, and Ghosts:
The Wangga of North Australia
by Allan Marett

Phat Beats, Dope Rhymes:
Hip Hop Down Under Comin' Upper
by Ian Maxwell

Some Liked It Hot:
Jazz Women in Film and Television, 1928–1959
by Kristin A. McGee

Carriacou String Band Serenade:
Performing Identity in the Eastern Caribbean
by Rebecca S. Miller

Global Noise:
Rap and Hip-Hop outside the USA
edited by Tony Mitchell

Popular Music in Theory:
An Introduction
by Keith Negus

Upside Your Head!
Rhythm and Blues on Central Avenue
by Johnny Otis

Coming to You Wherever You Are:
MuchMusic, MTV, and Youth Identities
by Kip Pegley

Musicking Bodies:
Gesture and Voice in Hindustani Music
by Matthew Rahaim

Singing Archaeology:
Philip Glass's Akhnaten
by John Richardson

Black Noise:
Rap Music and Black Culture
in Contemporary America
by Tricia Rose

The Book of Music and Nature:
An Anthology of Sounds, Words, Thoughts
edited by David Rothenberg
and Marta Ulvaeus

ABOUT THE AUTHOR

Matthew Rahaim is an assistant professor of music at the University of Minnesota. His research and review articles have appeared in *World of Music, Gesture, Journal of Asian Studies,* and *New Perspectives on Music and Gesture*. He has taught at the University of California, Berkeley; Stanford University; and St. Olaf College. Rahaim also is an avid performer of Hindustani vocal music, both in India and in North America.